RECEIVED

JAN 14 2022

D0398211

NO LONGER PROPERTY OF
SEATTLE PUBLIC LIBRARY

# THE NATURE OF TOMORROW

MICHAEL RAWSON

# The Nature of Tomorrow

## A HISTORY OF THE ENVIRONMENTAL FUTURE

Yale
UNIVERSITY PRESS
NEW HAVEN & LONDON

Published with assistance from the foundation established in memory of
Amasa Stone Mather of the Class of 1907, Yale College.

Copyright © 2021 by Michael Rawson. All rights reserved.
This book may not be reproduced, in whole or in part, including
illustrations, in any form (beyond that copying permitted by Sections 107
and 108 of the U.S. Copyright Law and except by reviewers for the public
press), without written permission from the publishers.

Yale University Press books may be purchased in quantity for
educational, business, or promotional use. For information, please e-mail
sales.press@yale.edu (U.S. office) or sales@yaleup.co.uk (U.K. office).

Set in Scala and Scala Sans type by Integrated Publishing Solutions.
Printed in the United States of America.

ISBN 978-0-300-25519-5 (hardcover : alk. paper)
Library of Congress Control Number: 2021936875
A catalogue record for this book is available from the British Library.

This paper meets the requirements of ANSI/NISO Z39.48-1992
(Permanence of Paper).

10 9 8 7 6 5 4 3 2 1

For my children,
for your children,
and for their children

It's a poor sort of memory that only works backward.

The White Queen in Lewis Carroll, *Through the Looking-Glass* (1871)

# CONTENTS

# PREFACE

THE SCIENCE FICTION WRITER William Gibson wrote a now classic short story that has special resonance for me. It is the tale of a photographer working on an illustrated history of futuristic architecture from the 1930s. All goes well with the project until the photographer, having dived too deeply into his work, finds himself beset by hallucinations of flying cars, enormous zeppelins, monumental art deco cities, and other icons of a future that never was. These "semiotic ghosts," fragments from the collective unconscious spilling into his reality, drive him half mad before he is finally able to exorcise them.

Having immersed myself in similar sources for over a decade, I cannot help but read Gibson's story as a cautionary tale. So I want to take advantage of my current mental equilibrium and say a few words about how this book evolved and the choices I have made along the way.

*The Nature of Tomorrow* explores a genre of Western ideas about the natural world that historians have largely overlooked: visions of the environmental future. I began my research with the intention of focusing on ecological utopias, imagined societies that exist in balance and harmony with the natural world, usually in some distant tomorrow. I was not surprised to find that such visions have been the exception rather than the rule. I was, however, surprised by what I discovered to be the rule itself: visions of tomorrow based on the single-minded expectation of endless growth on a finite planet, regardless of whether the end result was a utopia or environmental collapse. The theme of growth soon moved to the center of my research, resulting in a different book than the one I set out to write but perhaps a more relevant and urgent one. Stories about the future have reflected and promoted a widespread expectation of unlimited growth, an expectation that has, in turn, made a truly sustainable relationship with the earth more difficult to imagine.

One of the greatest challenges I faced in the early stages of writing this book was choosing the scale at which to work. I originally deferred to my training and planned to focus my research on the United States, only to find that the ideas I was pursuing kept escaping across national boundaries. The renowned historical geographer Clarence Glacken had once encouraged anyone studying environmental ideas to follow them wherever they led, even into areas patrolled by scholars who knew the terrain far better. Failing to do so, he warned, would leave the unadventurous researcher sipping a "thin gruel." So I took his advice to heart and briefly reimagined the project on a global scale. That, however, turned out to be too ambitious a structure, one that even the great Glacken steered clear of.

I finally decided to concentrate on the West, which proved a perfect fit for the themes emerging from my research. The West's progress and growth-fueled environmental dreams, while not the only way of imagining the nature of tomorrow, have formed a coherent tradition and been more than influential enough to merit a study of their own. I also became convinced that understanding the distant origins of the present-day fixation on growth requires a long timescale, leading me to take on the additional challenge of covering several centuries in a single volume.

The book focuses most closely on those countries that have had the largest impact on formulating the environmental ideas I explore: Britain, France, and later the United States, which has long been the land of frontiers and futures. Although readers will also come across the work of Danish economists, Italian futurists, and German science fiction writers, I have made no effort to be comprehensive in my coverage. The commonalities in attitudes toward human progress and expansion have been so strong across the West that, despite national differences in environmental thought, my story would look much the same no matter what countries I emphasized. Environmental imaginaries can and do operate on different levels: some are indeed national, like the distinctive set of ideas that gives meaning to forested landscapes in Germany, but others are transnational.

My sources are eclectic, and necessarily so, since Westerners have expressed their visions of the environmental future in a variety of different ways. I combed the literature on utopias and imagined futures for scientific, technological, and environmental themes, examining both fictional and nonfictional predictive literature as well as visual media, like advertisements and movies. As a result, the reader will encounter everything from Tommaso Campanella's seventeenth-century utopia *The City of the Sun,* to the nineteenth-century renderings of British illustrators, to the speculations of twentieth-century think tanks like the RAND Corporation. These various sources have intertwined with and influenced each other over time, together giving shape to a powerful tradition of environmental dreaming.

Some of the sources I discuss were influential, while others attracted far less notice. At a number of points in this book, I do not hesitate to give as much attention to the latter as I do the former. One of my primary goals is to reveal as much of this environmental imaginary as possible, and sometimes a little known work does more to illuminate its dim corners than a best seller. Some of the more obscure works also help me to emphasize what historians call contingency, the idea that the past could have unfolded differently and that there are multiple possible futures. To that end, these works uncover paths not taken and, in some cases, paths still open for exploration.

Since I am focusing on expectations of how human beings will transform the earth, certain genres of prophetic literature figure less prominently in the book. I look at stories that explore humankind's future in outer space only when the environments of distant planets are clearly intended to stand in for earth. Also, I include tales of natural disasters like unanticipated ice ages and collisions with comets solely when such events influenced how characters subsequently interacted with the natural world. Finally, I explore Christian-influenced visions of tomorrow so far as they represent future worlds designed and built by humans rather than by God.

The sources reflect a great deal of consistency in attitudes toward growth across lines of class, gender, and nationality. That is not surprising given that the vision of ever expanding abundance at the expense of nonhuman nature has always rested on the assumption that growth would lift all boats. The opening of new lands, new mines, new factories, new cities, and perhaps even new planets, along with the spread of labor-saving machinery, has long implied more opportunities and more wealth for everyone. It has been difficult to argue against that logic in the past, just as it continues to be today. The only people generally excepted from this projected abundance were the members of nonwhite races. The sources do not tend to depict this group as sharing in the growing pie until the late twentieth century.

The widespread expectation of growth-generated abundance should not be confused with the substantial level of social and political disagreement over how to achieve it and how to divide the spoils. The reality is that the push for human expansion and environmental development, while emphasizing control over the natural world, has always been a way to exercise control over people as well. Although this book is not a social history, I remain acutely aware of the social consequences of ideas like progress and growth. They have justified the displacement of some peoples, the enslavement of others, and the economic exploitation of still more. They are still used today to encourage the transformation of less industrialized parts of the world into objects of development.

Those, however, are more familiar stories. Less familiar is the history of how dreams of unlimited growth emerged and assumed a dominant place in the visions of the environmental future that so much of the world shares today. That is the story I tell in these pages.

# THE NATURE OF TOMORROW

# Prologue: Dreaming the Environmental Future

> The visions we present to our children shape the future. It *matters* what those visions are. Often they become self-fulfilling prophecies. Dreams are maps.
>
> Carl Sagan, "Dreams Are Maps" (1992)

IN 1995, A GROUP OF ENVIRONMENTAL activists traveled deep into the Amazon at the request of the indigenous Achuar people, whose lands—some two million acres of rainforest—straddle the border between Ecuador and Peru. Dreams play a prominent role in Achuar culture, and by the 1980s their elders and shamans were having visions that suggested their land and culture would soon come under serious threat. The peril was quite real: as the Achuar knew, Western oil companies were advancing through the lands of neighboring peoples and leaving environmental and cultural disruption in their wake. But when the activists arrived to help, they were surprised by what the Achuar had in mind. Rather than looking for assistance in organizing locally, they asked the activists to go back home and "change the dream of the modern world."[1]

Does the modern world, by which the Achuar mostly meant the industrialized West, actually dream about the future? The answer is an emphatic yes. In fact, Westerners are so thoroughly immersed in tales and images of tomorrow that the future often feels as real as the past. Science fiction stories appear regularly on television shows, in movies, and in print; news outlets supply a constant stream of speculation about the next development in artificial intelligence, space exploration, and life-extending medical procedures; advertisements stoke excitement about future forms of personal technology; think tanks make forecasts about which new weapons will win the next war. Stories, images, and predictions like these have long formed the building blocks of larger patterns of expectation, visions of the future that can be shared by a social group, an entire culture, or even billions of people around the world.[2]

Imagined tomorrows often emphasize the kind of fantastic scientific and technological feats that have become synonymous with the future. But visions of polished laboratories and gleaming machines often blind us to the fact that most such stories are, on their most fundamental level, environmental fables. They are stories about how science and technology will ensure ever greater human power over the natural world. The iconic animated sitcom *The Jetsons,* which originated in the United States in the 1960s and has since played in syndication on every inhabited continent, provides a good example. Although rarely examined from an environmental perspective, the show self-consciously depicts a future where every bit of the natural world has been replaced with something artificial. Yet that startling fact, which reveals all by itself how central environmental themes are to the show, is somehow harder to notice than the flying cars and robotic maid. Despite outward appearances, most fully imagined tales of tomorrow—even *The Jetsons*—contain a large measure of environmental dreaming.[3]

This book explores past visions of the environmental future over the last several centuries, but not for what they might reveal about the actual future. Instead, I am interested in what they reveal about the kind of environmental future the West has imagined itself working toward, what the Achuar called "the dream of the modern world." Where have the West's environmental expectations come from, how have they evolved over time, and to what kind of world were they supposed to have led? If dreams really do serve as maps, as Carl Sagan claimed, then it seems time to reexamine some of the most widely used maps to the future, if only to make sure that human civilization has not inadvertently gotten off at the wrong exit.

I have read through hundreds of stories and predictions produced across several centuries by scientists, fiction writers, government officials, and many others—each one a little map of the future in itself. Over time, I noticed that one particular expectation kept appearing, either implicitly or explicitly, in source after source: that humankind will expand endlessly, no matter the environmental consequences. This expansion might serve as a source of creation or destruction, depending on the story, but a force it would be. In short, it became clear that the West's long-term ambitions have been guided by the widely shared and paradoxical expectation of unlimited growth on a finite planet. That observation led me to a further and unsettling realization: humankind has not entered the Anthropocene, the age of human dominance over the environment, through some navigational error as many would like to think. It has, rather, been the West's intended destination for a long time.[4]

Given the severe environmental problems that human expansion has caused, the world seems in need of a better understanding of how the stories that people have told themselves about the future—and continue to tell themselves today—have helped to shape and sustain an expectation of limitless growth. That is the goal of this book. It is simultaneously a history of the future, a study of environmental dreaming, and, as the historian William Cronon might put it, a story about stories about nature. The book surveys a long chronological period, one that begins in the fifteenth century when Europeans first learned that the world was a far larger place than they had realized, and ends in the present day. Over the course of the journey through those centuries, the reader will encounter some familiar tales of tomorrow and many forgotten ones as well, all of them relevant in a time of ever-worsening environmental crisis. Stories like these have had a very real impact on human history, as the Achuar and their neighbors can readily attest, and continue to shape the future because they facilitate some paths forward while foreclosing others.[5]

Shared stories about the future emerge from an unexpected place: the past. More properly, they arise from social memory or collective understandings of past events. Memories, which often take the form of narratives, encourage certain expectations about the world of tomorrow. People then express those expectations through more narratives. In fact, stories about the past and the future share a crucial connection because they form two halves of a larger story about human affairs. And like the beginning and end of any story, they influence and shape each other. Karl Marx's prediction of a future worker's revolution and resulting communist paradise depended entirely on a particular view of the past that made modes of production the prime movers of historical change. Similarly, interpretations of the past that put technological advancement at the center of human history tend to suggest a future of even greater technological wonders. That is why modern futurists trying to make serious assessments of what tomorrow might be like tend to present their scenarios in the form of stories about past, present, and future: they understand that history and prophecy derive much of their meaning from each other.[6]

Stories about yesterday and tomorrow also share connections on a more fundamental level, for both are imaginative constructions of unknowable worlds. They are acts of invention that help us to understand our place in the time stream, to know where we have been and where we are going. Recording the past is not new: human societies have done so for thousands of years in an effort to build convincing and useful portraits of yesterday. Without a record of the past, a people would feel collectively unmoored, as if their society were suffering from amnesia. Recording the future—at least the secular future—is a much more recent and speculative affair. Once people began to believe that tomorrow would be materially different from yesterday, they needed to create stories that expressed their expectations. Those stories shape present identities as surely as the collective memories from which they grow, and people defend them with just as much passion.[7]

All of this applies to the West's dreams of endless growth and expansion, which gained considerable momentum when they became entangled with one of the core myths of Western culture: the idea of progress. The belief that human society has been moving in a positive direction, and will continue to do so indefinitely, goes back to ancient times. Such progress can come in many forms—moral, cultural, social, material, scientific—and connects stories about yesterday with stories about tomorrow. It is a theory, wrote the historian of progress J. B. Bury, that "involves a synthesis of the past and a prophecy of the future." It is also a theory that involves a considerable dose of faith, since it is impossible to be certain that changes heralded as progress are actually leading the world to a better place. The influence of progress as an idea waxed in the eighteenth century, which is when growth became an integral part of it, and waned in the latter part of the twentieth. But overall it has probably been the single most influential idea in all of Western history.[8]

Progress proved to be an excellent bedfellow for the idea of endless human expansion, for it too ignores limits. To claim, for example, that there are limits to the accumulation of knowledge or the evolution of human spirituality would suggest that improvement has an end point, and the existence of an end point would undermine the very idea of progress. Positive change, the idea of progress tells us, must move inexorably and forever forward toward a state of perfection that can be approached but never fully achieved. In an environmental context, progress became equated with ever-increasing material abundance and control over the earth, which requires constant expansion. A faith in growth and rejection of environmental limits has since served as the foundation for some of the West's greatest dreams and, more recently, some of its worst nightmares.[9]

Two related assumptions have been particularly influential in structuring visions of endless material growth. The first is the belief that science and technology will ensure that natural resources remain abundant and will continue to provide adequately for human needs, no matter how many people inhabit the earth or how large their appetites grow. The second is the faith that, again with sufficiently advanced science and technology at their command, humans can exercise complete control over the natural world and manipulate it in any way they choose. Together, these assumptions suggest that humankind has the potential to become so independent from nature, so thoroughly its master, that the term environmental limits is really no more than an oxymoron.

Over the past several centuries, the acceptance or rejection of these assumptions has helped to shape two distinct and opposing visions of the environmental future, visions so common and widely embraced that I treat them as consensus narratives. Other visions have existed and still do, but none have rivaled these for influence and longevity. Although the two have evolved and grown more complex over time, they will be familiar to most readers in broad outline. The stories they tell about the world of tomorrow are so compelling yet so fundamentally different from one another that they are, in effect, locked in a contest for the future. In fact, they are locked in a contest for the past as well, for where one stands on these deceptively simple assumptions can be the difference between radically different worldviews that structure past and future alike.

The first is a story that embraces these assumptions and foresees the complete development of the earth. It emerged during the Enlightenment and, over time, evolved into a vision of the future that science fiction writer Kim Stanley Robinson describes as "existence in great industrial city-machines, with people as the last organic units in a denatured, metallic, clean, and artificial world." The most widely recognizable example is probably *The Jetsons,* which represents a utopian version of this narrative played for laughs. Generally speaking, the development narrative portrays a world in which huge human populations house themselves in giant cities (often domed or underground), drive non-productive plants and animals to extinction, cultivate the sea intensively, consume largely synthetic foods, delve ever deeper into the earth for resources, control the planet's climate to produce the desired weather, and ultimately expand into outer space. It is a seductive vision of infinite material abundance delivered through glittering technologies on a world with no environmental limits in a universe of endless frontiers.[10]

The development narrative shares its general vision and assumptions with a way of environmental thinking often referred to as cornucopianism or Prometheanism, after the Greek god who gave fire to humankind. The Promethean perspective views the natural world primarily as a set of raw materials, embraces a faith in the ability of humans and their technologies to convert these materials to usable form, and holds that the human project should be to do just that. It has long held an influential place in Western political institutions and in the culture of capitalism, especially in the United States. Prometheans often express their visions of the future through what is called technological utopianism, which emphasizes machines as the key to a better human future. Technological utopias have usually embraced the dream of complete planetary development, but there have been exceptions, and there is no inherent reason why they have to.[11]

The second consensus narrative is a story of disaster built on an opposite set of assumptions: that resources are limited and that the natural world is not infinitely malleable or controllable. Humans, in short, are still part of the natural world and subject to natural laws. The resulting story of growth is a terrifying prophecy of environmental overshoot that often includes over-population, water shortages, exhausted soil, depleted resources, empty oceans, rising seas, and warming climate, often followed by war, famine, disease, and societal breakdown. The disaster narrative began to coalesce in the wake of World War I and gained strength after World War II with the rise of the environmental movement. Its apocalyptic vision presents an altogether dif-ferent answer to the question of what unceasing human growth and expan-sion will look like.[12]

The ideas that support the disaster narrative tend to overlap with certain schools of thought in modern environmentalism, at least where the exis-tence of limits is concerned. But this narrative does not reflect the preferred future of an environmentalist the way the development narrative might re-flect the preferred future of a Promethean. It is, rather, an environmental-ist's view of what the world will look like if the level of expansion favored by Prometheans actually comes to pass. Environmentalists have been largely unsuccessful in capturing the public's imagination with a vision based on something other than growth, mostly because social memory has not pro-vided enough support for one and because the development narrative effec-tively portrays any other way of life as backward. The costs of that failure have been considerable.

Although terms like Prometheans and environmentalists can be useful, there are advantages to thinking about different environmental attitudes as being embedded in competing stories instead of opposing groups. Scholars and commentators tend to favor the latter, organizing people into optimists and pessimists, cornucopians and conservationists, technologists and Mal-thusians, or boomsters and doomsters. But such labels are almost always misleading. Pro-growth advocates, for example, do not have a monopoly on optimism, and those concerned about overpopulation do not tend to reject technology. Such categories also suggest hardened group identities, when in reality people shift from group to group depending on the context. A per-son can be a boomster while reading a newspaper article about increased economic growth and a doomster after turning the page to find the latest news on climate change. In 2017, a Silicon Valley technology investor, whose job is anticipating future trends, admitted that his state of mind was "oscillating between optimism and sheer terror." People rarely fit comfortably and permanently into a single category but rather embrace different environmental narratives at different moments in time.[13]

Despite the strong expectation of growth embedded in Western culture, the West has also produced visions of the future that emphasize stable populations, cautious resource use, and steady-state economies. Collectively they form a loose countertheme that has tended to wax or wane depending on the historical context. Such visions have never been as common or widely embraced as the two dominant narratives of growth. But they have nevertheless represented significant and sometimes influential efforts to rethink the idea of progress and to venture outside the growth paradigm in search of alternative futures. They, too, have played a role in the larger history of environmental dreaming.[14]

It can be tempting to dismiss all of these stories about the future as the frivolous fantasies of a creative culture. But they could not be more important, for they carry causative weight and ecological force in the real world. This is easiest to see on an individual level. The rapidly developing field of prospective psychology is discovering that people are drawn by the future as strongly as they are compelled by the past, leading some scientists to suggest that a more appropriate name for our species would be *homo prospectus*. The ecological economist Kenneth Boulding has made a similar argument. "All decisions," he writes, "involve choices among images of alternative futures." Some people have even been able to recognize the power of these stories in their own lives, particularly the many scientists and inventors who have acknowledged that the writings of Jules Verne, H. G. Wells, and other visionaries inspired their choices of career. People are, in a sense, time travelers who need charts to find their way forward. Stories about the future often serve as those charts.[15]

It is a foundational principle of the field of futures studies that tales of tomorrow shape entire societies as well. The sociologist Fred Polak famously argued that visions of the future are the primary force pulling history forward. But one does not have to go that far to appreciate how important such images are to governments, businesses, and institutions, whether they are marketing and pursuing their preferred visions or reacting to forecasts produced by others. The Yale sociologist Wendell Bell has framed society itself as "a set of more or less shared expectations about the future and of the behavior based on them." The higher the level of consensus around a particular expectation, the more powerful a motivating force that expectation can be. In the West, growth has enjoyed such a consensus for centuries because it has been easy to imagine that an ever-expanding pie will benefit everyone, even if the slices are not cut to the same size. Although some of the prime contributors to growth, like industrialization and capitalism, have come under frequent and heavy attack from a variety of quarters, it has proven difficult to criticize growth itself for anything but environmental reasons.[16]

Narratives of development and disaster have not, of course, been the only forces steering humankind toward one of these possible ends. The world of tomorrow is not so easily planned and executed. As imagined futures have pulled societies forward, other forces—urbanization, industrialization, population expansion, advances in science and technology, and much more—have been pushing them in much the same direction. In fact, material change and cultural expectations have been deeply entwined for centuries, reinforcing and even creating each other as they work together to propel humankind toward its destiny. In that sense, these two narratives of the future are not just causes but also effects, projections of possible tomorrows arising from a long historical experience with unrelenting progress and growth.

It might seem strange for a historian to be writing about the future, even past futures. But historians are particularly well positioned to explore the uncertain terrain of things to come. "There is no other branch of learning," observed C. Vann Woodward, "better qualified to mediate between man's daydream of the future and his nightmare of the past, or, for that matter, between his nightmare of the future and his daydream of the past." The English diplomat E. H. Carr went even further, considering engagement with the future to be an unavoidable part of the historian's task. Good historians, he wrote, "whether they think about it or not, have the future in their bones."[17]

This book uses the tools of the historian to reconstruct the history of the environmental future. The story begins in the 1400s with the expansion of the West's environmental horizons and continues through the major phases in the evolution of the development and disaster narratives: the scientific advancement, economic expansion, and technological innovation that encouraged early visions of progress and growth; the invention of coal-powered machinery that made endless abundance seem like a real possibility; the use of Charles Darwin's ideas to frame unlimited human expansion as natural and inevitable; the emergence in the twentieth century of a new narrative that forecast environmental catastrophe; and the decline of the idea of progress when faced with mounting environmental problems.

The evolution of these two narratives, and the history of environmental prophecy in general, sheds considerable new light on the development of environmental thought. Set within the context of four centuries of imagined futures, twentieth-century environmentalism looks like not only a social and political movement but a new and distinctive way of thinking about tomorrow, one with roots that extend farther back in time and in different directions than historians have realized. The sustainability movement, rather than simply the most recent stage in the development of environmental thought, comes into focus as a vision of the future that has achieved widespread support by sidestepping what would surely be a polarizing discussion about growth and limits. And the idea that the world has entered a new geological age called the Anthropocene, which took many people by surprise, looks far less shocking in light of past expectations that such a period of domination over the natural world is exactly what humankind is working toward.[18]

The history of environmental dreaming also forces us to examine what we might call developmentalist thought. The fact is that many environmental dreams are painted more in cement grays and brick reds than forest greens. Exploring why individuals and groups choose to develop rather than conserve, and what environmental visions drive them, is just as essential to a full understanding of environmental history. Whether to use or preserve is a fundamental decision that humans have always had to make. It represents a choice between opposing impulses that cannot help but exist in tension with each other, like two sides of the same coin. So it makes sense to study the ideas that people have applied to the development of the natural world right alongside the ideas that have informed conservation, preservation, and environmentalism. They are best understood together.[19]

The history of past futures also provides essential context for present-day discussions about growth and natural limits. Most of those involved in the conversation are ecological economists hoping to adapt the ever-expanding world economy to environmental realities. But this history highlights an often-overlooked cultural dimension to growth that cannot be ignored. Human expansion is built into the Western vision of the future and has been for a long time. It is far more entrenched than a focus on economics might suggest. So adapting the world economy will require not just changes to the economy itself but also a major adjustment to the entire Western worldview, including the decoupling of growth from the idea of progress.[20]

Perhaps most importantly, the history of environmental dreaming speaks directly to the root of the current environmental predicament: the widespread rejection of natural limits. Although the idea of progress has lost much of its luster since the 1960s, the alluring vision of endless material abundance for an endless number of people lives on, with production, consumption, and population continuing to grow on a planet that does not. The failure to resolve that paradox, when seen from within the West's long tradition of environmental prophecy, begins to look like an extraordinary inability to reconcile memory and expectations with environmental realities. That failure has made it nearly impossible to develop a popular vision of tomorrow where people recognize environmental limits and live within them. Now, in the twenty-first century, we are called to rectify that failure by finding a new consensus about the past and a new set of expectations about the future. The first step is waking up to the fact that our dreams have consequences in the material world.[21]

# 1

# A Story of Progress and Growth

THERE HAVE ALWAYS BEEN DREAMERS, and Roger Bacon was one of them. A medieval English scholar and Franciscan friar, Bacon penned a letter around the year 1260 describing what he called "wondrous artificial instruments" that, he believed, had already been invented or at least designed in his own time. They included a seagoing vessel that moved without oars; a chariot that traveled without horses and at great speed; an airship that flew like a bird under the control of a single man; a machine that lifted enormous weights with ease; and a contraption that enabled people to walk on the bottoms of seas and rivers. Bacon assured his readers that these amazing machines were not the products of magic but rather technical marvels "achieved through the design and reasoning of art alone." His letter is striking not only because he was completely wrong about the existence of such machines, but also because his fantasies of technological achievement were centuries ahead of their time. Mechanical progress had not yet been rapid or impressive enough for many people to expect such advances.[1]

Bacon's letter is also noteworthy for what it does not contain: it makes no mention of people using these machines to expand human control over the earth and to increase material abundance. He could have imagined his oar-less ship conveying colonists to distant shores, or his horseless chariot rushing resources to newly built workshops, or his airship facilitating the discovery of unknown lands, or his powerful machine digging new harbors, or his breathing apparatus making it possible to build underwater cities. But

Bacon did not draw a direct line from technological achievements to human expansion like those in the industrialized world might reflexively do today. Since nothing in the past suggested that humans would someday master the forces of nature and use them to transform the globe and revolutionize material life, Bacon and his contemporaries assumed that environmental relationships and material culture would remain largely the same.

Some two hundred years later, those expectations began to change. New discoveries, inventions, and environmental knowledge made it possible for Western economies, populations, and power to begin expanding around the world. The present began to look quite different from the past, and science and technology seemed like the prime drivers of that change and perhaps even of human history itself. From this new understanding of yesterday emerged a radically different vision of tomorrow. Hopes for sufficiency, or having enough to satisfy material needs, gave way to dreams of endless abundance that became an integral part of how people in the West thought about human progress. By the end of the eighteenth century, growth and progress had moved to the very center of Western expectations and were finding expression in two competing narratives of tomorrow based on different environmental assumptions. One claimed that unrestrained growth would produce a utopia, while the other framed it as the path to global destruction.[2]

## Changing Expectations

Three interrelated events started Westerners down the road to a vision of the future centered on growth. The first was the dramatic expansion of the West's environmental horizons, which began in the 1400s with the "voyages of discovery." Island by island, coast by coast, the world outside of Europe came slowly into focus, and there was a lot of it. In fact, the world looked so big that the potential for trade in scarce resources and rare manufactures began to seem boundless. The real surprise, however, came in 1492 when Christopher Columbus stumbled on a new world previously unknown to the old one. European explorers were astonished by the natural abundance of the Americas, where they encountered larger forests, more plentiful game, and richer fishing grounds than anything they had experi-

This seventeenth-century engraving by Theodor de Bry appeared in various publications about New England, Virginia, and New Spain to illustrate the natural abundance of the Americas. (Courtesy of the John Carter Brown Library)

enced at home. As European diseases took their toll on Native American populations, precipitating an enormous demographic collapse, the vast American continents became even easier to imagine as sites for not only economic expansion but extensive colonization as well. From the perspective of Europe, the rest of the world was coming to look like an endless frontier.[3]

The invention of the telescope a century later enhanced the boundaries of that frontier even further. At the time, conventional wisdom held that the moon was perfectly smooth and unlike the earth. But when Galileo turned his newly built telescope toward the moon in the fall of 1609, he noticed features that looked like mountains, valleys, and seas, and thought that he might even be seeing evidence of an atmosphere. Once he published his findings the following year, word of this new world spread through Western Europe within weeks and expanded the West's environmental imagination outward toward the stars. Commentators immediately likened Galileo to Columbus and began dreaming of a day when Europeans would colonize the moon and exploit its resources. Later in the century, more powerful telescopes made it possible to speculate about the environments of the planets as well. The hope for human expansion across the unending cosmos had been born.[4]

The second event encouraging an expectation of growth was the Scientific Revolution. Beginning in the sixteenth century and accelerating in the seventeenth, scholars began to devote increasing amounts of energy to the systematic process of uncovering the laws of nature. The techniques used by these natural philosophers did not always constitute science as we understand it today, in part because scholarly thought still contained a lot of religious and magical ideas. But many of them were actively working to replace the traditional technique of searching for environmental knowledge in ancient texts with actual observation of the natural world. In many ways, their efforts set Europe's environmental imagination free to wander new paths.[5]

Among natural philosophers, expectations about the extent to which humankind could control and develop the natural world rose to unprecedented heights. René Descartes hoped that humans would someday know "the power and action of fire, water, air, the stars, the heavens and all the other bodies in our environment, as distinctly as we know the various crafts of our artisans." Through the application of such knowledge, he wrote, we could "make ourselves, as it were, the lords and masters of nature." Statements of such extraordinary ambition and confidence are hard to come by before the Scientific Revolution.[6]

The third event reshaping Western expectations was the acceleration of technological change. Pre-industrial Europe was no stranger to complex machinery like windmills and waterwheels. But the impact of recent advances— especially the introduction of the printing press, gunpowder, and the compass—had been profound. In 1620, the English statesman Francis Bacon claimed that "these three have changed the whole face and stage of things throughout the world, the first in literature, the second in warfare, the third in navigation." He recognized that they had, in turn, inspired other technological changes, and thought them so important that he gave them primacy of place in human history. "No empire, sect, or star," he wrote, "appears to have exercised a greater power and influence on human affairs than these mechanical discoveries." Bacon had essentially proclaimed technology the main force moving history forward.[7]

The idea that rapid innovation in the past foretold further innovation in the future began to spread widely in the middle of the seventeenth century. This was particularly true in Bacon's England, which developed a distinctive culture of improvement that held up material progress as the path to prosperity and happiness. The word improvement itself quickly became something of a national mantra, and those given to dreaming began to dream big. Bishop John Wilkins wrote about the possibility of developing submarines, flying chariots, and perpetual motion machines. The Marquis of Worcester, himself an inventor, published descriptions of one hundred inventions that he claimed to have perfected, including a mechanism for human flight and a very early description of a steam engine. Joseph Glanvill, an advocate of England's natural philosophers, believed that someday people would buy wings as easily as a pair of boots and take trips to the moon as effortlessly as to the southern seas. Such abilities might be many years away, but past accomplishments had made it reasonable to begin anticipating them.[8]

Seventeenth-century Europeans were of two minds about this technological turn. Some, like Francis Bacon, believed it would lead to the "great instauration" or renewal, a future time when humans would regain the mastery of nature that Adam and Eve had supposedly lost in the biblical fall. Others rejected the idea that machines were a form of divine compensation, seeing them instead as an unfortunate consequence of human sin and a barrier to restoring the close relationship with nature that had existed in the Garden of Eden. The two views are reflected in the competing ways that contemporaries interpreted the biblical story of the Tower of Babel and the mythical story of Icarus and his wings: sometimes they were told as stories of laudable ambition, sometimes as stories of tragic hubris. The tension between these two views, born in the Renaissance, still shapes Western attitudes toward technology and the natural world today.[9]

It was in these same years that dreamers began to link scientific and technological progress with human expansion. Wilkins expected that his submarines, if large enough, might serve as underwater colonies that spent enough of their time submerged to see children born who knew little of the world above the waves. The Marquis of Worcester hoped that his steam engine, once perfected, would vastly increase human control of water resources by draining mines, providing water to cities, and regulating the flow of rivers to improve the land along their banks. Glanvill, too, looked forward to the environmental transformations that such inventions would bring, including the conversion of deserts into lush slices of paradise.[10]

The new focus on growth, combined with the belief that the earth had the capacity to feed far more people than it did, encouraged the English and French to experiment with demographic forecasting. In 1696, an English statistician calculated that the population of England and Wales had doubled in the previous 435 years and predicted that such increases would continue far into the future. He estimated that the approximately five and a half million people of his own time would double to eleven million by the year 2300 and double again by 3500. In France, a military engineer calculated that, by the year 3000, the population of Canada would grow to fifty million inhabitants, far more than the France of his day. Estimates like these represented more than a simple awareness that population could grow. They expressed the expectation that it would, and for a thousand years or more to come.[11]

Some historians have argued that the primary root of the West's science and technology-fueled expansionism is the Christian tradition. They point in particular to divine commandments like "be fruitful and multiply and fill the earth and subdue it." Such passages undoubtedly reinforced the idea that all of nature is subordinate to human purposes. But observers at the end of the seventeenth century had a more sophisticated understanding of the forces transforming their world. The English minister John Edwards, writing in 1699, explained that "diligent Researches at home, and Travels into remote Countries have produced new Observations and Remarks, unheard-of Discoveries and Inventions. Thus we surpass all the times that have been before us; and it is highly probable that those that succeed, will far surpass these." New worlds, new technologies, and a new desire to know nature's secrets: those were the forces reshaping past, present, and future alike.[12]

## Science and Sufficiency

Half a century before the expectation of growth began to develop, natural philosophers produced the first comprehensive visions of a future built around increasing environmental knowledge. The most notable ones appeared in the first quarter of the seventeenth century and came in the form of fictional accounts of the ideal society. They followed the model set by Thomas More's *Utopia,* published in 1516, by setting their stories in lands that were distant in space rather than time. Thinking about the future as being substantially different from the present was still so unusual that future fiction would not become a literary genre for another century and a half. Until then, utopias set in unknown corners of the world stood in for tales of tomorrow.[13]

The early scientific utopias are particularly interesting because they emerged during a small window of time when increasing environmental knowledge was coming to seem like the key to the future but had not yet become linked to visions of expansion and abundance. So rather than putting such knowledge in the service of growth, these utopias applied it to other goals, such as satisfying present needs, fostering social harmony, improving the quality of human life, bringing people closer to God, and restoring the human place in nature to what it was before the biblical fall. The result is a series of steady-state societies with populations, production levels, consumption habits, and geographical ambitions that remain constant.

One of the earliest scientific utopias was *The City of the Sun,* completed by the Italian priest Tommaso Campanella in 1602. The fictional residents of the city, supposedly located on an island off the coast of India, live immersed in environmental knowledge and synchronize their lives with the harmonies of the natural world. They achieve much of this through the design of the city itself. Seven circular walls, one inside another, enclose a plain with a hill at its center. Each wall is named for one of the seven known planets, and with the exception of the outer surface of the outermost wall, all are covered with images that collectively depict the total sum of human knowledge, most of it about the natural environment. Some walls contain pictures of all known rocks and metals, supplemented with descriptions and specimens; others are covered with illustrations and samples of liquids, from oceans and rivers to wines and oils; still others contain images of all birds, reptiles, insects, and plants. On the hilltop at the center stands a circular open-air temple under an immense dome supported by massive columns. Only when Campanella describes the sun-shaped altar beneath the dome does the reader fully realize that the city's residents live inside a gigantic model of the solar system.[14]

The Solarians owe part of their contentment to their simple and egalitarian lifestyle. They own all goods in common; everyone works, resulting in a workday of only four hours; and there is no extreme poverty or excessive wealth. But they also benefit from their knowledge and command of the natural world. The priests look to the sky to divine useful information about the future, to calculate the proper days for sowing, reaping, and gathering the crops, and—more startlingly—to determine the best hours for breeding both animals and humans, for the Solarians are devoted eugenicists. In general, the Solarians display a remarkable appreciation for the interconnectedness of human and nonhuman nature, believing that "the earth is a great beast, and we live within it as worms live within us."[15] Campanella introduces advanced technologies only in passing, mentioning that the Solarians have learned to sail without wind or oar and to fly, and that they are developing telescopes and a device with which to hear the music of the celestial spheres. His main focus is on harmonizing the human world with the natural one and, by extension, with the rhythms of the divine.

In 1619, seventeen years after Campanella finished *The City of the Sun*, a German theologian and teacher named Johann Valentin Andreae published a utopian work that found a different way to integrate natural knowledge into society. *Christianopolis* describes a city of the same name populated by devout believers and situated on a remote island of unknown location. Andreae had read More's *Utopia* and Campanella's *City of the Sun*, and he drew inspiration from both. But his utopian vision also reflected his desire to establish a fraternity of Christians to safeguard knowledge about the natural and spiritual worlds and to restore social stability during a period of intense religious conflict in Europe. As a result, his utopia describes a Christian community that is dedicated to the pursuit of both environmental knowledge and social stability.[16]

Since Andreae believed that the key to social harmony was economic

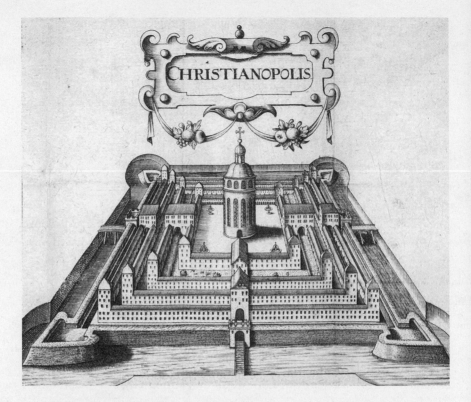

The residents of the fictional Christianopolis, seen here in an illustration
from Johann Valentin Andreae's book of the same name, used their increasing
environmental knowledge to improve living conditions in a society with a
stable population. (Courtesy of the Getty Research Institute)

equality and a simple existence, he imagined an almost monastic lifestyle
for the residents of Christianopolis. They wear modest garments of white
or gray, worship three times a day, live in small, unpretentious quarters, and
find leisure in quiet contemplation, although they are able to marry. The
focus of daily life is work, study of the natural world, and religious practice.
As in Campanella's City of the Sun, every citizen works, meaning that less
work is required of each individual. The city itself is square—a shape that
implied stability to the Renaissance mind—and a lavish public infrastructure that includes a council hall and temple filled with artwork and a well-
decorated college cloister supports the residents' simple private lives. The
environment surrounding the city feels just as secure, with a mixture of

open pastures, sown fields, and wild areas that remain unthreatened by other uses. The residents, according to the narrator, "have always managed by good fortune to maintain their community in a stable form, unchanging in all respects."[17]

The only thing that they do expect to expand is their knowledge about nature. Much of the city is dedicated to environmental research and to figuring out how to apply new discoveries to the Christian goal of improving human life. The community contains a striking number of laboratories with related departments of education. In the metal lab, residents closely examine everything they find in the ground, while elsewhere they study mathematics, natural science, anatomy, and other subjects. Unlike Campanella's Solarians, the residents of Christianopolis do not align their lives with astrological rhythms. Nor do they leave environmental research to the priests. Instead, they engage in it directly themselves and set skilled craftsmen to work implementing their new knowledge, making the city seem like "one single workshop, albeit with all sorts of different crafts in it."[18] The mechanical improvements that result, however, go unmentioned for the most part, and there is no evidence of futuristic technologies such as flight. Andreae believed that there were limits to human knowledge.

In 1624, a few years after Andreae's work appeared, Francis Bacon published the third and last major scientific utopia of the seventeenth century, *New Atlantis*. Bacon was a politician rather than a clergyman and one of the leading voices of the Scientific Revolution. It is not known whether he was familiar with the utopias written by Campanella and Andreae. But his turned out to be far more influential, going through multiple editions and serving as one of the primary inspirations for a very early and important research association, the Royal Society of London. The book has been a cultural touchstone ever since it first appeared in print. In 1939, the futurist and fiction writer H. G. Wells acknowledged its far-reaching impact when he wrote that Bacon's utopia "has produced more in the way of real consequences than any other Utopia that was ever written," including his own.[19]

Bacon never finished *New Atlantis,* but the focus of his ideal society is clear and occupies about a third of the book: a government-funded research institute "dedicated to the study of the works and creatures of God." Such organizations did not exist in Bacon's Europe, but it was the "very eye" and "lantern" of Bensalem, an imaginary island located somewhere in the Pacific. Founded almost two thousand years before the story begins, the institute houses a corps of natural philosophers or "fellows" who scour foreign lands for new knowledge, conduct experiments, and develop new technologies. Those who synthesize findings into useful generalizations are called "interpreters of Nature." The fellows have absolute control over what is done with the environmental knowledge they assemble, keeping even from their government sponsors any knowledge that they do not yet wish to release. Bacon originated the dictum that knowledge is power and entrusted them both to the fellows of his imaginary research institute.[20]

A large amount of the fellows' energy goes into devising ways to imitate nature. This would not have seemed unusual to a seventeenth-century reader, since it was widely believed that the best art could do was to produce an echo of God's creation. Renaissance-era magicians might imitate the sound of thunder with a small rocket, or cause it to snow by launching quills into the air and watching them waft slowly to the ground. But Bacon's natural philosophers produce the real thing. They create artificial metals by storing certain materials underground for years and then mining them; they build engines that can make wind; they construct special buildings where they can recreate weather patterns, colors, sounds, and smells; and they have machines that enable them to fly through the air like birds or swim beneath the water like fish. The fellows see themselves as doing the same work that God did. They are essentially recreating the creation.[21]

Bacon's fellows, however, do not stop at mere imitation. They find new applications for God's creations and even invent more useful versions of them. The fellows use deep caves and high towers on mountaintops for refrigeration, manufacture improved soil to increase agricultural yield, and create special bath waters and chambers with regulated air to improve health. Through their arts, they can force plants to grow faster and earlier in the season, make their fruit taste, smell, and look different, and even transform them into other plants. Animals are kept for experimentation and dissection, and the fellows have learned to manipulate their size, color, shape, and the number of offspring they produce. They have manufactured new kinds of food that promote health, including a drink made from meat that serves the purposes of both beverage and solid food and is often preferred by the elderly. The list of their abilities goes on at some length and even includes the making of entirely new plants and animals, a risky claim for Bacon to make at a time when Christians insisted that no plant or animal could exist that God had not made himself.[22]

Bacon's fellows are far more aggressive in their efforts to crack nature's code than Campanella's priests and Andreae's researchers, mostly because their ultimate goal is different. They seek not mere integration with God and nature, or the straightforward use of nature for human benefit, but such complete mastery of it that they can remake God's creation and even improve on it. The value of human intellectual abilities is maximized, the complexity and interrelatedness of the natural world minimized, and social, environmental, and even spiritual risks left unexamined. The book's most famous line not only sums up this ambitious spirit but would later become a slogan of sorts for scientists. "The end of our foundation," explains one of the natural philosophers, "is the knowledge of causes, and the secret motions of things; and the enlarging of the bounds of human empire, to the effecting of all things possible."[23]

Still, none of these utopias envisioned their societies growing in anything but natural knowledge and its practical applications. The City of the Sun and Christianopolis are utopias of sufficiency not because their residents are unable to produce more but because they have chosen to consume less. They plant only enough ground to satisfy their own needs, fabricate all of their own manufactured goods, and have little use for trade. Residents work less than their real-world counterparts and maintain simple material lives. Stable populations are essential to both. Even in Bensalem, there is nothing to indicate an ethic of growth besides a ceremony that honors elderly residents who have produced a large number of descendants. But all three utopias, especially Bacon's, were laying the foundation for a culture of scientific and technological innovation that Westerners would soon come to regard as the engine of growth.[24]

Some contemporary thinkers were less confident than Campanella, Andreae, and Bacon about the transformative potential of environmental knowledge. Bishop Joseph Hall's *The Discovery of a New World,* written in the first decade of the seventeenth century, describes a land called "Fooliana" where "Foolosophers" shave their heads to bring their brains closer to heaven and waste their time with useless experiments rather than devoting themselves to traditional Christian virtues. The people in Samuel Gott's *New Jerusalem* from 1648 do engage in worthwhile research, but Gott's narrator warns that the penetration of some natural mysteries is "beyond man's power; they lie too deep; the labour is too great." He also reminds his readers that the end of such study should not be knowledge and fame alone but the glory of God. Both writers feared the lesson of the biblical fall: that the unthinking pursuit of knowledge—reaching for the forbidden fruit—could lead to greater estrangement from things divine.[25]

Campanella, Andreae, and Bacon seem largely unconcerned with such warnings. Viewed through modern eyes, their utopias are remarkable not just for the absence of growth but also for a lack of awareness that scientific and technological progress have their dark sides. There is no unease about the moral implications of certain lines of research, no recognition that machines might have negative impacts on environment and society, no worries about the possible weaponization of scientific discoveries. Bacon alone seemed aware that such power could be misused, yet he remained confident that "sound reason and true religion" would rule the day. Their utopias only foresaw endless and unqualified benefits from the pursuit of natural knowledge. In that way, they would prove to be poor prophets.[26]

## Progress and Growth

In the next century, the idea of progress moved to center stage. Long an important idea in Western culture, progress became the dominant idea, imparting a sense of inevitability to scientific and environmental ambitions and to newfound Enlightenment goals like the perfection of human society through liberty and social justice. The idea of progress also became more secular and environmentally oriented, less about the will of God and more a historical process transforming the relationship between humans and nature on a global scale. With the idea of progress as their guide, historians writing during this period reimagined power over nature as the bedrock on which humans built civilization and redefined a society's relative level of civilization as the extent to which it was able to control the natural world.

Most importantly, the idea of progress became increasingly entwined with expectations of human expansion.[27]

This intellectual shift took place in the context of unprecedented economic growth in Western Europe. Wherever one looked, everything seemed to be expanding—population, agriculture, industry, transportation, commerce, mining—and each area of growth stimulated the others. Over the course of the eighteenth century, the population of Europe increased by fifty percent and the population of London doubled to almost a million people. Agricultural and industrial output swelled, in part with the help of a boom in canal construction and mostly without the mechanization that would come in the next century. Far-flung colonies provided new edible plants and raw materials to feed growing populations and industries, and trade and exchange were everywhere. Europe's experience was part of a worldwide pattern of growth, but thanks in part to its economic reach and the natural resources it gained from overseas colonies, Europe was the world's boomtown.[28]

New scientific knowledge and useful inventions continued to multiply and spread. Philosophers made advances in mathematics, chemistry, biology, and astronomy, and a method for vaccinating against smallpox reached Europe from the Ottoman Empire. Inventions like the seed drill helped to increase agricultural production, while innovations in weaving technology— the flying shuttle, the spinning jenny, the water frame, the spinning mule— dramatically increased textile production and paved the way for the industrial revolution. As the pace of change accelerated, ever larger slices of the population felt its effect.

The most astounding invention of the century, and perhaps the one with the greatest impact on visions of the future, was the balloon. In November 1783, the Montgolfier brothers launched the first manned, untethered flight of a hot air balloon on the outskirts of Paris, with the two passengers landing safely twenty-five minutes later. The new technology caused a psychological jolt that can be hard to imagine today, when balloons are regarded mostly as toys for children. But the Western world stood transfixed when balloons began going up over Paris, and confidence in science and its potential to alter the human relationship with the natural world soared with them.

Beginning in the late eighteenth century, balloon
flight became a symbol of humankind's conquest of
the skies. This engraving from 1788 shows Apollo,
god of the sun, crowning the pilots of the first
manned hydrogen balloon with laurel wreaths.
(Courtesy of the Library of Congress)

Although the practical implications were immediately apparent—Thomas
Jefferson foresaw the ability to cross deserts, mountains, and hostile territory, and even to reach the pole—it was their symbolic value that was most
important: human ingenuity had conquered the skies.[29]

The first to fit all of this change into a coherent ideology of progress was
the French economist Anne-Robert-Jacques Turgot, who published a brief
history of humankind in 1750. Turgot presented human history as a story
of progress, particularly in science and invention, and used that history to

predict more progress to come. He hailed a long list of innovations that set the modern world apart from the ancients, including "musical notation, our bills of exchange, our paper, window glass, plate glass, windmills, clocks, spectacles" and more. All of these, he explained, represented nothing more than human use of the natural world, for "the practice of the arts is a succession of physical experiments which progressively unveil nature." Turgot situated this unveiling as the very engine of human history and the key to the human future. It was no coincidence that Turgot, the first to articulate progress as a worldview, was also the first thinker in the modern period to promote economic growth.[30]

Later in the century, the noted mathematician and philosopher Nicolas de Condorcet expanded on Turgot's idea that humans shared a single past and a single globe-spanning future. In his *Picture of the Progress of the Human Mind*, published posthumously in 1795, Condorcet organized the human pageant into ten stages of progress that ranged from hunter-gatherer societies through the present and into the future. According to Condorcet, tomorrow would bring a world of free and well-educated peoples, governed by reason and no longer interested in colonizing their neighbors. Scientific advancements would make agriculture and industry more productive and improve human health to the extent that human lifespans would be without limit. Condorcet did ask whether, in a far-off day, the human population might outgrow its resources and bring an end to progress. But he believed that the advance of reason and the demise of superstition would somehow change sexual habits and prevent disaster. For Condorcet, the only obstacle to progress and growth was the duration of the universe itself.[31]

The English journalist and philosopher William Godwin also imagined progress toward a world-spanning human society, although he organized his vision of the future around the principles of anarchism. In his *Enquiry Concerning Political Justice*, first published in 1793, Godwin expressed complete faith in progress. "As improvements have long continued to be incessant," he wrote, "so there is no chance but that they will go on. The most penetrating philosophy cannot prescribe limits to them, nor the most ardent imagination adequately fill up the prospect." Godwin believed that institutions like property, marriage, and monarchy were standing in the way of human happiness but that they would, once people began applying reason to their lives, simply melt away. In the meantime, humans would develop the three quarters of the globe that remained uncultivated and extend their lifespans "beyond any limits which we are able to assign." Like Condorcet, Godwin reluctantly admitted that the earth is finite in size. But he believed that humans in the far future would grow more virtuous, become less interested in "the gratification of the senses," and perhaps stop propagating entirely.[32]

The connection between progress and growth became particularly strong in British America, where the primary occupation of the colonists was extending the frontier westward and developing the lands taken from native peoples. Migrating to thinly settled areas, founding new towns, breaking virgin ground, increasing the population: all were interpreted as signs of progress. The American Joel Barlow, who had extensive diplomatic experience in Europe and Africa, used an epic poem to portray the conclusion of such activities as a completely developed earth. Science was still at the center of such visions, as it had been in the work of the scientific utopians. But the idea of progress had transformed ambitions from simply controlling nature to transforming it for human use on a planetary scale. Accordingly, Barlow foresaw humankind not only gaining the power to walk under water, fly through the air, and make rain as needed—dreams that now went back for several generations—but also turning deserts into gardens, cultivating mountains up to their very peaks, and increasing agricultural production by a factor of ten.[33]

Not everyone was comfortable with the rapid pace of development and increasing dependence on machines that these visions implied. Those drawn to a smaller and simpler existence often looked to the native peoples of Africa and the Americas for models, although Enlightenment philosophers were of two minds about them. Sometimes philosophers derided them as degenerate savages and sometimes celebrated them as noble children of nature. In 1789, the Scottish writer William Thomson chose the latter approach and published a utopia set in central Abyssinia. There his narrator encounters the Mammuthians, a giant people that have developed advanced science but prefer a low level of technology. "They make it a rule," explains the narrator, "never to multiply mechanical invention where the purpose can be served by any of the simple contrivances or productions of nature."

As a result, they build their homes in trees, which they consider far more beautiful "than the proudest pillars." But few eighteenth-century thinkers would really have traded the benefits of European civilization for a return to the trees. The drumbeat of progress was hard to ignore, and it was leading in a different direction.[34]

By the end of the eighteenth century, the idea of progress was altering how people viewed time itself. Previous generations had embraced a cyclical understanding of history, in which prosperity ebbed and flowed, states expanded and contracted, and dynasties rose and fell. Such cycles would come to an end only with the Last Judgment. But the idea of progress replaced that circle with a line. Literate Westerners were coming to understand history as a story that began with people who were less advanced in their social thought and ability to control the natural world, and would end with people who were so advanced that they had achieved utopia. The Last Judgment might still come, but rather than walking in circles until then, humankind would be traveling a linear path to perfection that included using the power of science and technology to expand to all corners of the globe.[35]

## Debating Global Limits

The emphasis on progress and growth soon prompted two obvious but weighty questions: were there limits to growth on a finite planet, and if so, how might an end to growth affect progress? Condorcet and Godwin had anticipated these concerns and must have recognized that the stakes were high, because if progress and growth went hand-in-hand, then an end to growth might mean an end to progress. But their responses—that the problem would not present itself for many generations, and that future humans would become enlightened enough to find a solution for themselves—had dodged the issue by kicking it down the road. Other thinkers would soon tackle it more directly. Not long after the publication of Godwin's book, and in part because of it, the first serious debate about global environmental limits began.

The process of expansion, especially at the expense of forests, was already revealing environmental limits on local and national scales. Increases in population and economic activity in Europe had led to a serious decline in woodlands over the course of the eighteenth century, prompting the establishment of scientific forestry practices in France and the German states. Outside of Europe, rapid deforestation on colonized islands in the Caribbean Sea and the Atlantic and Indian Oceans had visibly altered hydrological systems, species compositions, and even climates. Both sets of changes kindled conversations about the need for more sustainable forestry practices. European naturalists also noticed that, despite nature's incredible fruitfulness, environmental checks on the advancement of individual species seemed to exist everywhere. No plant or animal anywhere in the world had a boundless range or infinite numbers.[36]

The first to put the pieces together and claim the existence of global environmental limits to human expansion was Robert Wallace, a Presbyterian minister in the Church of Scotland. Wallace argued in 1761 that the earth and its resources were ultimately finite in size and that, as a result, the human population would be too. "There are certain primary determinations in nature," he claimed, "to which all other things of a subordinate kind must be adjusted." One of those primary determinations was the fact that the earth was only so big.[37]

Wallace was particularly interested in how earth's limited size would affect the quest for utopia. His conclusion was grim. The existence of limits, Wallace argued, would ensure that the perfect government for which so many pined would unintentionally plant the seeds of its own destruction. Such a government, being perfect, would give its citizens the right to have as many children as they wanted. But as the population grew, humankind would eventually reach the limits of the earth's resources and space. Even if the earth could be made more fertile, or if someone invented an entirely new way to provide food, there still would not be room for an infinite number of humans unless the earth were "continually enlarging in bulk, as an animal or vegetable body." The world could be made a paradise, but only until "there was no longer any room for new colonies, and when the earth could produce no further supplies." Then, to avoid catastrophe, the perfect government would have to resort to inhuman measures to curb further population growth—restraints on marriage, the cloistering of women, the castration of men, the slaying of infants, the execution of all those over a certain age—that would themselves lead to war and the end of the perfect government. Mankind, he wrote, would be "reduced to the same calamitous condition as at present." In the end, the limits of the earth would ensure that utopia became dystopia.[38]

But the real debate over limits did not begin until over thirty years later, when the claims of Condorcet and Godwin attracted the attention of Thomas Malthus. An English cleric and professor of political economy, Malthus published a book in 1798 titled *An Essay on the Principle of Population* that set forth one of the most influential and controversial visions of the future ever articulated. While Malthus agreed with Wallace that nature places checks on the growth of plants, animals, and people, he disagreed that population pressure would only become a problem when the whole world was fully developed and incapable of producing more food. Instead, Malthus saw population and the food supply as constantly in tension with each other. He reasoned that unchecked population always multiplied faster than food production, and with predictable results. When a society had more food than it needed, population inevitably increased to match the supply; when it had less food than needed, famine, disease, and misery brought the population back in check. For Malthus, this never-ending oscillation between abundance and scarcity was an unavoidable law of nature.[39]

Malthus's argument presented a serious challenge to the idea of progress. It was impossible, he concluded, for any society to permanently achieve a state where all members could "live in ease, happiness, and comparative leisure; and feel no anxiety about providing the means of subsistence for themselves and families." Malthus would soften his position in subsequent editions of the book, embracing, for example, the possibility that prosperity might encourage the working classes to have smaller families like those of the middle classes. But he remained convinced that "a careful distinction should be made, between an unlimited progress, and a progress where the limit is merely undefined."[40]

For Malthus, Condorcet and Godwin's faith that humans could overcome a natural law was misguided. He considered it a flight of fancy unsupported by human experience but very much typical of the time. "The present rage for wide and unrestrained speculation," he wrote, "seems to be a kind of mental intoxication, arising, perhaps, from the great and unexpected discoveries which have been made of late years, in various branches of science. To men elate, and giddy with such successes, every thing appeared to be within the grasp of human powers." Malthus, in contrast, believed that some things lay outside of human powers and always would. Godwin's imagined utopia would therefore be destined to failure, since population pressure would force it right back into a state of misery, and not in a distant future but a near one. "I see no way," Malthus wrote, "by which man can escape from the weight of this law which pervades all animated nature."[41]

Malthus recognized the potential tension between his natural law and the biblical dictate to "be fruitful and multiply and fill the earth and subdue it." Like many Christians, he trusted that God would not have issued such a commandment without providing humans with the resources necessary to fulfill it. But Malthus saw no contradiction between natural law and biblical law. God had not made food as plentiful as air and water because he knew that doing so, on a finite earth, would drive the human population to impossibly large levels with unhappy results. Malthus found it difficult to imagine a divine gift that would have been "more likely to plunge the human race in irrecoverable misery, than an unlimited facility of producing food in a limited space." So, while God intended humans to be fruitful and multiply, he expected them to do so within the confines of the natural systems he had created.[42]

Godwin hit back hard against Malthus's ideas, although their positions were closer than they might have seemed. Malthus did believe in human progress, though he saw it as an uneven process. A closer study of history, he claimed, would show that civilization had experienced not just improvement but backsliding as well. He also shared the hope that human virtue would increase with scientific knowledge, if probably at a slower pace. And both believed, like most of their contemporaries, that human actions—far from causing environmental problems—improved the earth by turning a wilderness into a garden. They differed significantly, however, on what the end point of human expansion would look like. Godwin imagined the earth "all cultivated, all improved, all variegated with a multitude of human beings." Malthus believed that an all-consuming effort to maximize food production in order to stay ahead of population increases would also mean a world with no animals, no private property, and a population subsisting on nothing but potatoes.[43]

Malthus did not introduce anything approaching a modern environmental ethic into visions of the future. Nor did he make a comprehensive statement about environmental limits. But he did place humans firmly within nature, making them subject to natural laws just like other species. Rather than accepting the sometimes overheated claims made by the prophets of progress that painted future humans as virtuous gods wielding complete knowledge and command of natural forces, Malthus countered that humans would need to take environmental factors into consideration when building a better world. No scientific discovery, technological invention, institutional change, social reform, or revolution in human behavior would change that. Humans could never overcome natural laws, meaning that material progress faced environmental limits. This single claim, controversial from the day it first appeared in print, has shaped discussions of the future ever since.

## Narratives of Growth

Conversations about the environmental impact of science, technology, progress, and growth would reach a far larger audience once they were transformed into stories. That began to happen in the last quarter of the eighteenth century and the first years of the next, when the development and disaster narratives that we know so well today began to emerge in France. Their germination is worth exploring in some detail, for the earliest sprouts of these narratives reveal the outline of later themes and highlight the transition to more growth-oriented visions of tomorrow.

The development narrative first appeared in Louis-Sébastien Mercier's best-selling book *The Year 2440,* published in 1771. Mercier, a prodigious writer of plays and other works, has his Parisian narrator awaken unexpectedly seven hundred years in the future. Now an old man, the narrator is astonished to find a clean and enlightened city where social justice prevails. Its people enjoy liberty, political equality, and free education, and have shed the burdens of formal religion and standing armies. Although rich and poor

In this illustration from Louis-Sébastien Mercier's book
*The Year 2440*, the narrator learns from the date on a
pamphlet that he has slept for seven hundred years.
(Courtesy of the John Carter Brown Library)

still exist, a generous wealthy class freely shares with their less fortunate
neighbors. The book was the first utopia ever to be set in the distant future
rather than a secluded geographical spot in the present, making it a land-
mark contribution to Western visions of the future and Western literature
more broadly.[44]

Mercier drew heavily on Francis Bacon's vision of a society dedicated to science and the control of the natural world. Like Bensalem, Mercier's future Paris has an active research institute that has developed a host of remarkable innovations. Its members have doubled the size of some animals through interbreeding, exterminated the plague, invented an optical cabinet that shows scenes composed entirely of light, and created a wide variety of machines that increase the human ability to move large objects and generate power. They have even recovered lost knowledge from the past, like the engineering and embalming methods developed by the ancient Egyptians. The institute's goal is strongly reminiscent of Bacon's. "Our end is to know the secret causes of each appearance," a resident tells the narrator, "and to extend the dominion of man, by providing him with the means of executing all those labours that can aggrandize his existence."[45]

Also like Bensalem, Mercier's future France does not seek expansion abroad. Mercier believed that overseas colonies served only to oppress foreign peoples and that international trade simply enriched some at the expense of others. So his utopia has no colonies and focuses its economic energies on the domestic front. Its residents do, however, keep track of world events and—again like Bensalem—venture abroad to learn of new discoveries that might be of use to their people. They enjoy a degree of isolation from the rest of the world, although less than the scientific utopias of the seventeenth century.[46]

But Mercier's society reflects more contemporary thought in at least two key ways. First, Mercier became the first in a long line of future fiction writers to assume that science and technology—particularly in their ability to connect people through transportation, communication, and the shared language of science—would foster cooperation and peace on a global scale. This had already become a common theme in the writings of Turgot, Condorcet, and other Enlightenment thinkers. Mercier's characters explain that, by allowing freer communication between peoples, the printing press has ushered in a revolution of good feelings among nations. Scientific exchanges have helped as well by ensuring that "the opinions of one man have become those of the universe." Thanks to such advances, all of the world's nations are at peace, concentrating on running good governments rather than trying to control each other. Enlightenment reason, combined with science, has made brothers of all men.[47]

Second, Mercier's future France displays a newfound emphasis on growth and environmental change. Despite turning its back on colonial expansion and international trade, it has doubled the size of its population. Mercier, like other eighteenth-century thinkers, had come to see population growth as the sign of a healthy society, and since not just France but the entire world was flourishing in his story, he reported that the populations of London and Russia had tripled. He also notes that canals, the cutting-edge transportation technology of the day, crisscross France and even provide a direct transportation route from the North Sea to the Mediterranean. Mercier's future France was bigger, busier, and more intensively developed than the one that the author's readers lived in.[48]

When Mercier revised his book for a second edition fifteen years later, in 1786, growth and environmental conquest became even larger themes. Setting aside his previous rejection of trade and colonies for a desire to see France civilize the world, Mercier now described a future where his native country has extended itself around the globe through ocean-going commerce. Its wines and manufactured goods are particularly popular on the international market. The country also controls Egypt, Greece, several ports in India, a number of islands, and large swaths of Africa, which the French presence has transformed. Not only have the French installed enlightened governments in Africa, but they have changed the face of the countryside by widely disseminating European plants and animals. European trees now grow alongside native African ones, producing a high and dense forest cover that has successfully cooled the climate, while herds of European horses, oxen, and sheep thrive in the shaded pastures beneath the canopy. In Mercier's revised version of the future, the French have remade Africa's environment in the image of France.[49]

The passing references to canals in the first edition became an entire chapter on their importance and impact. Canals have dramatically expanded communication, commerce, and the amount of irrigable land, ensuring that there are "no more deserts within France, or miserable people on impoverished soil." Mercier believed strongly that all lands everywhere should be cultivated and attacked private country parks as wasted space. Reserved for special praise is a canal linking the Nile River to the Gulf of Arabia, since it has enabled the colony of Egypt to capture the combined trade of Europe,

India, and Africa. All of this, notes Mercier's spokesperson from the future, had been achieved through innovation in the mechanical arts. "We love these bold works," he gushes, "and, at the same time, honor the engineers because we see them as the authors of excellence whose inventions enabled a great and useful conquest of nature."[50]

Inspired by the balloons that had floated over Paris just three years before—Mercier himself had seen the first manned flight—he also added a chapter on international airship travel. The chapter opens with eight Chinese voyagers arriving in Paris by airship after an eight-day journey from Peking. "Looking up," reports the astonished narrator, "I saw an immense machine advancing at full sail at a prodigious height above the city." Such sites still excite the future Parisians as well, for the fact that humans "had conquered in its entirety the regions of the atmosphere" had not yet lost its power to amaze.[51]

Where Mercier's *The Year 2440* successfully introduced the development narrative, Cousin de Grainville's *The Last Man* articulated its disastrous counterpart. A teacher, author, and former priest, Grainville began writing his story in the same year that Malthus's *Essay* appeared. But as pessimistic as some found Malthus's work to be, *The Last Man,* published posthumously in 1805, proved a much darker work by several shades. Like some of his contemporaries, Grainville had fervently believed that the French Revolution was going to bring on the Christian millennium. Instead, it dissolved into unspeakable violence, and Grainville himself was imprisoned and nearly executed. *The Last Man* reflects his disappointment and loss of faith as well as a thorough knowledge of Milton's *Paradise Lost* and the Book of Revelation. From these influences, Grainville created something new and terrifying: the first fictional account of the end of humankind. Although his ideas about human population growth echoed those of Wallace and Malthus, he viewed environmental limits as part of God's plan for the end times.[52]

In Grainville's telling, the environmental apocalypse that ends human history has its origins in a divinely ordained link between the fates of humankind and the earth itself. God had decreed at the beginning of time that the earth would last only as long as humans were able to reproduce. Since then, humankind had used its ever growing knowledge and command of natural forces to spread around the globe, raise civilization to new heights, and transform the earth into a second Eden. But after humans had spent a few centuries at this pinnacle, the earth entered a pre-ordained period of old age inspired by the ancient theory of senescence, which held that the natural world would begin to decline just as people do. Soil fertility decreased, fields produced little but brambles, and wars erupted over ever scarcer resources.[53]

In a desperate attempt to save the natural environment on which they depended, humans drew on their immense scientific and technical knowledge to remake the earth. They revitalized exhausted soils, defrosted lands previously covered by ice, and rerouted major rivers like the Rhône and Ganges to cultivate the rich soils of their beds. When this proved insufficient, humans pooled their efforts in the greatest engineering endeavor of all time: to push back the oceans themselves in order to farm the seabeds. Engineers used powerful explosives to excavate huge channels and vast basins and developed moveable seawalls to help contain the water. But they never finished the project, for the sun began to cool, and human fertility—like that of the earth—began to decline. The inhabitants of northern lands fled south, and by the time portrayed in the book, the last organized remnants of human society are strung along the newly temperate coastline running from Mexico to South America. Most of the story is concerned with whether humankind, and the earth itself, can get second leases on life. Ultimately they cannot, and judgment day arrives.

Grainville makes clear throughout that, although the decline of earth is part of God's plan, humans have accelerated the process. One character claims of the human race that "their desires were never satisfied" and that, "by taking too much from nature, they have been spendthrifts with their power and have squandered their inheritance." Another recalls a time "when a thousand different species of flowers were in bloom" and criticizes ancestors who "had often looked on such good things with indifference" and "were often criminal in the use they made of them." When the fleeing northerners founded their South American colonies on virgin lands, they "cut down forests as old as creation" and "cultivated the mountains to the very peaks until they had exhausted happy fertile land," leaving fish as the only remaining food supply. In Grainville's future, the insatiable desires of humankind contribute heavily to the early exhaustion of the earth.[54]

The story displays a keen understanding of human dependency on the natural world and an outlook on the endpoint of human population growth similar to that of Robert Wallace. When Philantor, the greatest natural philosopher in human history, discovers the secret of immortality, he refrains from sharing it broadly when he realizes the environmental implications. "He acknowledged," reports one of the characters, "that the almighty had set the term of human life in accordance with the size of the earth and the fecundity of its inhabitants," and that "if men prolonged their youth, the earth would not be capable of supporting their too numerous descendants who would fight to the death for living space." Too many people making too many demands on the natural world would inevitably bump up against environmental limits. Like Malthus, Grainville insisted that God had planned it that way.[55]

In such a light, death appears to be more gift than curse. Toward the end of the story, the Spirit of the Earth, deep in an underground laboratory filled with scientific instruments, fights desperately to keep the world limping along a bit longer. His only hope is to coax children from the last two fertile humans on earth. Angry and losing hope, he turns to Death, now standing at his elbow, and criticizes him for the damage he has wrought on humankind throughout the ages. But Death will have none of it. "Had I not saved earth from an over abundance of children," he claims, "they would have exhausted all her resources. . . . Had it not been for me, the end of the world which you dread would have happened long ago." Death's work had paradoxically delayed the coming apocalypse, while humans had hastened it. In Grainville's future, it is human beings—through their excessive numbers and profligate resource use—that bring about the end of all things.[56]

Grainville's *The Last Man*, while appreciated by critics, was not widely read, and his theme of human-induced environmental apocalypse had little influence on other contemporary tales of the future. The theme's presence is significant because it reflects early anxieties about the long-term consequences of human progress and expansion and highlights the transition from viewing the end of the world as a wholly religious event to imagining it as a secular one. Scholars also credit the book with having introduced the "last man" theme into literature and art. That theme subsequently appeared in works such as Lord Byron's poem "Darkness" from 1816, in which an individual watches civilization collapse as the fading of the sun freezes the earth, and Mary Shelley's novel *The Last Man* from 1822, which portrays a future world so wracked by plague that only a single character remains alive by the end of the story. But Grainville's idea that humans might contribute to a world-ending environmental disaster themselves would lie dormant for a time.[57]

Mercier's book, in contrast, played a large role in spreading the much more attractive development narrative across the West. It went through countless print runs, was translated into Dutch, English, German, and Italian, and found readers throughout Europe and across the Atlantic, where both George Washington and Thomas Jefferson had copies on their shelves. In fact, *The Year 2440* became one of the most widely read books of the eighteenth century, with an estimated sixty-three thousand copies in print by the time of the author's death in 1814. The book also inspired a wave of futuristic fiction in France, Germany, Denmark, and the Netherlands that clearly showed the influence of Mercier's work. *The Year 2440* had tapped into a growing curiosity about what tomorrow would bring and an expectation that science, technology, and growth would pave the way to utopia. By translating that curiosity and expectation into a successful narrative, it gave concrete shape to the West's increasingly progress- and growth-steeped dreams.[58]

# 2

# Industrializing the Plot

DESPITE MERCIER'S ENTHUSIASTIC EMBRACE of technology and growth, his future world contained few machines. Less than half a century later, however, machines would become so central to the imagined future that no vision of tomorrow was credible without them. The author Jane Webb displayed a keen appreciation for that fact in a popular work of fiction that she published in 1827. Her story, set in twenty-second-century Egypt, described the Nile valley as a place where "steamboats glided down the canals, and furnaces raised their smoky heads amidst groves of palmtrees; whilst iron railways intersected orange groves, and plantations of dates and pomegranates might be seen bordering excavations intended for coal pits." In Webb's future Egypt, as in so many other visions of tomorrow produced in the first half of the nineteenth century, machines provided the muscle for developing the natural environment at a fantastic pace and on a global scale.[1]

The catalyst for this transformation was the industrial revolution. Beginning in Great Britain in the late eighteenth century, the West experienced a gradual transition from hand production to mechanization and from renewable sources of energy like wood, wind, and water to nonrenewable coal. Industrialization happened differently in different places, but the general result was that production increased, costs declined, markets expanded, consumption rose, populations boomed, and cities swelled. By mid-century, much of the West was experiencing an unprecedented level of economic growth, and for the first time in human history technological change was

driving the world economy. Industrial capitalism also brought a host of social, economic, and environmental dislocations—increasing disparities in
wealth, urban slums, the deskilling of labor, the formation of antagonistic
classes, industrial pollution, environmental degradation. But many expected
that the rising tide would eventually lift all boats and wring universal and
permanent abundance from a plentiful earth.[2]

The development narrative crystallized during this period, transforming
from a vague sense of environmental mastery to more specific visions of
reshaping an infinitely malleable and abundant natural world. By the 1820s,
forecasts of population growth, human expansion, and dramatic alterations
to the earth's surface and climate had become common in the most economically advanced nations. The sense of rapid progress, according to a
contemporary, extended "down even to the wholly uneducated classes." In
the following decade, future fiction emerged as a small but recognizable
literary genre capable of bringing the future to life for an ever wider audience. Although the first half of the century also saw criticisms of growth
begin to emerge, the world still felt too large for a fully developed narrative
of global environmental disaster to coalesce. As a result, with mechanical
wonders promising unlimited plenty from a seemingly boundless earth,
eighteenth-century fantasies of growth and progress became nineteenth-
century expectations.[3]

## The Mechanical Path to Abundance

The futuristic fiction of the early nineteenth century overflowed with mechanical inventions. Airships carrying thousands of passengers dominate
the skies; steamships, sometimes with additional pull from giant kites, turn
the oceans into lakes; trains traveling hundreds of miles an hour defeat
time. Machines dry hay faster, bore deeper tunnels, and shield cities from
inclement weather. The more machines, the more futuristic the story felt.
Jane Webb's book was so packed with imaginative innovations in science
and technology that the famous English landscape architect J. C. Loudon
went out of his way to meet the author, assuming it was a man. They were
married later that year.[4]

Authors did not include fantastic machines in their tales of tomorrow just for their novelty value. The machines demonstrated human control of the natural world, something writers did not hesitate to point out. "So many new inventions had been struck out," wrote Webb of her future England, "so many wonderful discoveries made, and so many ingenious contrivances put into execution, that poor Nature seemed to be degraded from her throne, and usurping man to have stepped up to supply her place." The fiction of the future was in general agreement that machines would transform dreams of growth and progress into reality.[5]

Most of those contemplating the future saw particular potential in steam, which was the most transformative technology of the day. Steam's power to remold the material world and fuel expansion appeared to be boundless. When the great French scientist François Arago delivered an address to commemorate James Watt, who made important refinements to the steam engine, he foresaw a future liberated from the bonds of nature through steam. With such power at its command, he claimed, humankind could bring more land under cultivation, grow more food, increase its population, expand its cities, and cover the earth with elegant mansions, even those parts previously considered uninhabitable. Future generations, Arago assured his listeners, would remember this time as the Age of Watt.[6]

Possible applications for steam multiplied so quickly that, as early as the 1820s, parodies of future steam technologies began to appear. One future world sped up the delivery of mail by using steam-powered cannons to shoot it from town to town. Another featured a "steam concert" in which the performers were steam-powered machines that achieved greater technical accuracy than their human counterparts, and without being subject to "colds, loss of voice, and bronchitis." Still another contained a ballroom that enabled guests to dance a quadrille without the trouble of having to move their feet: they simply stood on circles set into the floor (blue for the gentlemen, pink for the ladies) while the steam-powered circles moved them around in the necessary pattern.[7]

British illustrators joined in, projecting the cutting-edge technologies of the day into comical futures. Henry Alken's images show the roads and parks of London crowded with a dizzying variety of fast-moving steam-powered vehicles that fill the air with smoke and occasionally run out of control or explode. Charles Jameson Grant's image of the year 2000 depicts a long

CONCERT A LA VAPEUR.

In J. J. Grandville's drawing of a "steam concert,"
which he included in his book *Another World* (1844),
a human hand turns on the steam in the lower left
corner of the image and technology does the rest.
(Courtesy of the Getty Research Institute)

chain of moveable houses traveling by rail and people making shorter trips
using mechanical wings fastened to their backs. William Heath's series of
images shows a vacuum tube that provides a direct trip to India, a steam-
powered horse long enough to accommodate five riders, and machines
doing a variety of household chores. Most illustrators of future worlds filled
the skies with every kind of aerial device imaginable, usually kept aloft by
balloons, kites, steam, or some combination of the three.[8]

Faith in the speed of technological change ran so high that the reading public could be easily fooled into believing advances had taken place that, in fact, had not. In April 1844, the New York *Sun* ran a front-page article claiming that a manned balloon had just made the first crossing of the Atlantic Ocean, and in a mere seventy-five hours. The article, a hoax written anonymously by Edgar Allan Poe, used convincing details from actual balloon voyages to describe a trip that would not actually take place until 1978. Steeped in the idea of progress and eager for stories of human advancement, much of the reading public—especially the more intelligent, thought Poe—accepted the account without question. So many people wanted copies of the paper, Poe later wrote, that "the whole square surrounding the *Sun* building was literally besieged."[9]

The fascination with new discoveries arose partly from the growing appreciation that applied or "useful" knowledge could enhance national power. As early as 1774, Great Britain began enacting laws preventing the export of cotton machinery, the golden goose of the British economy, and forbidding the emigration of artisans who knew how it worked. Later, it became clear that the traditional sources of national power were undergoing a broader shift. "Henceforth," wrote an American futurist in 1833, "it is no more the strength of the human arm, or the number of men, nor personal courage and bravery, nor the talents of military commanders, nor the advantages of geographical situations, that give power to a nation; but it is intelligence (knowledge of useful things)." The French utopian Claude-Henri de Saint-Simon would have agreed, as he looked forward to a day when the citizens of the world invested authority in a technocratic elite.[10]

The true promise of industrialization and mechanization, however, was material abundance. There was widespread hope that the application of mechanized production to earth's natural resources would produce so much material wealth that most of humanity's problems would simply vanish. Why steal from others when goods were so cheap that they might as well be free? Why make war with another country when yours was awash in plenty? Why envy your neighbor when everyone could live the life of the rich? Why deal sharply to achieve wealth when it was readily at hand for everyone? In such a world, money and private property might become entirely unnecessary, and most conflicts would end before they began.

Promises of abundance appealed to both capitalists and utopian socialists, an early wave of socialist thinkers. The utopian socialists saw capitalism
as a failure but were sold on the productive benefits of industrialization. In
Britain, Robert Owen advocated the creation of model industrial communities in the countryside and believed that, if properly organized, industry
could produce more wealth "than the population of the earth can require
or advantageously use." In France, Étienne Cabet began a popular movement based on the fictional utopia he portrayed in *Travels in Icaria,* assur-
ing his readers that "the current and limitless productive power by means
of steam and machines can assure equality of abundance." Industrialization, if guided by a socialist society, could set humankind free.[11]

Their socialist successors, Karl Marx and Friedrich Engels, also looked
forward to a world of unprecedented material abundance driven by scientific and technological advances. But their prophecy of a communist future,
which would become one of the most influential visions of tomorrow ever
articulated, showed more awareness of the harmful environmental consequences of growth. They worried about soil exhaustion, forest depletion,
water contamination, and air pollution, recognized the connection between
exploiting workers and exploiting nature in the rush for development, and
explicitly stated that humankind has a responsibility to hand the next generation an improved environment rather than a squandered one. Marx and
Engels erred, however, by insisting that environmentally destructive behaviors are largely a product of capitalism and that a socialist society would
manage the environment in a much more sustainable manner. When socialist states finally appeared in the twentieth century, their approaches to
the natural world proved to be just as damaging as those of their capitalist
counterparts.[12]

Many of the utopian socialist futures also carried an implicit critique
of consumption, the flipside of industrial production. Despite their whole-
hearted embrace of the factory, Cabet and Owen foresaw simple material
lives, though not nearly as spartan as in the earlier scientific utopias. The
French utopian socialist Charles Fourier, who was far less enamored of industrial expansion, attacked the growing consumer culture more directly.
He rejected the dominant economic idea that "if every individual could be
made to use four times as much clothing as he does, society would quadru-

ple the wealth it derives from manufacturing work." Instead, Fourier hoped to keep consumption low by, first, shifting from individual household consumption to more efficient communal consumption (a move that he believed would also reduce waste) and, second, producing manufactured goods of such a high quality that they would rarely need to be replaced. Although industrialization would help to ensure that everyone had enough, consumption was rarely an end in itself in the socialist utopias.[13]

The same was not true in capitalist circles, where increased consumption came to have a far more positive connotation. By mid-century, economists had built their understanding of resource use on the assumption that human wants are unlimited. That idea, combined with the expectation of boundless plenty through continued growth, suggested that increasing personal consumption was a positive good that would promote progress. "The number of artificial wants amongst a people," wrote the London author and barrister Michael Angelo Garvey, "and the estimate they form of what constitutes comfort, are the infallible measure of their advance from barbarism." As a result, any attempt to suppress material wants was "a monstrous error" that would "extinguish science, destroy all the arts by starvation, put an end to commerce, and erase every vestige of civilisation from the face of the earth." Growth-driven consumption became associated with civilization and self-denial with savagery, helping to drive the West away from the classic utopia of sufficiency and toward a new utopian vision of abundance.[14]

## Settling and Transforming the Planet

With machines promising endless material wealth, it was easy to believe that humankind had escaped traditional limits on population. Fourier, who had worked out the future in impressive detail, claimed rather off-handedly that the human population would reach its "full complement" at three to five billion people. John Adolphus Etzler, a German-American utopian, made a more careful calculation of the earth's carrying capacity based on the amount of land he believed would sustain a single human being under ideal circumstances. Confining his estimate to the areas between thirty degrees north and south latitude, Etzler calculated that the earth could nourish one trillion human beings. But he considered that number to be conservative, since further knowledge about the workings of nature might raise it even higher. The existence of less densely settled areas in Australia, Africa, and the Americas helped to make such numbers feel more believable than they might otherwise have been.[15]

Fiction writers were just as eager to see an expanded human population. Some, like Cabet, overestimated the rate of future growth. His fictional Icaria had doubled its population in fifty years, a growth rate far higher than the global population or Cabet's native France would actually experience. Other writers erred in the other direction, projecting growth rates that must have sounded fantastic at the time but either fell short of reality or were achieved much sooner than expected. A French story from 1810 portrayed the world a century later with a population one third larger, which underestimated the true gain over that period by half. In 1821, clippings from a fictional newspaper supposedly published in the year 4796 gave the population of New York City as five million, a number it actually reached before 1920. Most agreed, however, that whatever the actual future numbers might be, the warnings of Thomas Malthus could safely be ignored.[16]

Tales of tomorrow often illustrated future population growth with visions of colonization and urban expansion. Cabet's Icarians developed colonies expressly for housing their surplus population, and the fictional memoirs of Lord Moresby, supposedly written around the year 1920, report that future England has purchased parts of Colombia so that it no longer has to send its emigrants "to be bewildered and lost in the woods and snows of Canada." Cities like London are portrayed as greatly expanded, and one account of a future Russia imagines the region closest to Europe developed into a single, enormous city. A visitor flying over it reflects on "the legendary account that once there were two cities, one called Moscow, and the other St. Petersburg, and they were separated from each other by a great open plain."[17]

Ultimately, this surging human population would require that every inch of the earth's surface be put to practical use. In 1824, the Russian writer Faddei Bulgarin described what the world might look like after a thousand years of human expansion. "At the present time," said one resident of Bulgarin's future, "there aren't any uninhabited lands: the whole earth is populated, fertilized and adorned by the hands of men who have multiplied to an unbelievable extent. Even naked rocks in the midst of the ocean, thanks to soil brought in or made out of rock, have been transformed into luxuriant gardens." Such predictions did not envision crowding: Garvey, who foresaw a shift of Europeans to less populated areas, explicitly hoped that population density would decrease. But escaping the creations of man would no longer be possible.[18]

Even the surfaces of the seas would become home to humankind through the construction of floating islands. Fictional versions ranged from a modestly sized island with hills, trees, and a house, all inhabited by a single elderly man and pulled by whales, to a "great floating village" several kilometers long that toured the world and offered each passenger a private cottage, farmyard, and vegetable garden. More ambitious still was Etzler's description of what he hoped would be a series of very real artificial islands. They were to be "constructed of logs, or of wooden stuffs prepared in a similar manner as it is to be done with stone, and of live trees, which may be reared so as to interweave each other and strengthen the whole." Buildings, machines, and gardens would cover them, and steam engines would propel the islands and convert seawater into drinking water. Each island would house thousands of families and travel the seas in search of trade and the most favorable climates.[19]

Settling the entire planet also meant transforming it in unprecedented ways. The literature of the day is filled with grandiose plans to flatten inconvenient mountains, raise new ones to provide views, excavate valleys, create lakes, drain swamps, deepen sea channels, sink bottomless mines and wells, and cover the earth with a network of roads. Fourier believed that socialist utopian communities could accomplish such feats by pooling their resources to field enormous "industrial armies." Ten or twenty million strong, these workforces would undertake large-scale natural improvements like land reclamation, reforestation, and even the greening of the Sahara Desert. "Instead of having devastated thirty provinces in a campaign," he wrote, "these armies will have built thirty bridges, leveled thirty mountains, dug thirty canals for irrigation, and drained thirty marshes." Jane Webb's story took place in a time when "the whole earth was brought to the highest pitch of cultivation; every corner of it was explored; mountains were leveled, mines were excavated, and the globe racked to its centre." In fact, the earth has been so completely hollowed out beneath her future England that any-thing falling to the ground produces a deep and resonant sound like the striking of a drum.[20]

With the population in these future scenarios constantly growing, hu-mankind would have to replace every green plant not in the service of man with one that was. Mercier's future Parisians have swapped elms and chest-nuts for fruit trees along their public walks. In Cabet's Icaria, farmers brag that there are no useless trees or hedges in their fields. "Wherever a fruit tree would be more useful than anything else," a visitor is assured, "you will see a fruit tree." By taking advantage of every inch of land, the Icarians have doubled the area devoted to agriculture and increased food production by a factor of twelve. No place, even those intended for leisure or located on the very margins of cultivated lands, would escape the relentless effort to refashion the globe in support of production and growth.[21]

As in Mercier's utopia, canals often found a place in the imagined fu-tures of the early nineteenth century. In 1810, the German author Julius Von Voss imagined twenty-first-century Berlin as a major port city, despite that fact that it was located about eighty miles from the sea. The widening and deepening of rivers and canals had given it easy access to deeper wa-ters, and engineers had used some of the excavated material to raise the height of mountains along the Elbe River for scenic purposes. Fourier was one of several people to foresee construction of the Suez and Panama ca-nals, and he predicted that canals would also link the Aral and Caspian Seas with the Sea of Azov, and Quebec with the Great Lakes. Another fictional future world included a system of canals that ran from Antioch to the Eu-phrates River, connecting the Mediterranean Sea with the Persian Gulf.[22]

Visions of a world crisscrossed by an array of ambitious canals took their cues from actual reports and proposals. Among the most widely discussed was a study published in 1811 by Alexander von Humboldt, a German nat-uralist who would later go on to much acclaim. Humboldt studied nine possible routes for a canal through Central America connecting the Atlantic with the Pacific, eventually concluding that a route through Nicaragua would be the most practical. Gigantic and transformative projects of this kind cap-tivated the public imagination and increased excitement about the great technological accomplishments that would mark the triumph of human empire. In 1827, the aging German writer Johann Wolfgang von Goethe expressed disappointment that he would not live long enough to see canals on the scale envisioned by Humboldt. "It would be worth the trouble," he wrote, "to last some fifty years more for the very purpose."[23]

Many futurists also expected human expansion to produce a warmer climate that was less subject to temperature extremes. A common belief at the time held that removing forests and marshes and extending agriculture made climates more temperate. Such changes already seemed under way in the United States and Canada, and if warming on a regional scale was possible, then warming on a continental or even global scale might be too. With that in mind, the German author A. K. Ruh—writing in 1800 but looking five hundred years into the future—imagined that the reduction of forests and the filling of swamps had left his homeland's climate "extremely pleasant, gentle, mild," and capable of growing lemon, orange, and almond trees alongside the usual chestnut, birch, and fir. Bulgarin's story takes place a thousand years in the future in a Siberia made tropical through the same process. Not only has the melted North Pole become a major transportation route, but the warming of northern regions has drawn the earth's internal heat northward as well, altering climate worldwide. "Now cold reigns in India and Africa," explains a future professor of history and archaeology, "and the Polar Lands have become the richest and most fertile on Earth."[24]

Fourier developed a more complex theory of climate change that was simultaneously prescient and bizarre. He, too, expected that the continued extension of cultivation into new areas would warm those parts of the earth. But once cultivation reached the sixty-fifth parallel, which is north of Hudson Bay, Fourier expected the northern lights to coalesce into a crown around the arctic region. The combination of human cultivation and the heat reflected by the crown would melt the northern icecap and raise the temperature enough to permit settlement of Siberia and northern Canada. Lands closer to the equator would become more temperate as well, although the South Pole, which would not have the benefit of a crown, would remain cold. Heat from the warmer north would also dramatically change the composition of oceans worldwide, which would become more acidic and eventually come to taste like lemonade. This last claim was one that Fourier's critics never tired of quoting. His science—if it can even be called that—was of course completely invalid. But his prediction of a warming world climate, melting polar region, and acidifying oceans comes surprisingly close to twenty-first century realities.[25]

Less frequently, a writer might suggest a more technological means for warming the climate. In the late 1830s, the Russian author Vladimir Odoevsky imagined that, in the year 4338, Russians use a series of massive pipes to transport warmer air from the equator to northern latitudes. The air is used to heat both interior and exterior spaces. At the same time, the country's industrialists have entered into negotiations with the Chinese to transport colder air into the streets of Peking. The expectation of a warmer future was so widespread that some authors did not even bother to give causal explanations, like the French writer who mentioned off-handedly that the future Paris "will enjoy a temperature quite similar to Naples." Although the late twentieth century would find itself surprised by a warming climate, many in the late eighteenth and early nineteenth centuries expected and even looked forward to it.[26]

Humankind's newfound control of natural forces would also enable it to breed more useful kinds of plants and animals. In the spirit of Francis Bacon, one of Cabet's farmers brags of vegetables that have tripled in size and new breeds of cattle and sheep that "bear no more resemblance to their former selves than do our grain, vegetables, fruits, and flowers." Odoevsky imagined different kinds of fruits created by grafting existing varieties together. "I noticed a fruit which was something between a pineapple and a peach—nothing could be compared to its taste," wrote his main character, a Chinese student visiting Russia. "I noticed figs growing on a cherry tree and bananas growing on pear trees. It is impossible to count all the new varieties invented, so to speak, by Russian gardeners." Fourier, ever the quirky prophet, not only looked forward to advances in animal breeding but also predicted the domestication of zebras, beavers, reindeer, and other wild animals.[27]

Animals that were troublesome or no longer useful might be driven to extinction. This was a new idea, since the connection between human activity and the permanent disappearance of certain kinds of animals had not been obvious to earlier generations. Most people had considered it impossible for any of God's creatures to disappear entirely. But fossil evidence was

beginning to paint a different picture. By the 1820s, most scientists accepted the idea that an entire world of largely unknown animals had once
existed and since become extinct. Fourier had already predicted back in
1808 that future humans would save the most useful aquatic species from
the acidifying oceans by bringing them to unaffected bodies of water while
leaving the less useful ones to perish. Cabet's Icarians take a more direct
approach: they have destroyed most local wildlife by converting habitats
into productive land and work to eradicate the remaining bird and insect
pests by organizing massive one-day hunts that span the entire republic.[28]

Particularly common was the expectation that steam-powered modes of
transportation would lead to the disappearance of the horse. Equine extinction appeared in several short stories and was often played for laughs in
caricatures and comic songs. At a time when mechanical progress was rapid
but horses remained absolutely indispensible, the idea that humans would
someday do without them must have seemed both reasonable and slightly
ridiculous. Horses manage to avoid extinction in Odoevsky's future, but
only because people have bred them down to the size of lapdogs for use
as pets. Once transformed, they become part of the radically changed fauna
of the future. "How many species," marvels Odoevsky's visitor from China,
"have disappeared from the face of the earth or changed their forms!"[29]

## The Limits of Coal

Those who dreamed of the distant future in the early years of industrialization rarely worried about global limits to growth in the way that Grainville had. Concerns about overpopulation or resource exhaustion on a planetary scale are unusual, although Faddei Bulgarin's story of a thousand years
into the future was an exception for its brief passage about deforestation.
Oak, pine, and birchwood are valued more than gold and silver, he writes,
"because without any foresight our ancestors destroyed the forests and took
no concern for growing or preserving trees; finally they became rarities and
objects of great value." But this transformation seems to have caused only
slight inconvenience, if any, since the world simply switches to iron as a
primary building material.[30]

The one resource that attracted widespread fear of exhaustion was coal, which powered both the West's machines and its dreams. In Great Britain, the cradle of the industrial revolution, the rate of coal production had been accelerating for centuries. By the 1850s, it was fourteen times greater than it had been just a hundred years before, and coal accounted for ninety-two percent of all energy consumed on the islands. This represented a sharp break with the traditional organic economy, which depended on the solar energy invested in current living things, like plants and the animals that fed on them. An organic economy had definite and obvious limits. But coal tapped into the stored solar energy of past geological ages, freeing economies from traditional energy limitations. As a result, the industrial revolution would be unlike the many previous economic expansions in human history that had eventually petered out. This time, powered by coal, the expansion would keep going.[31]

Coal achieved a special, almost mystical place in Western culture because it seemed the very source of the West's power over nature. "By the help of a few bushels of coal," wrote Arago, "man will vanquish the elements; he will play with calms, and contrary winds, and storms." The American philosopher Ralph Waldo Emerson spoke of coal as the essence of industrial society. "We may call it black diamonds," he wrote. "Every basket is power and civilization. For coal is a portable climate. It carries the heat of the tropics to Labrador and the polar circle; and it is the means of transporting itself whithersoever it is wanted." Even the smoke belched by coal-burning factories and railroad engines, smoke that coated buildings and blackened lungs, became a welcome and iconic symbol of progress. The historian Lewis Mumford later captured the centrality of coal's cultural place at this time when he wrote that "the reek of coal was the very incense of the new industrialism."[32]

Coal, however, had a weakness that earlier sources of energy like wood and water did not share: it was not renewable. As a result, dreams of abundance gave birth almost immediately to fears of scarcity that introduced a broad public to the idea of resource exhaustion and the social collapse that might follow. As early as 1789, the mining engineer and natural historian John Williams made a study of Great Britain's coal deposits and predicted their eventual exhaustion. He believed that the country had excavated half of its available coal in just the past eighty years and that failure to use the remaining deposits wisely would result in the resource's complete exhaustion and the collapse of British civilization. Commerce and manufacturing would fail, cities would become "ruinous heaps," and "the future inhabitants of this island must live, like its first inhabitants, by fishing and hunting." French officials considered coal deposits to be uncommon and already in decline, and some Scots advocated the planting of more trees in anticipation of the day when the coal mines were exhausted. Others, however, like the Scottish economist John Ramsay McCulloch, saw little reason for worry. Writing in 1837, McCulloch declared that the coalfields of South Wales alone could supply Great Britain "for 2,000 years after most of the other coalfields are exhausted." The debate, of course, has never ended. But the eventual exhaustion of coal became a common expectation and a regular theme in tales of the future.[33]

Some were already looking to the next energy horizon. Etzler believed that coal's scarcity allowed wealthy industrialists to monopolize the energy supply, making it necessary to find a source of free and limitless energy outside of market mechanisms. His search led him to what we today refer to as renewable energy sources: wind, tidal, and solar power. Writing in 1833, Etzler advocated the founding of subscription-based associations that would build windmills, develop machines to translate tidal motion into power, and construct mirrors to concentrate sunlight and boil water for steam engines. Etzler believed that he had found the Holy Grail: free and boundless supplies of power for society's machines that would enable humankind to fully develop the earth's resources and house themselves comfortably in communities designed around the ideas of Fourier. His future would not be one of mere abundance but of "superabundance." But for better or worse, Etzler's inventions failed in public demonstrations and coal remained king.[34]

The idea of progress, however, suggested that worry was unnecessary because the discovery of coal's replacement was just a matter of time. So fiction writers often solved the problem by simply inventing a previously unknown process or material. Cabet's Icarians have just discovered "sorub," a raw material more plentiful than coal that produces a "chemical agent" stronger than steam; Bulgarin's society relies on an "illuminating gas" made directly from the atmosphere; and Mary Griffith's future America employs an unspecified "power" that is safer than steam. Even the British economist

William Stanley Jevons, who lived very much in the real world, speculated that someday "some source of force now unknown may be detected." Fear of coal's exhaustion was often met with confidence that either human ingenuity or nature itself would solve the problem when the time came.[35]

Even those who accepted the argument that Britain would eventually run out of coal did not necessarily advocate the conservation of existing stocks. In his much-read book *The Coal Question,* published in 1865, Jevons self-consciously extended Thomas Malthus's principle of population to resources. The country's accessible coal supplies were limited, he warned, and would last only another 110 years if consumption continued to grow at an exponential rate. So what to do? Believing exhaustion to be inevitable, Jevons outlined two paths forward: Britain could continue to pursue economic growth, or it could slow or even trim back its expansion. "We have to make the momentous choice," he wrote, "between brief greatness and longer continued mediocrity." For Jevons, the choice was clear. Given that Britain's past accomplishments were built on its lavish use of energy, that it had more gifts to give the world, and that the torch of civilization would eventually pass to other countries with untapped coal deposits, he advised the pursuit of brief greatness built on continued growth. Anything else seemed a betrayal of progress.[36]

## The Stationary State

There was at least one group that doubted the ability of economic and population growth to continue forever: economists. The late eighteenth and early nineteenth centuries saw the development of modern political economy as economic thinkers strove to understand the industrial revolution, the acceleration of European growth, and the rapid transformation of Western economies. The school of thought that developed—referred to today as classical economics—envisioned economies and their societies as existing in one of three possible stages of expansion: progressing, declining, or stationary. The stationary state had a constant population and stock of capital and an economy that did not grow. For the classical economists, the stationary state was not only a very real stage of economic development but the likely and perhaps inevitable end point of capitalism itself.[37]

In general, a country would reach a stationary state when its economy bumped up against environmental limits. Adam Smith addressed the stationary state as early as 1776 in his *Wealth of Nations,* which remains one of the most influential books on economics ever written. Smith defined a stationary state as occurring when a country "had acquired that full complement of riches which the nature of its soil and climate, and its situation with respect to other countries, allowed it to acquire." For David Ricardo, another founder of classical economics writing a generation later, the limit to growth would be set by the available amount of natural resources, particularly agricultural land. He argued that as population grew, and increasingly marginal and less productive lands were put under the plow, a country's ability to continue expanding would decrease.[38]

Neither Smith nor Ricardo saw the stationary state as a happy place to be. According to Smith, wages and profits would be extremely low and competition for jobs and business opportunities high. Smith considered contemporary China to be settled into a stationary state and painted the resulting conditions of life as bleak. In China, he claimed, laborers worked an entire day for a small quantity of rice, artisans spent more time trying to drum up business in the streets than working in their shops, the poor were far worse off than anywhere in Europe, and infanticide was common. Historical records suggested to Smith that such conditions had prevailed at least since the days of Marco Polo. Smith allowed that it might be possible for a country to stabilize at a higher level of wealth than China's, and he suspected that inadequate laws and institutions were holding the country back from its true potential for growth. But however a country reached the stationary state, once it got there, life became "hard" and "dull" compared with the progressive or growth state, where "the great body of the people, seem to be happiest and most comfortable."[39]

Of all the classical economists, John Stuart Mill thought most deeply about the social and environmental implications of the stationary state. Mill was the intellectual successor to Adams and Ricardo, one of the great theoreticians of capitalism, and for much of the nineteenth century the most influential political economist in the English-speaking world. His 1848 book, *Principles of Political Economy,* served as the standard text in the field of economics through the end of the century. Mill devoted an entire chapter of his book to the stationary state, which he considered to be the inevitable endpoint of a capitalist economy. Even in his day, he explained, only technological advancement and the economic opportunities provided by less developed parts of the world were postponing its arrival. When those came to an end, so would growth.[40]

Unlike his predecessors, however, Mill thought the stationary state would be an improvement over the growth state in a number of ways. First, it would put less emphasis on the consumption and acquisition of material goods. "I know not why it should be matter of congratulation," he wrote, "that persons who are already richer than any one needs to be, should have doubled their means of consuming things which give little or no pleasure except as representative of wealth." Similarly, he saw no social advantage to moving large numbers of people from the middle class to a working wealthy class, or from the working wealthy to a class so affluent that work became unnecessary. He believed, rather, that "the best state for human nature is that in which, while no one is poor, no one desires to be richer, nor has any reason to fear being thrust back by the efforts of others to push themselves forward." In the stationary state, he claimed, people who already lived comfortably would spend less time competing for superfluous material rewards.[41]

The second advantage of the stationary state was that, by reducing the focus on accumulating wealth, it would free the industrial arts to fulfill their true purpose: making life easier for people. "It is questionable," Mill wrote, "if all the mechanical inventions yet made have lightened the day's toil of any human being." They had, of course, made large fortunes for manufacturers and enhanced the comfort of the middle classes. But otherwise they had simply "enabled a greater population to live the same life of drudgery and imprisonment." Mill saw new mechanical inventions as having the potential to alter human destiny in much more positive ways. Doing so, he claimed "is in their nature and in their futurity."[42]

Third, the arrival of the stationary state might prevent population from rising to levels that hampered social development. Mill imagined a possible future that was able to adequately feed and clothe its population yet suffered from a harmful degree of crowding. "It is not good for man to be kept perforce at all times in the presence of his species," he wrote, explaining that solitude gives people the space they need to think and helps to mold good character. Being alone in a natural setting imparts another kind of benefit, he claimed, for it is "the cradle of thoughts and aspirations which are not only good for the individual, but which society could ill do without." Population only needed to be large enough to establish a viable social community, and Mill felt that the more developed countries had already achieved those levels.[43]

Finally, Mill worried that letting growth go on for too long would produce enough environmental damage to diminish the quality of life for future generations. He found little satisfaction in contemplating the kind of world that so many contemporary futurists desired: every inch of land cultivated, every useless animal eliminated, every wild shrub and flower labeled a weed. For Mill, the earth owed much of its pleasantness to the kinds of things that excessive growth would eliminate "for the mere purpose of enabling it to support a larger, but not a better or a happier population." He not only wanted future generations to embrace the stationary state but hoped they would do so long before social, economic, and environmental conditions forced them to.[44]

Mill, in short, saw the stationary state as anything but stagnant and dull. He claimed that "there would be as much scope as ever for all kinds of mental culture, and moral and social progress; as much room for improving the Art of Living, and much more likelihood of its being improved, when minds ceased to be engrossed by the art of getting on." Science would also continue to progress, with Mill suggesting that growth in knowledge of the natural world might be one of the few things that is actually unlimited. With judicious foresight and just institutions, scientific discoveries could, for the first time, become "the common property of the species, and the means of improving and elevating the universal lot." For Mill, the path to utopia led straight through the stationary state.[45]

Mill's greatest departure from the thought of his intellectual predecessors, then, was in decoupling moral, intellectual, and scientific progress from never-ending material growth and associating them instead with growth's end. This was an uncommon view at the time, but Mill was adopting an uncommon perspective. By attempting to look more broadly at what brought happiness to human beings, he recognized the importance of hard-to-measure factors like the needs for community, solitude, and access to the natural world. "The desire to engross the whole surface of the earth," he wrote, "in the mere production of the greatest possible quantity of food and the materials of manufacture, I consider to be founded on a mischievously narrow conception of the requirements of human nature." Intangible factors that went beyond wealth and material comfort were important too.[46]

Despite its well-established place in economic thought in the early nineteenth century, the idea of the stationary state left almost no mark on popular visions of the future. The world still felt far too large for ongoing growth to spark many serious conversations about its end. Mill himself admitted that even well settled countries still had space for "an immense increase of population." Plus, like Grainville's vision of environmental apocalypse, the idea of a stationary state ran too contrary to the dominant narrative of progress and growth. In fact, by the end of the century, concerns about the natural world would largely disappear from economic thought, and attention to the stationary state would go with it. Economists would not seriously reconsider the idea until the second half of the twentieth century, when questions about the environmental consequences of growth would gain a much greater sense of urgency.[47]

## Grappling with Growth

For many of the same reasons, those gazing into the distant future in the early nineteenth century did not tend to see environmental exhaustion on the horizon. But a few did use the space of the future to participate in a larger cultural conversation about the negative consequences of urban industrial growth. It had escaped no one's attention that the relentless expansion of Western cities was eating up fertile and scenic countryside at an astounding pace; that cities themselves were awash in human, animal, and industrial filth; that industrial economies consumed an enormous amount of resources; and that scientific and technological change had put pressure on individuality, spirituality, and the human connection with the natural world. As a growing number of thinkers turned their gaze toward the distant future, they brought new ideas to ongoing discussions about these problems. Some speculated about alternative ways to structure the human relationship with the natural environment, while others highlighted the long-term problems that growth and industrial values might cause.[48]

In a direct response to the sprawl of industrial cities, Owen and Fourier devised the first plans to organize industrialization around self-sufficient communities that did not grow. The details of their proposals differed, but each included a central complex housing a maximum population of a few thousand people and a surrounding area with farms and factories within easy walking distance. Owen's plan emphasized industry more than Fourier's, which privileged agriculture and horticulture. But both sought a synthesis of urban and rural that would restore the community of the small town and render huge cities unnecessary. Owen insisted that his urban designs would provide "superior habitations surrounded by gardens, pleasure-grounds and scenery," thereby saving people from both the crowded conditions of the city and the isolation of the countryside. Such plans, however, really substituted one kind of growth for another. While they would keep individual cities from growing too large, both Owen and Fourier expected their followers to keep founding new communities indefinitely as older ones reached their maximum allotted populations.[49]

In the United States, the philosopher and naturalist Henry David Thoreau criticized supporters of the development narrative for trying to improve nature rather than working with it. "How little have we cleared and hedged and ditched!" he wrote, mocking the Promethean perspective. "Let us not succumb to nature. We will marshal the clouds and restrain tempests; we will bottle up pestilent exhalations; we will probe for earthquakes, grub them up, and give vent to the dangerous gas; we will disembowel the volcano, and extract its poison, take its seed out. We will wash water, and warm fire, and cool ice, and underprop the earth." Thoreau argued that such an aggressive approach was entirely wrong-headed and would yield fewer dividends than a kinder and gentler touch. He suggested the keeping of bees as a model, since it required no more than "directing the sunbeams." The key was to refocus society's attention from reforming nature to reforming people, who in Thoreau's opinion needed it far more.[50]

Félix Bodin, a French historian, politician, and admirer of Fourier, put the threat posed by growth and progress to familiar landscapes and traditional

Robert Owen wanted to replace endlessly sprawling cities with towns of limited
size and population. This engraving from 1838 shows what his model communities
might have looked like once completed. (Mary Evans Picture Library)

ways at the center of an ambitious work of fiction. *The Novel of the Future*,
published in 1834, portrays a late-twentieth-century world society that is
well on its way to a triumph of Western-style capitalism, industrialization,
and democracy, all of which the narrator equates with progress. People move
freely around the globe, making populations more heterogeneous, and gov-

ernments have given up their rivalries and disbanded their armies, choosing instead to collect modest taxes to support local services. Efforts to colonize new lands, undertake large commercial speculations, or fight wars like the one waged worldwide to abolish slavery have fallen to heavily armed private corporations, or associations of people who share common interests.[51]

But there is a conflict brewing in Bodin's future world. On one side is the Association of Civilization, which supports the progress made by Western nations over the prior century and a half. On the other is the Poetic Association, which works to preserve the nature, history, and culture that is rapidly disappearing in the relentless march forward. It is a collection of affiliated groups with very different agendas, including monks who fear the disappearance of their religious beliefs, manufacturers vulnerable to new technologies, princes and aristocrats turned out of power, an assortment of writers, poets, artists, and philosophers, and many more. The various groups are united by a sense that history has taken a wrong turn, particularly with industrialization. To accommodate the various views of its members, the organization's Central Committee holds its general meetings in natural or historic places and deliberates by candlelight while arrayed in historic dress.[52]

The Poetic Association has been fighting an uphill battle. The organization has spent large sums to reintroduce hares and foxes into the English countryside, to encourage traditional costumes in rural areas, and to save dying languages like Gaelic and Basque, all to no end. Its members have also watched wild areas disappear entirely from England, including Sherwood Forest, now planted with barley, hops, and turnips and plowed by steam. After conducting a careful study of coal reserves in the British Isles, the organization offers its members "the consoling perspective of a future exhaustion of that odious aliment of mechanical industry, that powerful agent of a dismal, uniform and monotonous civilization destructive of all poetic life." The report also concludes, however, that coal will last for at least another century, long enough for steam to drive the noble horse to extinction.[53]

Yet the organization has enjoyed some successes as well, managing to preserve a variety of threatened sites around the world from development. "One cannot contemplate without admiration," admits the narrator, "the enormous amounts it has expended in Europe and Asia to save curious ruins of churches, mosques, pagodas, châteaux and abbeys, and to conserve entire ancient monuments of which industry was on the point of taking possession, in order to convert them to its own use or demolish them." The Poetic Association not only acquires significant sites but restores them as well. It has even reassembled Stonehenge. One of the organization's financial committees reports a partial list of the various landscapes it owns: "The association now includes in its domains 59 subterranean caverns and

77 grottoes open to daylight; 36 rocks of bizarre form have been preserved from mining, and, thanks to you, 44 waterfalls, some of them nearly 100 feet in height, which would have been muzzled as captives of industry and ignobly set to operate mills."[54]

Bodin's book did not find a wide readership, perhaps because it is frustratingly incomplete: the story brings his competing associations to the brink of open warfare and then abruptly stops. Its importance lies less in its immediate influence on visions of the future and more in its prescience, for organized efforts to preserve nature, history, and culture were almost nonexistent when Bodin wrote it. The West was only just beginning to wake up to the loss of significant landmarks and natural areas to development. The oldest national preservation group, Britain's Commons Preservation Society, was not founded until 1865, over thirty years later, and the United States did not form the first national park until 1872. Stonehenge, reassembled by Bodin's fictional association, had to wait until 1882 to gain a degree of legal protection in the real world and remained in private hands until 1918. Although Bodin's epic battle would not come about in actual historical time, the strong urge to preserve natural areas threatened by growth would in fact develop into a movement.[55]

A more influential attempt to project industrial values into the future came from the popular French writer Émile Souvestre. Published in 1846, *The World As It Shall Be* went through three editions in French, one each in Spanish and Portuguese, and was excerpted in the widely read American periodical *Harper's Magazine*. Generally considered to be the first industrial dystopia, it pushes the urge for mechanization, consumption, efficiency, and utilitarianism to their extremes. The main characters, a young married couple, ask a time traveler named Monsieur Progrès to transport them to the future so that they might see all of its glories. They awake in the year 3000 on the island of Tahiti, now the center of a worldwide industrial civilization devoted entirely to personal acquisition. Everything is commodified, even the couple themselves when a professor purchases them as if they were antiquities. Chiseled above the door of his house is the inscription: "Every man's home is his castle. Every man for himself." That, the professor tells the couple, "sums up the entirety of human law."[56] Souvestre's dystopia focuses largely on the negative social implications of industrial values, envisioning a world that feeds babies en masse by machine, educates children in sharp business tactics, and breeds its workers to be more proficient at particular jobs.

But Souvestre also explored some of the potential environmental consequences of industrial values, such as the application of utilitarianism to public spaces. Aiming his satirical sights at Mercier and Cabet's utopias, where people have replaced ornamental trees with more useful fruit-bearing ones, Souvestre has his main characters visit a public garden where "colossal cabbages took the place of flowering chestnuts, and alternate rows of tree-sized lettuces replaced groves of acacia and sweet-smelling limes. As for the flowers, they had been replaced by tobacco, rice, and indigo." In fact, the entire system of forestry in Souvestre's future society is based on enlarged versions of edible plants. "Thus," concludes the proud tour guide, "everything has been tailored to the needs of man, who has reduced the whole of creation to the proportions of his stomach."[57]

Souvestre also suggested that utilitarianism and the quest for industrial-scale efficiency, if pushed too far, would take a terrible toll on animals. Like Cabet's Icaria, Souvestre's society has bred its domesticated animals to yield more meat and milk. But rather than being impressed with the results, his visitors from the past recoil in horror. "Bulls, bred to put on a great deal of weight, had lost their bones," they observe. "Cows were no more than animated machines that turned grass into milk; pigs were no more than masses of flesh, growing larger before one's very eyes." The animal kingdom, they conclude, has become a set of monstrous creatures so transformed from their original beauty and proportion that God himself would not recognize them.[58]

Souvestre aimed another satirical arrow at the commodification of landscapes. In his corporatized, profit-driven future, a company has purchased the entire country of Switzerland to exploit the leisure value of its natural attractions. To deter anyone trying to avoid the price of admission, the company has surrounded the country with a stone wall passable only through twelve huge gates. Each gate bears the inscription: "NO MONEY, NO SWITZERLAND." Once inside, visitors encounter pay stations at every waterfall, glacier, and view, making it "impossible to admire the Rhine Falls without buying a ticket and depositing your umbrella." Like so much else in Souves-

A professor of zoology in Émile Souvestre's *The World As It Shall Be* (1846) cares for a small menagerie of animals that have largely vanished from the wild.

tre's industrial dystopia, the beauties of nature are seen primarily through the lenses of consumption and utilitarianism.[59]

## The Ruins of the Present

Despite such concerns, there was only one widely known image of tomorrow in Western literature and art during these years that projected a disastrous end to progress and growth. It was the image of a person from the future contemplating the ruins of the present. Although the use of ruins to encourage reflections on mortality went back to ancient times, it did not become closely linked to musings about the future of civilization until the late eighteenth century. One of its earliest appearances in print was in a book published in 1791 by the Comte de Volney, a French philosopher who traveled to Palmyra in Syria to see the ruins of its ancient and long abandoned city. As his mind wandered over the view, Volney began to wonder about the long-term fates of modern cities like Paris, London, and Amsterdam. "Who knows if some traveller, like myself," he wrote, "shall not one day sit on their silent ruins, and weep in solitude over the ashes of their inhabitants, and the memory of their greatness?" Another early appearance, this one in art, came in 1798 with Joseph Gandy's completion of two renditions of the recently completed Bank of England's rotunda, one showing the space in all its present glory and the other as a future ruin.[60]

The image of contemporary society in ruins became increasingly popular, even though the West was still very much on the ascent. Writers produced a variety of stories that explored Europe's return to a primitive state through the eyes of tourists, explorers, or archaeologists visiting from whatever part of the world had inherited the mantle of civilization. Brought to life by authors such as Edgar Allan Poe and Hans Christian Andersen, the characters pass up wild rivers once known as the Thames and the Seine, search out the remains of ancient cities, try to interpret the ruins, and occasionally meet barbaric survivors who evoke the theme of the last man. In 1840, the British historian and politician Thomas Babington Macaulay introduced one of the most influential and best-remembered motifs: a figure from New Zealand sketching the remains of St. Paul's Cathedral from the wreckage of London Bridge.[61]

Future ruins owed part of their appeal to the mystery of why the collapse had occurred, since authors and artists usually left the reasons to the reader or viewer's imagination rather than spelling it out. Was it war? Moral failure? The end of coal? The presence of civilized visitors implied relative decline rather than worldwide collapse, and the increasingly frequent comparisons of the British Empire with ancient Rome, along with the destruction caused by the French Revolution, were undoubtedly present in the minds of both the producers and consumers of these images. But since the ruins did not speak, the reader or viewer had to speak for them, making them effective vehicles for exploring almost any anxiety about the durability of modern society.

This engraving from 1872 by Gustave Doré depicts a
distant future in which a visitor from New Zealand
contemplates the ruins of London.

The popularity of future ruins ran directly counter to the narrative of
progress, replacing the linear arrow of time with the much older cyclical
model where civilizations rise and fall in a predictable pattern. These were
the years when the great American painter Thomas Cole created his five-
panel "Course of Empire" series, which portrays the development of a great
civilization from the wilderness and its eventual collapse back into it. Cole
had himself been inspired by a contemporary poem of Byron's that set the
cyclical view of time in two memorable lines: "History, with all her volumes
vast, / Hath but *one* page." Works like these made a gloomy argument: that
decline is the unavoidable destiny of all human societies. But they also of-

fered some comfort by suggesting that the relentless striving and bewilder-
ing change brought on by progress and growth would some day give way to
calm, quiet, and a resurgent natural world.[62]

Nothing, however, could shake the increasing confidence in a future of
seemingly endless progress and growth. Even Bodin's narrator, who tried to
portray the preservation-oriented Poetic Association in an understanding
light, assured his readers that progress was no mirage. He criticized those
"embittered individuals" who insisted that "humankind has merely been
repeating the same cycle since the beginning of time, elevating itself from
barbarity to civilization and then falling back from civilization into barbarity." He also condemned the pessimists who maintained that environments
were declining, "that rivers have been less beautiful since canalization has
drained them somewhat, that mountains no longer raise summits as proud,
and that pears and peaches are less tasty despite being larger." One can almost feel the sweep of the narrator's arm as he brushes such views aside.
"In spite, I say, of all these dismal theories," he concludes, "progress does
exist and is continuing: that is as clear as daylight."[63]

# 3

# An Evolutionary Tale

IN THE TWENTY YEARS BEFORE World War I, no single person influenced visions of the future more than the British author H. G. Wells. Many of his tales of tomorrow became instant classics, including *The Food of the Gods,* a powerful paean to the role that growth would play in the human pageant. Wells called it "a fantasia on the change of scale in human affairs." Published in 1904, the book tells the story of a synthetic growth-enhancing substance that escapes from two careless chemists. It quickly spreads through the countryside, dramatically enlarging plants, chickens, wasps, and eventually human children. The latter grow into forty-foot giants who resist belated attempts by the British government to reestablish control over the rapidly changing environment. "We fight not for ourselves," says one of the giants, "but for growth, growth that goes on for ever. To-morrow, whether we live or die, growth will conquer through us. That is the law of the spirit for evermore." The book ends with the giant gesturing toward the stars, suggesting that the earth alone can no longer satisfy humankind's spirit of expansion.[1]

Wells's work was not only building on the now well-established development narrative but also riding a growing wave of interest in futuristic fiction that had begun in the 1860s. One source of this surging popularity was a recent flood of astonishing technological achievements, including the transatlantic telegraph cable, the transcontinental railroad across North

America, and the Suez Canal. More important, however, was the publication in 1859 of Charles Darwin's *On the Origin of Species*, which enabled the idea of progress to fuse with the concept of evolution. Together, progress and evolution made it seem as if humankind was experiencing more than a simple increase in scientific and technological discoveries: it was traveling on a rising evolutionary path sanctioned by nature itself, one that began in the primordial muck and would end with some grandiose destiny. Evolution reframed all of human history as a journey of progress.[2]

By the 1890s, nonfiction prediction was also becoming increasingly common as scientists and inventors, long a prime source of ideas for fictional futures, began to make more frequent public forecasts themselves. These were the "high priests" of science, wrote *The Strand Magazine,* and although little known to prior generations, they had now decided to speak out and "become prophets." To the readers of the newspapers and magazines that spread their ideas, these experts seemed uniquely qualified to speculate about how their work might advance the evolution of human society in years to come. As a result, by the early twentieth century it looked to the general public as if the study of the future had become a rational and scientific endeavor. It helped that fiction and nonfiction predictions tended to be in remarkable agreement with each other.[3]

Despite all of the optimism, a sense of uneasiness about the growth-oriented future had developed by the end of the century. The world had begun to feel smaller and more fragile. Geographers were close to mapping the few places still unknown to the West, the United States announced the closing of its frontier, and the French geographer Jean Brunhes pondered "the material limits of our earthly cage." At the same time, concerns began to surface that human expansion or the unwise use of science and technology might provoke large-scale environmental crises. A new taste developed for stories about environmental disasters and for utopias that abandoned growth for more sustainable environmental relationships. Nevertheless, most of those looking ahead continued to use progress and evolution as their guides, imagining futures that would remake and even transcend the natural world. Right up until the start of World War I, the triumph of human empire seemed at hand.[4]

## Evolution as Progress

Evolutionary theory opened a new frontier of optimism for the human future because it mapped so neatly over the idea of progress. By demonstrating that humans, though beginning as lower forms of life, had biologically surpassed all other animals, evolution suggested that they would continue that upward trajectory. "We are proud of having so immensely outstripped our lower animal ancestors," wrote the German Darwinist Ernst Haeckel in 1867, "and derive from it the consoling assurance that in future also, mankind, as a whole, will follow the glorious career of progressive development, and attain a still higher degree of mental perfection." Humanity could now be assured not only of endless scientific and technological advances and boundless growth, but also of unlimited improvement to the species. In fact, evolutionary thought was so malleable that it quickly became popular to apply it to social and technological change as well. H. G. Wells argued that Darwin's thought had even transformed the idea of utopia itself. Once a static and permanent state, utopia now looked to Wells like a dynamic one, "a hopeful stage, leading to a long ascent of stages."[5]

Futurists often pondered how evolution would shape the racial composition of the human species. Since this was a time when Western scientists endorsed the racial hierarchies that justified imperial expansion, it should not be surprising that Anglo-Saxon authors often forecast the evolutionary demise of everyone who was not Anglo-Saxon. "In 'the survival of the fittest,'" explained a guide from the year 2882, "we English, along with the races kindred to us, have everywhere carried the day, and everywhere all others have been crowded off the world's too narrow surface." Indigenous peoples in the Americas, New Zealand, the Arctic, and elsewhere routinely vanish. Such an end would have come as no surprise to anyone visiting an anthropological exhibit at a world's fair, which displayed non-white peoples in human zoos that suggested they were not only technologically primitive but biologically so as well. Even when fiction writers portrayed races interbreeding at the borders of different populations, sometimes forming new races, everyone ended up looking more or less white. One visitor to the future is surprised to find that his guide is part Eskimo, since the man looks so much like a Welshman.[6]

The faith that evolution would inevitably whitewash the world sometimes provided the justification for incredible, if fictional, atrocities. The naturalist William Delisle Hay depicted the world's Anglo-Saxons assisting the process of evolution by annihilating the populations of Asia and Africa. Hay's fictional twentieth century, unlike the real one, had been a century of peace in which ideas about universal fraternity and brotherhood reigned supreme. But by the twenty-first century, the Anglo-Saxon population found itself on the verge of outstripping its food supply. The crisis clarified just how inferior the other races were and how difficult it was "to understand exactly what sphere of usefulness in the economy of Nature was filled by the Chinaman and the Negro." Provocations by a Japanese-Chinese alliance and the black population of Africa eventually provided convenient excuses for wars of extermination. "What we chiefly learn from this page of history," concludes a future historian, "is the inevitable certainty of nature's laws, and the futility of resistance to them. The duty of a rising race is either to absorb or to crush out of existence those with which it comes in contact, in order that the fittest and best may eventually survive." It would be hard to find a more brutally frank application of evolutionary principles to human relationships.[7]

Animals were expected to suffer much the same fate, in part because Westerners were beginning to observe the process of extinction right before their eyes. Naturalists had gradually pieced together the stories of several island-bound birds that had come under tremendous pressure from hunting and could no longer be found. The moa of New Zealand, the great auk of the North Atlantic, the dodo of Mauritius: all, it appeared, had been driven to extinction by human activity. By the 1870s, North Americans were witnessing first-hand the catastrophic decline of the passenger pigeon and bison, animals that had once existed in awe-inspiring numbers. Writing in 1892, the great French scientist Charles Richet predicted matter-of-factly that "the complete cultivation of the soil will cause the almost total destruction of certain animal species."[8]

Long before Richet's pronouncement, writers of future fiction had begun to clear their imaginary worlds of all wild animals and often domesticated ones as well. Sometimes their stories depict the survival of animals that were useful for food or some kind of labor, or relegate small numbers of selected species to zoos, national parks, or hunting preserves. More often, humankind makes a clean sweep of it—often through systematic programs of extermination—and turns to vegetarianism. Although naturalists were just beginning to promote animal conservation, fiction writers remained in broad agreement that virtually all animals would disappear, from elephants and dogs to serpents and kangaroos. "The whistle of machinery and the hum of motors have taken the place of the song of birds," notes a visitor to the year 2011. "The forests are deserted and the fields without moos, whinnies, or larks."[9]

Many futurists offered no justification for the mass extinctions, as if the reasons should be obvious to readers. Those who did seek to rationalize it offered one of two explanations. The first was utilitarianism. A large human population must use land efficiently, and agriculture produces more food per acre than hunting and husbandry. "We needed the land and we needed its productions," writes a historian looking backward from the year 2180. "We could not afford to retain animals." The other justification was evolution. The nineteenth-century British geologist Charles Lyell had explained that human beings, in extirpating other forms of life, were simply participating in a fundamental law of nature in which one species conquers territory from another. Extinction was simply nature's way. So when a visitor to the year 2907 questions the loss of the horse, his guide is able to offer a simple explanation: "It was his fate in the process of evolution." Both rationales suggested that animal extinction represented progress. Regret was unnecessary and rarely expressed.[10]

The theory of evolution also suggested that the human species itself could be improved. Utopian writers had been advocating the selective breeding of humans since Plato, and earlier in the nineteenth century Cabet had depicted his fictional Icarians as working hard "to perfect the human race." But On the Origin of Species directly inspired Darwin's half-cousin Francis Galton to found the field of eugenics, which applied the scientific method to the making of better human beings. Eugenic thought spread around the world and into the fictional future, where many societies required the screening of couples for biological compatibility before marriage and euthanized unhealthy babies as well as the sick and the old. Authors opposed to eugenics painted such futures in dystopian hues, often portraying them as civili-

zations in which Christianity had gone extinct. Visitors from the past sometimes find themselves striving to revive the idea that society must take care
of all God's children, reminding readers that Jesus healed the sick and lame
rather than eliminating them from the breeding stock.[11]

Fiction writers were just as capable of imagining scenarios in which evolution worked to the human race's disadvantage because humankind was
out-competed in the Darwinian struggle to survive. The idea that humans
might not actually be "the fittest" emerged as early as 1871 in Edward Bulwer-
Lytton's immensely popular *The Coming Race*. The main character finds his
way deep underground through a mine and discovers a subterranean world
that houses a technologically advanced race called the Vril-ya. Once much
like humans, they have since evolved into larger, stronger, and more intelligent beings. They have also developed an extra nerve in their hands that
allows them to control an immensely powerful electro-magnetic force at
will. The main character, telling the tale many years later, is convinced that
the Vril-ya will someday emerge from their subterranean home and take the
place of humankind.[12]

Evolutionary competition did not have to be organic. It took only four
years after the appearance of *On the Origin of Species* for someone to apply
Darwin's ideas to technology. In 1863, Samuel Butler published a letter
titled "Darwin among the Machines" in a New Zealand newspaper. He
claimed that machines were accelerating in complexity at a worrisome rate
and would someday be the masters of men. To ward off future disaster,
Butler recommended—tongue-in-cheek—that humans immediately declare
a "war to the death" against their machines. Almost a decade later, Butler
pursued this idea further in a now classic satirical utopia called *Erewhon, or
Over the Range,* in which a society has done just what he suggested. Centuries before the time of the story, a learned professor had written a wildly
influential book warning against the rapid evolution of machines. "Though
our rebellion against their infant power will cause infinite suffering," the
professor wrote, "what will not things come to, if that rebellion is delayed?"
The professor's book sparked a devastating civil war, after which the victors
destroyed all technology created in the past several centuries and passed
laws against further innovation.[13]

Sixteen years later, an English writer explored the risks of failing to make such a preemptive strike. The result for his future humans is the "great disaster of 1948." One day, a group of American engineers finds that the most sophisticated train in their shed has created, or perhaps given birth to, another smaller train. Other trains do the same thing, with the new trains being even more advanced than the old ones. The machines were reproducing themselves and evolving with each new generation. "It portended a war between the marshaled forces of nature," observes the narrator, "the entrance of the Inorganic world into unnatural rivalry with the Organic." Panic ensues as the trains begin to arm themselves, learn to move off their tracks, and work together to annihilate humankind. The group of people at the center of the story fights its way down the Mississippi River to New Orleans and eventually to a deserted Honolulu, where they form a new settlement. For all they know, they are the last surviving humans in the world.[14]

Even without the sudden appearance of a superior race or a dangerous rise in machine intelligence, evolution could still thwart human ambitions. Such was the case in one of the period's most striking and far-seeing applications of evolutionary theory, H. G. Wells's *The Time Machine*. Published in 1895, the book simultaneously made Wells an international literary figure and cast a doubtful shadow on the idea of endless progress. Wells's unnamed Time Traveler uses a machine of his own design to journey to the year 802,701, where he finds many of the environmental changes that his generation liked to imagine: the world is warmer, animals are extinct, insect pests are gone, diseases have been eliminated, and the world is as tame as a garden. "One triumph of a united humanity over Nature had followed another," marvels the Time Traveler. "Things that are now mere dreams had become projects deliberately put in hand and carried forward."[15]

But the Time Traveler soon finds the appearance of environmental perfection to be deceiving. The human species, he discovers, has evolved into two branches: the Eloi, who live like children in a pastoral paradise, and the Morlocks, who maintain the Eloi's infrastructure but prey on them at night like wolves. Even worse news lies ahead, for additional jumps into the still farther future reveal that humans have become extinct. The few forms of primitive life that remain will likely follow suit as the sun continues to cool and the earth freezes. The lesson that Wells wanted to convey to his generation was this: humans are not traveling along a path of guaranteed betterment, and even if they do achieve utopia someday, it is unlikely to last because nature cannot be held permanently in a particular state. Enduring social and environmental progress is an unattainable goal.

## The Human Hive

Visions of whole peoples dying out and animals going extinct, although explained with evolutionary theory, ultimately emerged from the widespread expectation that human population would continue to grow. At some point, there just would not be enough room for everyone and everything. But in stories that adopted a narrative of beneficial development, human population usually manages to stabilize with little trouble. Some future societies find that moral suasion yields the desired result, while others benefit from birth control or even a rising standard of living, with the authors noting that the wealthy tend to have fewer children. One overcrowded society learns how to choose the sex of a baby and finds its unexpected salvation in the fact that parents prefer boys at a ratio of twenty to one. The population drops precipitously, and with no adverse social consequences. In other cases, nature helps out by lessening the human desire to have children or revealing a new law that "nature never produces life without there being a corresponding supply to meet its needs." Such stories suggested that nature itself desires the largest possible human population and will be willing to help further that goal when the time comes.[16]

To keep up with the rising population, food production would have to expand as well. Earlier in the century, fiction writers had imagined agriculture spreading over every inch of cultivable land. Now they extended farming into the oceans and beneath the ground. The people of the future enclose large bays with breakwaters to farm lobsters, crabs, and oysters, and build huge floating factories that trawl the seas like giant grain harvesters, catching fish as they go and either canning or freezing them onsite. They also cultivate fields of edible sea plants on the ocean floors. "Enlightened science threw its bread on the waters," reports the president of the Tenth World-Republic, "and we are reaping the fruits." Agriculture even spreads to underground caverns, where people grow fungi that serve as the foundation for synthetic animal food. The optimism of fiction writers was inseparable from the forecasts of scientists like Charles Richet, who insisted that "even if humanity grows ten times larger, the land and sea will feed everyone: we can be completely confident of it."[17]

Many saw the future as an urban one, partly because cities have the potential to concentrate huge populations, thereby maximizing the area available for food production, but also because urbanization was a major contemporary trend. The acceleration of urbanization in the developing West extended back into the eighteenth century and possibly earlier. But the most impressive growth took place between 1830 and the eve of World War I, a period that saw tremendous economic expansion and population growth with related increases in the number and size of cities. The West began the period with twelve percent of its population living in cities and ended with thirty-four percent. It began with one city containing over half a million people and ended with forty-seven cities of that size. By mid-century, London had a population of two and a half million people, probably making it the largest city in human history, and was devouring the surrounding countryside at an astonishing pace.[18]

Two popular approaches emerged for envisioning the city of tomorrow within a completely developed world. The first embraced and celebrated urban growth. Drawing on the invention of skyscrapers and passenger elevators at the end of the century, it often found expression in visions of a monumental city that appeared cut from one piece, a vertical metropolis so tall, complex, and multileveled that it seemed to stand in opposition to nature itself. "Instead of individual buildings, disunited and independent in architecture," wrote the American inventor Hudson Maxim, "that great city of the future will be as one enormous edifice. . . . Stupendous banks of streets, arcades and corridors, parks and playgrounds will rise one above another, tier on tier, to eye-tiring heights, supported by vast columns several blocks in diameter at the base, traversed by great streets and thoroughfares and rising to a height of two thousand feet or more." Dramatic cities like this one lent themselves to visual representation and appeared in newspapers and magazines and on travel guides and postcards. But despite Maxim's mention of parks and playgrounds, such images rarely show any greenery. To do so would have worked against their most powerful message: humankind has out-done nature and no longer needs it.[19]

The American artist William Robinson Leigh produced this
striking image of a monumental future city around 1908.
(Courtesy of the University of Chicago Library)

The second approach to the urban future looked for ways to address the severe environmental problems that growth had caused in contemporary cities. In general, large Western cities suffered from overcrowding, pollution of the air, water, and soil, and a lack of public green space. Most had grown in the absence of significant planning and government regulation and catered more to the needs of industry and commerce than to the people living in them. As a result, Western cities were simultaneously celebrated as symbols of cultural and economic achievement and condemned for the appalling environmental conditions they produced. The cultural mecca of Paris was packed with dense slums; the commercial hub of New York City contained almost a million people before turning serious attention to park construction; and London, the center of world finance, suffered from smoke-induced fogs so thick that people sometimes walked blindly into the Thames and drowned. To urban planners and fiction writers alike, the solutions would come mostly from science and technology.[20]

Futurists often solved the problem of excessive urban density by moving the residential population to more spacious garden suburbs and having them commute daily to work in the city. This kind of decentralization was already happening in a number of countries with the help of trains and streetcars, particularly in Britain and the United States. It also seemed like a logical evolution of the city, since futurists foresaw even greater improvements in transportation technology on the horizon—pneumatic trains, high-speed airships, and so on—that would make commuting ever faster and cheaper. In many of these fictional visions, little more than commerce and industry remains in central cities, which are noticeably smaller as a result. Various fiction writers portrayed the population of Boston shrinking by three quarters, northern Manhattan returning to agriculture, and workers commuting to a smaller Paris from all over the world via inexpensive air transportation. In one story, a traveler from the past visiting New York City in the year 2199—not yet aware of the migration to the suburbs—is so struck by the city's diminished size that he begins to wonder how Thomas Malthus would explain the decrease in population.[21]

Science and technology would also play a key role in solving problems of pollution and public health. The air is clear and fresh in the city of tomorrow because electricity has replaced coal. Rivers run clean and bright because sewage is chemically treated and shipped to the countryside as fertilizer. Public health is improved due to the widespread adoption of vaccines, cremation, and new habits of cleanliness. Jules Verne contrasted this kind of hygienic utopia with the industrial dystopia in his 1879 book, *The Begum's Fortune*. "Frankville," built by a Frenchman in the northwestern United States, employs a number of sanitary innovations: brick houses, low density development, subsidized water, the removal of particulate matter from smoke, and washable floors and walls in place of carpets and wallpaper. "To clean, clean unceasingly," wrote an observer, "so as to destroy the miasmas constantly emanating from a large community, such is the principal work of the central government." In contrast, the industrial city of "Stahlfeld," or "Field of Steel," built forty kilometers away by a German armaments maker, is true to its name and devastates the surrounding landscape.[22]

To add greenery to the city, futurists looked less to science and technology and more to planning. The international urban parks movement, which gained momentum mid-century, emphasized large pastoral parks connected by parkways. But some fiction writers went even further, completely surrounding urban residents with trees, plantings, and greenswards. Emile Calvet's utopian Paris placed the city's streets behind the buildings so that their fronts could open onto broad greens, and the terraced buildings of Chauncey Thomas's future Boston were covered in foliage during the milder seasons. Luxuriant roof gardens were particularly popular in the imagined futures of the time. They usually serve as pleasure gardens (sometimes with grass engineered to grow no taller than an inch) but occasionally double as vegetable gardens to feed the urban population. When a visitor from the past marvels at how garden-like the urban future is, his guide cannot help but agree. "The roof gardens are the flower beds," she explains, "the parks are the turf spaces, and the streets and avenues are the gravel paths."[23]

The nineteenth century's most influential urban utopia appeared in Edward Bellamy's *Looking Backward: 2000–1887*, published in 1888. Bellamy's book was one of the century's best sellers. It was popular on both sides of the Atlantic and inspired the founding of several utopian communities and a social reform movement. His vision of Boston at the cusp of the twenty-first century depicted an almost entirely urban society centered on the production and consumption of factory-produced products by a population organized into an industrial army. Bellamy spent little space describing the city itself, except to say that it had broad streets, large squares, and colossal buildings set in park-like enclosures. But his book gave the definite impression that a huge, technology-driven, consumer-oriented city had completely eclipsed town, village, and country life.[24]

Bellamy's vision of an urban world troubled H. G. Wells, who subsequently used the space of the future to explore the negative consequences of extreme urban concentration. Between 1897 and 1899, Wells wrote two stories set in a twenty-second-century England where the population is clustered in a handful of glassed-in, hive-like mega-cities. Over time, smaller settlements had disappeared: new electrical technologies had made it more desirable to live in fully wired cities, and transportation between cities had become so fast and cheap that stops in towns and villages along the way became unnecessary. As a result, the countryside, though given over entirely to human uses like agriculture, pasturage, and wind turbines, has no permanent residents. Even the few remaining agricultural workers live in the cities and commute to the countryside. "The city," writes Wells, "had swallowed up mankind."[25]

To explore the resulting isolation from the natural world, Wells follows a pair of newlyweds who leave London to pursue their fantasy of a more romantic and adventurous past. Once in the uninhabited countryside, Denton and Elizabeth stumble into a deserted village and take up residence in a rundown building. Things go well at first. They spend a night marveling at the moon and stars and awaken to birdsong. But despite a promising beginning, they quickly find themselves entirely unprepared for their engagement with the great outdoors. The two lovers catch colds, grow bored, and work hard to turn over a garden only to realize that they have nothing to plant. Within a few days, they find themselves running from a hailstorm and plunged into absolute darkness for the first time in their lives, "as if they were in some other world, some disordered chaos of stress and tumult." The next morning, after being set upon by a pack of sheep dogs that watch the nearby herds of a giant food corporation, they decide it is time to go home. "Ours is the age of cities," admits Denton. "More of this will kill us." Before leaving, Elizabeth stoops to kiss the petals of a small flower that represents everything she desires and everything she cannot have.[26]

However fiction writers of the time felt about the city of the future, they invariably powered it with electricity rather than steam. Practical applications like the telegraph, telephone, phonograph, arc light, and incandescent bulb had followed one upon the other, and electrical power plants, especially those that harnessed the might of Niagara Falls, had become points of fascination and common tourist attractions. The century's many world's fairs often dedicated entire buildings to electricity or even made it the fair's main theme, staging fantastic light shows that vanquished the night at the flick of a switch. Silent, invisible, and poorly understood, electricity evoked an almost tangible sense of wonder. Not only did it seem to offer unlimited power, but many also considered it the source of the human soul or even of life itself. By its very presence, electricity promised to speed up the pace of human existence and bring about what the French illustrator Albert Robida called "the electric life."[27]

Since it was still widely predicted that coal would grow increasingly scarce and expensive over time, scientists and fiction writers expected renewable sources to generate electricity for the cities of tomorrow. Many scientists favored one over the others: the illustrious Scottish physicist Lord Kelvin preferred wind power; Samuel Langley of the Smithsonian Institution liked solar; and Charles Richet predicted the extensive development of water power. Fiction writers, for their part, embraced them all and more. In their hands, the people of tomorrow harness tides, rivers, and waterfalls; sink copper rods deep into the ground to extract geothermal energy; electrify water to create hydrogen fuel; collect and focus sunlight using giant mirrors and lenses; cover the roofs of buildings, the crests of hills, and the masts of ships with wind turbines; and maintain huge magnets in orbit where they gather electricity from the atmosphere and conduct it back to earth through the wires that tether them. "No true engineer," wrote an editorialist in the magazine *The Electric Age*, "will believe that with so many sources of energy around us the progress of mankind and the work of the engineer will cease with the exhaustion of the coal fields."[28]

## Promethean Dreams

By the 1870s, Western mastery of the natural environment had grown extensive enough that geologists began proclaiming a new geological age in which humankind had proudly taken its place alongside other forces of nature. In Italy, Antonio Stoppani coined the term "Anthropozoic" with the future very much in mind. "When we say the Anthropozoic era," he wrote, "we do not look to the handful of centuries that have been, but those to come." In the United States, Joseph Leconte coined the term "Psychozoic," which emphasized how the power of the human mind had made humans "one of the chief agents of change" in the world. These terms did not provoke ambivalence, as "Anthropocene" would in the twenty-first century, but rather pride in the human accomplishments of past and future.[29]

In this atmosphere of great expectation, futurists devised ever more ambitious plans to alter the earth for human convenience. Such schemes embraced a profound level of interference with the makeup of the planet and represented the outside margin of what Western culture dreamed might be possible. They were usually inspired by the latest scientific research and were sometimes the subjects of serious consideration. But they often found more traction in the world of fiction, catching the imagination of a public convinced that, even if such things could not be achieved today, they surely would be tomorrow.

As climatologists abandoned the idea that clearing forests and marshes would warm the West, futurists began to imagine more technological means for transforming the climate. In 1874, the Scottish medical doctor Andrew Blair wrote of a future society that drills through Greenland into the earth's core, releasing enough geothermal energy to spark a "caloric revolution" that introduces the earth's subterranean heat into every part of the globe. In Blair's future, the last snowfall anywhere in the world is recorded in the year 2800. American fiction writers imagined the construction of tremendous climate-altering barriers, for one author a wall almost two miles high that strategically directs atmospheric currents, for another a series of artificial reefs sunk in the Atlantic to redirect warmer water toward Europe and North America. The latter echoed the ideas of Harvard geologist Nathaniel Shaler, who proposed in 1877 that the United States consider widening the Bering Strait to guide warmer Pacific water toward the pole. In France, Albert Robida imagined the use of electricity to capture cold northern winds and redirect them to warmer areas. Humans, he wrote, would command the atmosphere and redesign the seasons to their liking.[30]

Making the Sahara Desert bloom, long a popular fantasy, finally gained

To illustrate the ability of future humans to control the climate, the French
artist Albert Robida drew the Great Sphinx of Giza surrounded by water
and lashed by heavy rains. Weather control machines crown the pyramids,
and three travelers with umbrellas trudge toward a café tucked behind
the Sphinx. (Courtesy of the Getty Research Institute)

some scientific backing in the 1870s. Based on information acquired through
exploration and surveys, the French geographer François Elie Roudaire and
the British engineer Donald Mackenzie both proposed plans to introduce
seawater into low-lying parts of the Sahara. The French wanted to extend
their control deeper into North Africa from the Mediterranean, and the British desired an easier route from the Atlantic to the Sudan. With the recently
completed Suez Canal up and running, it seemed that the technology might
already exist to cut the necessary channels. The idea attracted serious attention into the twentieth century, when a writer for *Scientific American* embraced another French plan to create a huge inland sea, despite objections
that it might plunge Northern Europe into a new ice age or even alter the
planet's equilibrium by shifting so much water weight to a different part of
the globe. Needless to say, fiction writers loved the idea and put a number

of different spins on it. Jules Verne published the best-known treatment in 1905, in the last of his books released before his death.[31]

Futurists also liked the idea of leveling the earth's mountains. All of them. The world government in Hay's *Three Hundred Years Hence* begins destroying the ranges in New Zealand and South America to create more agricultural land. It eventually halts the work, however, because it comes up with a better idea for achieving the same goal: moving the entire human population to cities built on piles driven into the seabeds, an event remembered by later generations as the "Terrane Exodus." In contrast, the future society created by Andrew Blair to represent the Christian millennium sees the work to its completion. Blair devoted large sections of his book, and many military metaphors, to describing how humans destroy the great mountain chains by smashing them with battering rams, dissolving them with acids, and blowing them up with electrical bolts. Once the mountains are gone and the valuable minerals collected, engineers begin to re-sculpt the earth's surface into more useful and pleasant forms. "Chaos had been disinherited of all his former earthly possessions," reflects the narrator. "We had rendered the crust of the globe but one large piece of artificial topographical sculpture—one large Eden."[32]

Just as ambitious were fictional efforts to create new land masses to accommodate the growing human population. In Albert Robida's *The Twentieth Century,* capitalists tackle the problem by financing the construction of an entirely new continent in the Pacific Ocean. Engineers work to connect far-flung islands by cutting blocks from the Himalayas and the Rocky Mountains, sinking them to the ocean floor, and constructing columns and frameworks on top of them. They complete the work by importing soil from India, the Americas, and the bottoms of the world's rivers and transplanting useful species of plants and animals from all over the globe. Another future society in a more distant year has filled in all of the world's oceans, leaving only a few large and deep canals that function as sewers. Future population growth, the reader learns, might necessitate the eventual filling of these areas as well.[33]

The Russian writer Alexander Kuprin came up with a Promethean plan for supplying the world with energy after the exhaustion of coal: converting the entire planet into an electromagnetic induction coil. By the year 2906, the world's scientists have labored for an entire generation to wind three billion miles of steel cable around the earth from north to south. They then constructed massive terminals at both poles and ran secondary cables to everywhere on the globe that needed power. After a single year of operation, the earth's "inexhaustible magnetic power" was successfully driving every factory, agricultural machine, train, and ship, and lighting every street and home, all without causing the kind of environmental damage that coal had. Although many had initially eyed the project with doubt and fear, it had forever solved humankind's energy problems and promised permanent abundance. A single line from the story could serve as a slogan for all imagined projects with similarly Promethean ambitions: "Glory to the only god on Earth—Man."[34]

Fiction writers also began searching for untapped resources beyond the earth. The idea that Westerners might treat extraterrestrial environments like extractive colonies went back to the seventeenth century, when Galileo first noticed that the moon had earth-like features. But Jules Verne's *From the Earth to the Moon,* published in 1865, and other works of science fiction had begun spreading such a vision to larger audiences. By the end of the century, future humans were routinely crashing asteroids into earth's surface so they could be mined or turned into new continents; battling alien space empires over resource-rich planets; and making "considerable havoc of Jupiter's gaseous envelope" by extracting massive amounts of oxygen and nitrogen. Scientists usually play a prominent role in the stories. "Exulting in their might," wrote Robert William Cole in *The Struggle for Empire,* "the gray-haired scientists steered their vessels through the dark depths of space, while they ransacked worlds for treasures and luxuries; some even towed great masses of valuable rock or precious metal behind their ships. Rare and beautiful plants were uprooted, and strange animals were captured and stowed away in the interior of the ships, and finally deposited in London or the other great cities of the world." The conquest of space, it seemed, would look a lot like the conquest of earth.[35]

Among the most ambitious of the environmental projects imagined during this period was the straightening of the earth's axis relative to the sun. It was well known that the earth's tilt produced the seasons, and scientists had been exploring possible connections between fluctuations in the

earth's orbit and tilt and past changes in climate. But Jules Verne transformed this natural process into a human ambition. In 1889, he published
a humorous adventure story about a private corporation that purchases the
North Pole for the coal reserves thought to lie beneath it. The company an-
nounces that it will melt the ice by shifting the earth's axis to make it perpen-
dicular to the sun, thereby increasing the annual amount of sunlight on the
poles. A big selling point for the public is a seemingly beneficial side effect:
the creation of a single, yearlong season everywhere in the world.[36]

At first, the world greets the news with enthusiasm. Agriculture could
take place all year in the most favored climates, and people could choose
to live in whatever season they liked best. But the public soon realizes that
the process of shifting the earth might produce disastrous displacements
of the oceans, inundating some areas while leaving others permanently high
and dry. As tensions rise, the police raid the company's offices and learn
that it is constructing a gigantic cannon with sufficient recoil to move the
world. The race is on to find the cannon, which has been secretly constructed at the base of Mount Kilimanjaro. Although the authorities are too
late to stop the blast, the damage is only local: the company's mathematician had inadvertently dropped some zeros from an early calculation and
underestimated the size of the force required to do the job. Subsequent study
finds that altering the earth's axis would require more cannons than the
planet's surface could possibly hold. "The world's inhabitants could thus
sleep in peace," Verne concludes. "To modify the conditions of the Earth's
movement is beyond the powers of man."[37]

John Jacob Astor, an American businessman and one of the richest men
in the world, did not share Verne's doubts. Astor published a work of fiction
in 1894 that describes the United States in the year 2000 and discusses a
plan by the Terrestrial Axis Straightening Company to do exactly what its
name implies. Where other writers tended to follow Verne's lead in portraying such a scheme as environmentally dangerous and the work of greedy
corporations, Astor presents it as all benefits and no risks. One reason
might be that his mechanism for tipping the planet does not involve explosives, as Verne's did, but works instead on the principle of ballast: his fictional company is building massive holding basins at both poles and pumping water into and out of them as needed to adjust their weight and tip the

globe. "Never in the history of the world," he concludes, "has man reared so splendid a monument to his own genius as he will in straightening the axis of the planet." Astor's enthusiasm lived on in a later and quite real proposal by a respected New York City engineer, who advocated melting the North Pole to increase the earth's tilt and thereby improve the climate of the Northern Hemisphere.[38]

## Escaping the Bonds of Nature

At the extreme end of these dreams was the fantasy that humans might go beyond the conquest of nature and transcend it entirely. In Western culture, the "higher" civilization was not just the one with more scientific and technological knowledge but the one that had used that knowledge to remove itself farthest from the natural world. In many ways, the idea of civilization served as a yardstick for measuring a society's distance from nonhuman nature, with progress describing the passage from one rung to the next on the climb away from it. The highest of all possible civilizations would therefore be entirely unencumbered by the natural world, especially organic nature.[39]

For food, the next step up the ladder was abstraction from its original natural sources. Many futurists expected that scientists, through the magic of chemistry, would someday be able to synthesize any kind of food from any kind of vegetable matter. In a utopia written by the Scottish-American academic John Macnie and published in 1883, the key vegetable was maize. "Our milk," explains a guide from the ninety-sixth century, "is an artificial product prepared from maize: so, to a large extent, is our beef, as you call it, and similar articles of food. . . . From maize alone, as a basis, every variety of food could be prepared." Such scientifically advanced accomplishments were invariably a source of pride. "Needless to say," boasts a resident of an early twenty-first century future, "no hen laid those eggs; they are an admirable composition of artificial albumen. No cow gave the milk from which this cheese was made; no vine grew grapes to make this wine."[40]

Even higher up civilization's ladder was food manufactured directly from inorganic material. Some future societies mined nitrogen from the air to make entirely synthetic food, while others subsisted on processed coal or gravel. "When you can . . . eat of the stones of the earth," the Preceptress of a feminist utopia advises her visitor, "poverty and Disease will be as unknown to your people as it is to mine." Making nutritious and delicious food from rocks, chemicals, and gases represented progress not only because it reflected a high level of scientific sophistication but because it also indicated a lack of dependence on organic nature. Such a diet gave the appearance of almost complete freedom from natural constraints.[41]

Portrayals of synthetic food in fiction, often in the form of food pills, emerged directly from the food science of the day. The most famous advocate was Marcelin Berthelot, a French chemist renowned for his research in synthesizing organic compounds. In the 1890s, he expressed absolute certainty that chemically produced food would someday be on the menu. "I do not say that we shall give you artificial beefsteaks at once," he cautioned, "nor do I say that we shall ever give you the beefsteak as we now obtain and cook it. . . . But it will be a tablet of any color and shape that is desired, and will, I think, entirely satisfy the epicurean senses of the future." The University of Chicago chemist George Plumb agreed, predicting a time when kitchens would be stocked with nothing but hot water and food tablets. One of the founders of nutrition science, Wilbur Olin Atwater, expressed a bit more caution. He suspected that synthetic food still lay far in the future, if it was possible at all. But the potential existed, giving him hope that he need not fear for humanity's food supply.[42]

To its advocates, synthetic food offered all kinds of advantages. First, by arriving tasteless though packed with nutrition, it could be flavored by cooks or individual consumers in any way desired. Second, one could eat it quickly. The German science fiction writer Kurd Lasswitz wrote of how busy business people in the year 2371 "swallowed the universal-strength-extract pills of various dishes that allowed them to consume a meal of several courses in a few seconds." Third, synthetic food was so inexpensive that governments could offer it free to the poor and banish hunger forever. Some writers did depict synthetic food in a less rosy light: the American journalist Anna Bowman Dodd portrayed the liquid and pellet food served in her socialist dystopia as being just as gray, lifeless, and boring as the society itself. But she was bucking the trend.[43]

Given enough time and the right evolutionary nudge, humanity might

Evolution, wrote H. G. Wells in "The Man of the Year Million" (1893), would
eventually liberate humans from their dependence on the natural world.
This illustration from the article shows future humans deriving all their
required nutrients from a chemical bath. (Courtesy of the University
of Illinois at Urbana Rare Book and Manuscript Library)

be able to outdistance its own roots in the natural world. By the 1890s, fiction writers were often portraying people of the far distant future as biologically different, usually with larger heads to house more developed brains
but with smaller and weaker bodies. H. G. Wells pushed this evolutionary
trend to its logical conclusion, publishing a description of humans in the
year one million that would go on to influence many others. Toothless and
hairless, with only vestigial ears, nose, and mouth, Wells's future humans
nourish themselves not with organic food but by swimming in a chemical
nutritive fluid. Only their hands remain strong and well developed. Otherwise, "their whole muscular system, their legs, their abdomens, are shriv-
eled to nothing, a dangling, degraded pendant to their minds." Wells worked
on the principle that humankind's evolutionary trajectory would, in time,

suppress most of the traits that linked humans to animals. The irony was that, by relinquishing this kinship, the people of his future seemed to lose their humanity as well.[44]

One of the best ways for a fiction writer to maximize the distance between nature and civilization was to migrate human society underground into an entirely manufactured environment. Even then, subterranean life often ended up looking similar to surface life. A story set in the year 2882 imagines the human population so large that it has constructed countless subterranean levels to accommodate itself. But the ceilings of most levels are set at five hundred feet, since "a sky of about that elevation is considered to give a fairly natural effect over one or two or a few square miles." Deep beneath the surface, artificial green spaces abound. Sparkling streams tumble through landscapes filled with fragrant if artificial vegetation, designed in at least one case to evoke the Scottish Highlands. Residents consider the artificiality of such places to be an advantage because it gives them the opportunity to improve on nature. Imitation plants woven from synthetic material will not decay or turn yellow, and fake flowers with enhanced scents can perfume the air in all seasons. "We enslaved ourselves at first by a needless fidelity" to "nature's exact forms," explains a resident of the time. "But now we give free play to imagination." Life underground provided one more opportunity for humankind to outshine nature.[45]

The most thoughtful accounts of underground life, however, recognized that such a profound separation from the natural world would come with costs. In E. M. Forster's classic short story, "The Machine Stops," most of humanity has migrated to underground cities governed by a totalizing technological system called "the Machine." Individuals live entombed in technology: everything they need, from food to entertainment to medical care, is available with the push of a button reachable from the single chair in their private rooms. Although people communicate with each other constantly, even obsessively, through a system remarkably like twenty-first-century social media, they have grown afraid of direct experiences of all kinds and remain physically isolated. When the Machine begins to malfunction and eventually stops, the underground civilization collapses and its inhabitants die overnight.[46]

The cost of this overreliance on an artificial environment is not only social decay but also biological degeneration. Hints appear throughout the story that humanity has evolved into a fleshy, pale, hairless, toothless, and weak creature with big eyes and ears and a tendency toward subservience. The machine has encouraged this transformation, in part by euthanizing infants that showed promise of physical strength. A vigorous child "would have yearned for trees to climb, rivers to bathe in, meadows and hills against which he might measure his body," explains the narrator. Since the Machine did not make such surroundings available, it adapted humankind to those that it did provide. The lesson spelled out toward the end of the story is that the quest for comfort and the exploitation of nature had gone too far. "Progress had come to mean the progress of the Machine," writes the narrator. The result for humankind was decadence rather than godhood.[47]

In 1896, the great French sociologist Gabriel de Tarde wrote a remarkable story about an underground future that explored the psychological toll of long-term estrangement from nonhuman nature. Translated into English as *Underground Man,* with a preface by H. G. Wells, the book describes a subterranean society forced from the surface centuries before by the rapid and unexpected cooling of the sun. Tarde intended the book to serve as a sociological experiment. He wanted to answer the question: what would happen to human society if it retained its technological and cultural accomplishments but was cut off completely—for the first time in its history—from the influence of organic nature? Previous generations might have struggled to even formulate such a question. But by the end of the nineteenth century, the growth of Western accomplishments and ambitions had made it possible to dream about a complete escape from the natural world.[48]

The answer given by Tarde's narrator, speaking after six hundred years of adjustment to underground life, was that the transition had given humankind the freedom to achieve its full potential. Life on the surface had been life as a slave to nature. Now, humankind enjoyed complete liberty from unpredictable rainstorms, cyclones, lightning strikes, animal attacks, and a capricious sun that shone only when it wanted to and dictated the hours of night and day. The lack of contact with a larger natural world was not to be regretted. Plants and animals had merely been "rough drafts in creation" and the "fumbling experiments of Earth in quest of the human form." Besides, the discovery of ancient audio and video recordings of the natural world—a thunderstorm, a mountain torrent, a nightingale's song—revealed its wonders to have been far less impressive than poets and novelists had led people to believe. In contrast, humanity's subterranean galleries are so splendid in design and decoration that they evoke the sublime, making people feel "like the traveller of yore when he entered the twilight of a virgin forest." Now focused entirely on its own works, humankind can only be impressed with itself.[49]

Despite all of the self-congratulation, however, people remain deeply attached to the natural world they have lost. Even after the passage of six centuries, artists and architects incorporate more natural imagery into their work than they did before the destruction of the world's surface. Natural scientists continue to troll through mountains of old environmental data and, like the long dead Beethoven who continued to compose despite the loss of his hearing, construct new theories about the natural world without the ability to observe it directly. And poets, reports the narrator, "make us weep when they speak to us now of azure skies, of the sea-girt horizon, of the perfume of roses, of the song of birds, of all those objects that our eye has never seen, our ear has never heard, of which all our senses are ignorant, yet our mind conjures them up within us by a strange instinct."[50]

In fact, Tarde's future humans experience nature's absence so profoundly that it almost seems to unsettle their minds. In what seems like a desperate attempt to find fellow travelers, scientists conclude that molecules have ideas and desires and construct a "psychology of the atom." Thanks to their work, says the narrator, "we are no longer alone in a frozen world. We are conscious that these rocks are alive and animated," that "these living stones have some message for our heart." Even more revealing are the "malcontents" who "persist in condemning as monotonous our day devoid of clouds or night; our year, devoid of seasons; our towns devoid of country-life." The narrator admits that, come May, the same feeling of restlessness is widespread among the general population. He prefers to think of the sensation as having external origins, as if spring's "wandering ghost returns at stated seasons to visit us and tantalise us by her haunting presence." But its origins are clearly internal, arising from the fact that humans cannot outrun the natural part of themselves. In light of such passages, the true results of Tarde's sociological experiment become clear: complete freedom from organic nature succeeds only in producing an endless and incurable sense of disconnection and loss.[51]

## Imagining Environmental Disaster

The increase in the West's environmental ambitions coincided with a rising fear of scarcity, especially of forest products. The British began instituting forest conservation laws in India mid-century, and in 1864 the American conservationist George Perkins Marsh published his carefully researched and now classic call-to-arms, *Man and Nature*. "The earth is fast becoming an unfit home for its noblest inhabitant," he warned. "Another era of equal human crime and human improvidence . . . would reduce it to such a condition of impoverished productiveness, of shattered surface, of climatic excess, as to threaten the depravation, barbarism, and perhaps even extinction of the species." Rapacious and wasteful forestry practices continued to be the rule, however, and it would be a full generation before the American conservation movement kicked into full gear and began to influence federal management of national forests. Even then, the goal of conservation was to manage resources so they would continue to feed future growth.[52]

Equally frightening was the prospect that industrial activity might be damaging the planet in some wholly unexpected way. Lord Kelvin created a stir in 1897 by announcing that human activities would deplete all of the breathable oxygen in about five hundred years. Kelvin began his calculation with the amount of oxygen in the atmosphere and concluded that the extensive burning of coal, which consumes oxygen, and the destruction of forests, which replenish it, would eventually reduce the amount of naturally occurring oxygen to nothing. Kelvin's claim received media coverage on both sides of the Atlantic and prompted an American scientist to predict a day when breathable air would be a manufactured product. People would go about with diving bells on their heads and purchase whatever quantity of air they needed. Fiction writers quickly picked up on the theme of metered air, but the larger point was not lost on the reading public: human activity had the potential to cause environmental destruction on a planetary scale.[53]

As environmental anxieties increased in the last quarter of the century, so did the publication of stories describing environmental disasters. Most drew on recent advances in astronomy and geography to imagine catastrophes triggered by random acts of nature rather than human actions. In the hands of fiction writers, the world of tomorrow was repeatedly unsettled by stray comets, asteroids, planetoids, and nebulae; frozen by a waning sun or cooling earth; inundated by rising oceans; dried by their recession; or suffocated by volcanic gases. In stories like these, the forces of nature were arbitrary, vengeful, or simply weakening due to old age. But human actions caused about a third of the fictional environmental catastrophes published before World War I and reflected a growing discomfort with the expanding human impact on the earth.[54]

Some of these disaster stories mulled the big-picture, long-term environmental consequences of growth, with Mars becoming a popular stand-in for earth after the astronomer Percival Lowell portrayed the red planet as a drying and dying world. Lowell claimed that his telescope had revealed an extensive network of canals extending from the frozen poles that must have been created by intelligent inhabitants desperate for water. Alexander Bogdanov's classic socialist utopia *Red Star*, published in 1908, was one of several books to elaborate on the idea. Bogdanov's Martians have waged a relentless war of conquest with their planet's environment, believing that "there cannot be peace with the natural elements." That approach has produced a surge in population and exhausted the planet's coal, wood, and iron. When the story begins, the Martians are anticipating food shortages within the next thirty years. But they remain unwilling to curb their birthrate, since such a move "would mean denying the unlimited growth of life." So instead, they begin debating whether to search for additional resources on Venus or the more hospitable earth. The latter choice, of course, would require that they first exterminate its inhabitants.[55]

The French writer Eugène Mouton also took a long-term, large-scale view, trying to imagine what would happen if the process of planetary warming went too far. Writing in 1872, Mouton envisioned a future world that contained many familiar elements from the period, including growing populations, spreading suburbs, expanding industry, and ever more intensive agriculture. But Mouton kept his eye on the inexorable release of stored solar energy that accompanies these processes. In order to feed its population and industry, humankind burns all of the world's forests and fossil fuels and gets started on atmospheric hydrogen and oxygen. The tremendous increase in human bodies also contributes to the escalating release of energy. In time, the ever increasing heat passes a tipping point and begins to dry the wells, boil the oceans, and kill all of the planet's life, including humans. Mouton had the science dreadfully wrong, perhaps intentionally so, since he meant the story to be at least partly humorous. But it was likely the first tale ever written of catastrophic human-induced climate change.[56]

In contrast to these broader meditations on growth, many of the disaster stories produced during this period focused on the unfortunate environmental consequences of a particular kind of human expansion. The long-standing dream of constructing a canal through the Central American isthmus, for example, reminded several authors of Alexander von Humboldt's warning that such an effort might inadvertently divert the warm Gulf Stream away from Europe. One book tracks the immediate aftermath of the canal's completion, which causes part of the Central American isthmus to sink and the Gulf Stream to begin flowing from the Atlantic Ocean into the Pacific. Great Britain and Northern Europe are plunged into a deep freeze, and King Edward decamps to Australia. Another book takes up the storyline a thousand years later after a long exodus of population to new colonies in Canada, Africa, and Australia has left Britain in a semi-primitive state. British culture has survived, but outmigration has reduced the great metropolis of London to a mere ten thousand inhabitants.[57]

Other cautionary tales explored the risks of mining the atmosphere on an industrial scale. The idea had been partly inspired by Nikola Tesla, who had suggested that scientists make fertilizer directly from nitrogen in the air. In one story, an inventor discovers a process for hardening air, enabling him to freeze large volumes of it into bricks for use in construction. But the removal of too much air eventually causes the barometric pressure to drop, leading to excessive rainfall and crop failures around the world. In another, a corporation begins extracting massive amounts of nitrogen from the atmosphere to make synthetic food for the growing human population. Eventually, the ratio between nitrogen and oxygen becomes unbalanced, people begin to act strangely, and the excess oxygen in the atmosphere ignites and burns civilization to a crisp.[58]

A short story published in 1909 suggested that disaster might await cities that have grown too large and heavy for the earth to support them. Informed

In a story published by Robert Barr in *McClure's Magazine* (April 1900), corporations remove so much nitrogen from earth's atmosphere that the remaining oxygen ignites, searing the surface of the planet in a worldwide conflagration. This illustration from Barr's story shows the Brooklyn Bridge reduced to a pile of fused stone.

by the discovery of a real-world geological fault line running beneath 125th Street in New York City, the story tells how the incredible weight of the buildings at the heavily developed tip of Manhattan causes the fault to snap, tilting the whole island south of the fault like a plate. Water mains break, gas lines snap, elevated rail lines collapse, buildings crumble, and thousands die in the streets. "Like Babel we have built," explains a professor of geology watching the island list. "Who thought that we little things could have made an island, a whole island tilt?" Salvation comes in the form of another fault line running across the island farther to the south. When that fault gives way, the area north of it tips back into place, while the heavily developed area to the south, with its "huge mass of skyscrapers with their cyclopean walls, their glistening summits and their deep canyons of shade," slides into the harbor.[59]

Many other kinds of human-induced environmental catastrophes appeared as well, ranging from mad scientists releasing designer plagues to industrial fogs that destroy entire cities.[60] But they did not coalesce into a single, coherent, and memorable vision of the future that could challenge the dominant narrative of human expansion. They remained scattered speculations about the limits to growth, many probably written more as entertaining diversions than serious warnings about the environmental future. As a group, fiction writers were not very worried about the specter of environmental limits, mostly because scientists were not worried about it. At least not yet.

Still, admissions of environmental limits were beginning to come from unexpected quarters, like the technological triumphalist Jules Verne. One of his lesser-known books contains a revealing dialogue between two characters touring an exhausted coal mine. "It's a pity that all the globe was not made of coal," one muses. "Then there would have been enough to last millions of years!" His older and wiser companion, however, expresses relief that most of the world's material is not flammable. "The earth would have passed to the last bit into the furnaces of engines, machines, steamers, gas factories," he explains. "Certainly, that would have been the end of our world one fine day!" The conversation quickly moves on to other topics, making it easy for readers to overlook Verne's suggestion that the West's long-term expectations might be incompatible with environmental realities.[61]

## The Pastoral Alternative

Toward the end of the century, a new vision of the environmental future emerged that backed away from the idea of growth. Instead, it imagined simplified human wants and explored ways that humans could work with rather than against the natural world. Fiction writers articulated this vision through what scholars sometimes call pastoral utopias. Their stories picture a world with stable population and production levels, low consumption rates, smaller and greener communities, simpler or fewer technologies, and less aggressive and more immediate relationships with the natural environment. Although these imagined futures usually rejected growth, they were not motivated by a fear of limits. Nor were they naive exercises in rural nostalgia or simple outgrowths of anti-capitalist sentiment, although they sometimes contained elements of both. They were, rather, responses to the human and environmental costs of living in a competitive, materialistic, heavily technologized, and constantly expanding society. The result was a series of innovative efforts to redefine progress and to redesign the human relationship with the natural world.[62]

One of the earliest and most radical of these pastoral utopias was *A Crystal Age,* published in 1887 by the naturalist W. H. Hudson. The story takes place several thousand years in the future, long after the single-minded pursuit of control over nature has destroyed urban industrial society. Life in a thinly populated Britain now centers on isolated houses governed by all-powerful mother and father figures, who alone are allowed to reproduce. Otherwise the residents of these houses live together as equals, producing whatever they need from the local environment and celebrating nature through decorative artwork that covers the houses and all of the books, furnishings, and decorations inside them. There is no machinery, no money, and no economy to speak of. Despite its beauty and simplicity, however, the society's harsh and arbitrary punishments and taboo on sex mark it as heavily repressive. The main character, an unintentional visitor from the nineteenth century, never fully adjusts to his new circumstances.[63]

Almost as green but far more appealing was William Dean Howells's fictional Altruria, a pastoral utopia located on a little-known continent in the Pacific. Howells, a distinguished writer and editor in the United States, drew heavily on the earlier utopias of More and Campanella to create an updated version of the utopia of sufficiency. Altruria had once been as competitive, urban, and technology-oriented as the West but had since evolved into an egalitarian society that emphasizes the agricultural life. The inhabitants perform three hours of obligatory labor in the morning but have their afternoons free. Consumption is low, in part because fashions rarely change; beauty and artistry are prized in all things; and population remains stable through some unspecified means. The Altrurians have replaced the filthy industrial cities of the past with smaller regional capitals surrounded by villages, which is where most people live and work. They have also reorganized their relationship with industrial technology: the Altrurians have cleaned it up by replacing coal-powered steam with water-powered electricity, and they engage with mechanical transportation less, since they enjoy village life so much that they find little reason to take the high-speed electrical conveyances to the capitals. In general, life is simple, needs are few, and the Altrurians immerse themselves in nature.[64]

The best known and most influential of the pastoral utopias was William Morris's *News from Nowhere; or, an Epoch of Rest,* published in 1890. Morris described himself as a man "with a deep love of the earth and the life on it, and a passion for the history of the past of mankind." Both expressed themselves in his life as an artist, poet, conservationist, and leading light of the international Arts and Crafts Movement, which emphasized traditional craftsmanship over industrial production. Morris had little respect for how Western society was using its advanced technologies. He believed that such knowledge would be more beneficial to humankind if used to prevent pollution and make work more satisfying, rather than to design more destructive weapons and increase the production of goods that nobody needed. Morris looked backward in time to find a period that did not emphasize self-interest as strongly as his own and settled on the Middle Ages as a model for his future society. Although he undoubtedly romanticized medieval life, Morris recognized its limitations and sought only to borrow what he thought the period did better than his own: value the hand-made and the beautiful, embrace a smaller scale and a slower pace, and appreciate the natural. His pastoral utopia was, in part, a response to Edward Bellamy's urban and industrial one.[65]

Morris's twenty-second-century England is a creative and contented utopia set in a newly rural society. Class war has overturned capitalism and eliminated all formal government as Marx predicted, but it has also led to the abandonment of industrialization. The population of England has remained stable since the nineteenth century, and most urbanites have migrated to the countryside and abandoned the cities, which have since contracted. Housing developments have returned to meadow, and the residents of London use the former Houses of Parliament to store manure. Large factories are a thing of the past, since the population produces whatever it needs by hand. There is no money or mass production for market. England, explains one resident, "is now a garden, where nothing is wasted and nothing is spoilt." Residents prefer simple technologies that are easy to repair and add beauty to the landscape, although they have retained a few more sophisticated ones that they find useful. There are no efforts to invent new machines, no organized scientific research projects, and no incentives for economic growth.[66]

Underlying Morris's society is a new way of relating to nature. The inhabitants have replaced the nineteenth century's desire to control and exploit the natural world with an "intense and overweening love of the very skin and surface of the earth on which man dwells." Although they still remain dependent on the natural environment for all of their basic needs, they have developed an expanded sense of their relationship with it. In fact, they do not even use the term "nature" anymore, since it obscures the connections between the human and nonhuman worlds. Residents of the nineteenth century, explains one of Morris's characters, tried to make nature their slave because "they thought 'nature' was something outside them." Her society had learned otherwise.[67]

Less well known but unique in its vision was Algernon Petworth's *The Little Wicket Gate*, published in 1913. Rather than reducing the level of technology and emphasizing agriculture, the author imagined a technologically sophisticated society that retains an intimate relationship with wilderness. The inhabitants of this future Great Britain live in beautiful houses arranged in garden settings and organized into towns. Their advanced technology includes solar-powered lighting and anti-gravity vehicles, although machinery serves humanity rather than the other way around. But rather than embedding the garden towns in agricultural landscapes, the author surrounds them with an immense and completely wild region of indefinite size. "There are great forests and rivers," explains a resident, "and salt and fresh-water lakes; deep valleys, wide plains, and high mountains, some so high that they are crowned with snow. It extends hundreds and hundreds of miles, how far I know not."[68]

Where a society based on growth and progress would have pounced on this land for its untapped resources, Petworth's town dwellers refuse even to map it. Since their society is based on service to others rather than self-ishness, they find it beneficial to surround themselves with spaces that exist outside of humankind's natural sense of competitiveness. The wilderness areas also satisfy the occasional need to leave civilization behind and re-connect with one's wild roots. They consider the satisfaction of this need to be the "fourth necessity," after food, clothing, and shelter. Whenever the mood strikes them, people light out, live in the wild on their own for a time, perhaps seeking inspiration, and then return. The reason for leaving these areas in their wild state is therefore completely utilitarian: the concern is not for the welfare of the area's plants and animals. But it is a different kind of human need that this society is trying to fulfill, one that is psychological or spiritual rather than material. By leaving the wild untouched, and pre-serving its mystery by leaving it unmapped, they have nurtured a space where "Nature seems to hug your soul."[69]

John Ruskin and his followers in the English Lake District tried to put some of the principles of the pastoral utopia into action in the real world. One of the most prominent British thinkers of the nineteenth century, Ruskin was convinced that coal-fueled industrial society was depleting finite resources and damaging the global climate. He considered it unsustainable in the long term and expected that people would someday return to a life of handmade manufactures and lower consumption, if not by choice then by necessity. Encouraged by Ruskin's writings, like-minded friends and neigh-bors created gardens that showed special reverence for native plants and revived traditional crafts and industries using local materials. Ruskin him-self founded the Guild of St. George to purchase land and encourage its cultivation using traditional methods. In Ruskin's mind, such efforts would prepare for the day when the British people would plow the railroad embankments back into their fields. But these were all small-scale experiments, and most were quickly forgotten.[70]

The great French illustrator Albert Robida recognized that it might not be desirable or even possible to make such radical changes to social and environmental relationships. So he imagined the creation of a pastoral space within a future industrial society. In his 1892 book *The Electric Life,* which portrayed a technologically advanced 1950s, the people of France exult in the many benefits that science and technology have brought to humankind but also recognize the costs. The rapid pace of life has exhausted the population; a lack of physical activity and a diet of artificially manufactured food have damaged public health; overpopulation has strained resources; and industry has polluted the soil, air, and water. Robida portrays the future French as struggling to solve problems of their own creation and making matters worse by stubbornly believing that all scientific and technological change is for the best. The challenge they face is to balance a relentlessly growing and changing world of cities and technology with a seemingly biological need for a slower pace, a simpler life, and a greener environment.[71]

Robida's future society finds a partial solution in setting aside a vast national park along the coast of Brittany to preserve not only the rural landscape but traditional culture as well. It is "a region forbidden to all the innovations of science, barred to industry. At the fence marking the frontier, progress stops and does not pass." Permanent residents live beneath thatched roofs, spin thread on wheels, and herd animals. Visitors enter the area in horse-drawn stagecoaches and must communicate with the outside by post, since there is no electricity. Just a short distance from cities where "our scientific civilization reigns in triumph and full intensity," notes the narrator, it seems as if "the clock of time has broken down."[72]

Robida's approach was more patently nostalgic than some others and easy to push to a humorous extreme. Just the year before, the Scottish poet and novelist John Davidson had imagined a future in which the British government has empowered a corporation to purchase all of Scotland, clear it of structures built after 1700, and turn it into a history-themed resort for the wealthy. Steam, electricity, and water power are banned, native vegetation makes a comeback, and visitors are charged by the month to dress and act as if they are living in former ages. The highly profitable venture is heralded

Workers in traditional dress oversee one of the entrances
to Albert Robida's fictional national park in *The Electric
Life* (1892). By turning back the cultural, technological,
and environmental clocks to an earlier period, the
park provides the population a much needed
haven from unrelenting progress and growth.
(Courtesy of the Getty Research Institute)

as "the salvation of a fragment of the Old World from the jaws of Civilisation" and inspires similar projects all over the world. In an earlier book,
Robida himself had included a tongue-in-cheek subplot in which a corporation purchases all of Italy and resettles seventy-five percent of its population
in Uruguay. The remaining residents stay behind to dress in traditional garb
and serve as innkeepers, cooks, and gondoliers in the carefully maintained
cities, ruins, and other tourist spots.[73]

But when Robida published *The Electric Life* ten years later, he was ready to take the idea more seriously. He presents his national park as a necessary escape from "the great scientific and industrial movement that was then turning everything upside-down so rapidly and radically transforming the surface of the Earth." Immersing themselves in the rural landscape and provincial life of the past enables his otherwise urban and modern characters to renew their strength. The park is therefore not a frivolous playground but a psychological necessity, serving "all those enervated and overworked by electric life" by providing natural surroundings "far from any absorbent and enervating machine or apparatus, with no Teles, no phonos, and no Tubes, beneath a sky empty of all traffic." In order to survive life in the endlessly innovating and growing industrial cities of the future, people have to spend part of their time in the simpler, unchanging, and rural environment of the past.[74]

Although it appeared in some widely read works, and had real world reflections in the urban and national park movements, the pastoral vision remained a minor note at the turn of the twentieth century. Most of those peering into the future continued to see endless development supported by evolution itself, and their growth-oriented optimism was spreading rapidly around the world through translations of futuristic works into Arabic, Chinese, Japanese, and Turkish. Even the prospect of a European war, widely predicted by futurists since the 1870s, gave prognosticators little pause. If war came, a united world and an age of peace would emerge from the destruction; if it did not, communication and transportation technologies would serve as unifying forces and bring about the same beneficial results. "Everything seems pointing to the belief," wrote H. G. Wells in 1902, "that we are entering upon a progress that will go on, with an ever-widening and ever more confident stride, forever." Western faith in science, technology, growth, and progress was at an all-time high. But that was about to change.[75]

# 4

# Narrating the Apocalypse

THE WEST'S FAITH IN PROGRESS suffered a serious blow on the battlefields of the First World War. "The consequence of applying science to the ancient methods of war was not expected in 1914," explained a British futurist over twenty years later, "and produced a horror from which we have not yet recovered." The millions dead and maimed from poison gas and other advanced weaponry put the old assumption that moral progress would naturally follow scientific and technological progress permanently to rest. Instead, it seemed as if humanity's new power over natural forces would become instruments of domination and destruction. "Men sometimes speak as though the progress of science must necessarily be a boon to mankind," wrote the philosopher and mathematician Bertrand Russell seven years after the war's end. "But that, I fear, is one of the comfortable nineteenth-century delusions which our more disillusioned age must discard." Concern about humankind's ability to wield its science and technology responsibly would grow even deeper after the dropping of the atomic bombs a generation later.[1]

The idea of progress, along with the expectation of continued growth, nevertheless remained strong into the 1960s. Periods of incredible scientific and technological innovation and unprecedented economic expansion followed both wars, suggesting that immense abundance was still to come from the further mastery of nature. "Look around," wrote the well-known American science writer Victor Cohn in 1956. "Penicillin, jet planes, nylon

stockings, dacron suits, automatic washers . . . all were unknown or laboratory dreams fifteen years ago; all will be outdated twenty-five or thirty years
from now, or ten years, or five." The image of a streamlined, technological
future became a common and highly successful marketing device. Sometimes companies even sold the future itself in the form of aluminum Christ-
mas trees or foods that used artificial coloring and gelatin to go beyond the
hues and textures found in nature. The development narrative would reach
its high point after World War II in what is now remembered as the golden
age of futurism.[2]

But during those same decades, scientists began to question more directly the environmental implications of growth. They reflected on the role
that competition for scarce resources had played in sparking the world wars,
and they wondered whether surging human populations and expanding
economies would exhaust key resources. Such concerns finally crystalized
into a new narrative of the environmental future. Like an inverted reflection of the cornucopian view of growth, the new vision accepted the idea
of environmental limits, treated environmental factors rather than human
progress as the prime drivers of history, questioned the value of scientific
progress, and claimed to see environmental apocalypse looming on the horizon. By the late 1960s, narratives of development and disaster existed side-
by-side in the public imagination, each resting on a different set of assumptions about nature and history, each embracing radically different stories
about past and future.

## Progress as Dystopia

The development narrative survived the First World War, but not un-
changed: the new climate of doubt unwound its story into utopian and dystopian strands. In the former, growth and the mastery of nature produced
a familiar technological utopia, but one that also reflected an ever-greater
fascination with the machine. Science fiction, its popularity on the rise,
found new media outlets like pulp magazines, radio shows, comic books,
and movies through which to spread the vision. Modernist architecture
reinforced it as well by embracing a machine aesthetic that emphasized the
technological control of the natural world: a lake controlled by a modern

dam, a river spanned by a suspension bridge, or a meadow improved by a freshly paved parkway. And the two great American world's fairs of the interwar period placed the celebration of the West's scientific and technological progress at their very center. Nothing better expressed the philosophy informing these fairs than an epigram in one of the official guidebooks: "Science Finds—Industry Applies—Man Conforms."[3]

The utopian strand still made little room for animals that did not have some practical value. Fortunato Depero, one of the leaders of Italy's literary and artistic "Futurism" movement, looked forward to a day when "civilization will have swept all the lower forms of animal life off the face of the earth." The idea of ultimate animal extinction was so much a part of mainstream thought that, in 1926, a full-page article appeared in a number of American newspapers claiming that every wild animal would need to prove its usefulness to humankind or would have to go. The article explained that any animals unable to pay their way "will be 'junked' because they are not of sufficient use to man to live in the same sphere with him." That was also the future envisioned by H. G. Wells in *Men Like Gods,* his utopia from 1923. Set three thousand years into the future, the book imagines humans closely scrutinizing every species to determine its level of utility and ultimate destiny.[4]

The new human habitats expected to overrun the animal ones would have been recognizable to the previous generation. Dreams of low-density development spreading to the horizon continued in designs like Frank Lloyd Wright's Broadacre City and in the sprawl of actual suburbs. The monumental city centers imagined by commercial artists endured in the more carefully sculpted if still heroically proportioned designs of professional architects like Hugh Ferriss. And the small, self-contained cities of Robert Owen and Charles Fourier reemerged in Ebenezer Howard's garden cities. Before World War I, Howard had proposed cities of limited size surrounded by agricultural greenbelts: when populations reached a certain level, new cities would be founded on virgin land. His idea eventually blossomed into a Garden City Movement that saw the construction of a number of such towns in Great Britain and the United States into the middle of the twentieth century. All three models of the future city were striving to accommodate growth, either by extending existing cities outward, building them upward, or constructing entirely new ones as needed.[5]

The utopian strand of the development narrative continued to enjoy enormous appeal into the 1960s. In fact, the decade produced two of the narrative's most memorable interpretations. The General Motors Futurama exhibit at the 1964–1965 New York World's Fair took visitors on a ride through miniaturized landscapes that showed humanity extending its domain on a number of environmental frontiers. On the ocean floor, "aquacopters" searched for precious metals, drills extracted oil, and tourists enjoyed a stay in Hotel Atlantis. In the Amazonian jungle, a pair of machines used laser beams to fell ancient trees while a third followed behind, grinding up trunks with its front end and extruding a paved highway out its back. In a desert, reclaimed seawater nourished crops on automated farms. On the moon, rovers glided around crater rims on their journeys from one lunar base to another. At every turn, Futurama proclaimed that technology—much of it manufactured by General Motors, of course—would continue to unlock the doors of nature's endless larder. As visitors exited the ride, they received metal lapel pins that read: "I have seen the future."[6]

Even more enduring was the animated television sitcom *The Jetsons*. Although its American creators produced only a single season of the show from 1962 to 1963, decades of international syndication ensured that its vision of a technological utopia complete with jet packs, flying cars, and robot servants would spread around the world. Every aspect of the Jetson family's life in the year 2062 is simultaneously saturated with futuristic technology and alienated from the natural world: they live, work, and play in buildings that rise above the clouds when it rains; vacation on dude ranches with mechanical horses; rocket to the moon for wilderness experiences; and dine on synthetic food prepared instantaneously by machines. The cartoon family seldom encounters anything that is not artificially made and rarely sees the surface of the earth or encounters other animal species. Yet their abundant leisure time and automated lifestyle have retained their appeal, and the show remains a popular culture touchstone.[7]

But with the idea of progress severely shaken by the wars, the development narrative also evolved a second, more dystopian strand that quickly came to rival its utopian counterpart. In this version, humankind fully develops the natural world and achieves a fantastically high level of science and technology, only to find that it lacks the ability to wield its power wisely. As a result, the people of the future engage in devastating wars, use technology to dominate each other, suffer from scientific accidents, endure rifts between the human and natural worlds, and lose the things that made them human to begin with. The end point is often discontent or authoritarianism at best, barbarism or extinction at worst. The age of scientific and technological dystopia had begun.

Feeding the dystopian mood was a revival of the idea that history is more circular than linear. The most powerful articulation of this view appeared in the German historian Oswald Spengler's *The Decline of the West,* published just months before the end of World War I. Drawing on the history of past human societies, Spengler rejected linear history and the idea of endless progress and argued instead that history moves forward in unrelated cycles of rise and fall. Western civilization, he claimed, had moved beyond its highwater mark and was now on the downward side of an unavoidable curve. Spengler's ideas about cyclical history and inevitable decline influenced a broad audience of thinkers, sank deep into the public consciousness, and stoked fears that the best days of the West might be behind it.[8]

Dystopian novels proliferated, with many exploring how future humans might misuse their power to manipulate natural forces. Among the most influential was Aldous Huxley's *Brave New World,* published in 1932. Huxley painted a chilling portrait of a twenty-sixth-century World State where the greatest good is social stability. To ensure it, the state uses genetic engineering to breed five distinct castes of people. Each group is biologically designed and socially conditioned to accept its place in the social order, eliminating the possibility of dissent. Life for the upper caste revolves around consumption and sex, with critical thinking and individualism strongly discouraged. The lower castes, who live comparatively dull lives, are nevertheless content because they are bred and trained to be. It is difficult to read Huxley's book and not come away convinced that humankind should never be trusted to guide its own evolution.[9]

The interwar years produced a number of other now classic dystopias filled with warnings about human hubris, fallibility, and misuse of science and technology. Karel Čapek's play *R.U.R.*, which premiered in Prague in 1921, takes place about a generation into the future when the world has come to rely on the labor of artificial people manufactured from chemicals. In time, these "robots" (Čapek created the term) realize that they are superior in strength and intelligence to humans and revolt against them, taking their place as the dominant species. Yevgeny Zamyatin's *We*, completed in Russia the same year, portrays an authoritarian, industrialized society of the future so attracted to the idea of absolute control that it has built a wall to separate the machine-like lives of its people from the spontaneity and chaos of the natural world. In Germany, Alfred Döblin published an ambitious, multi-century account of the future entitled *Mountains, Seas, and Giants* that describes an effort to create new land for settlement by melting Greenland's icecap. Removing the ice, however, frees huge and monstrous creatures that rampage through Europe and drive the human population underground.[10]

Concerns about machine civilization were so widespread that prominent figures felt a need to defend it. Lewis Mumford cautioned against "scrapping the machine and returning to a bare subsistence level in little island utopias devoted to sub-agriculture and sub-manufacture." Rather than a new adventure, he considered such a future "a bedraggled retreat" and "a confession of complete failure." Lord Birkenhead, Britain's Lord Chancellor after the First World War, warned that it was impossible to go backward. "There can never be an industrial counterrevolution," he claimed. "Nothing could transform Britain into a nation of forty million yeomen farmers and peasant proprietors; the acreage of the British Isles could not support such a swarm of agriculturalists. Starvation and a frantic return to the factories would be the inevitable conclusions of any large-scale 'Back to the Land' experiment." Both would likely have agreed with Nikola Tesla, who believed that "the solution of our problems does not lie in destroying but in mastering the machine." Building a better future would require more technology, not less.[11]

## The Return of Malthus

While the development narrative was sprouting a dystopian branch, a new narrative of growth-induced environmental disaster began to coalesce, in part around fears of overpopulation. After World War I, biologists, chemists, demographers, and economists began to ponder the role that overpopulation might have played in sparking the conflict. Their efforts shed a harsh new light on several centuries of staggering growth in human numbers. In the three hundred years between the first European encounter with the Americas and the early years of the industrial revolution, world population had doubled to about a billion people. After little more than a century of industrialization, it had doubled again, with some two thirds of the population undernourished and the rate of growth still increasing. Daunting numbers like these, combined with a shaken faith in progress, made it easier to imagine that humankind might have misjudged its ability to manage growth.[12]

Malthusian concerns about population outstripping its food supply quickly began to gain strength. In 1923, the Harvard chemist and geneticist Edward East warned that "if world saturation of population, which approaches speedily, is not prevented, in its train will come more wars, more famine, more disease." The prominent English journalist Philip Gibbs agreed, writing that the world would need to increase food production, rationalize its distribution, and alter industrial life in radical ways if it wanted to avoid "a fierce conflict for the fertile places of the earth." Similar worries inspired the formation of the International Union for the Scientific Investigation of Population Problems, founded in Paris in 1928. The population movement that developed in these years was diverse, attracting those interested in eugenics, racial purity, and family planning as well. But it was largely the shock of the war that explained the surge in public and scientific interest.[13]

World War II further heightened concerns about overpopulation. In 1948, two best-selling books by American scientists, Fairfield Osborn's *Our Plundered Planet* and William Vogt's *Road to Survival*, blamed the war directly on overpopulation and resource scarcity and foresaw conditions worsening in the future. "Unless, in short," Vogt concluded, "man readjusts his way of living, in its fullest sense, to the imperatives imposed by the *limited* resources of his environment—we may as well give up all hope of continuing civilized life." Their warnings about a worsening environmental crisis and its link to famine and war, which had become unthinkable in the atomic age, were echoed in newspapers, magazines, and radio shows around the world.[14]

Visions of what an overcrowded world might look like began to appear in short stories, books, television shows, and movies in the early 1950s. Two of the most common themes were the rise of authoritarian governments, which many believed to be inevitable on a planet jammed with people, and their ruthless efforts to cull their populations. Fictional methods of future population control included forced relocation to less populated areas; re-settlement to fishing fleets that are forced to stay permanently at sea; en-couragement of homosexuality; compulsory euthanasia on reaching a par-ticular age; the intentional introduction of new diseases; and the staging of trumped-up wars in which a single government sends its own unsuspecting citizens to fight on both sides. A third theme, often the source of hope, was the possibility that space exploration might reveal new places to live on other worlds.[15]

Despite such frightening visions, many postwar experts insisted that hu-mans would find ways to increase the food supply as needed. The countries of the world could put more land under the plow; expand irrigation, using desalinization plants where necessary; explore new sources of nutrition; im-prove food plants, perhaps by bombarding seeds with atomic radiation; and intensify existing agriculture by increasing the use of machinery, fertiliz-ers, and pesticides. At Oxford University, the agricultural economist Colin Clark calculated that the world could support as many as twenty-eight bil-lion people by using all of the available arable land and cultivating it with the same intensity as the Dutch. In Denmark, the economist Ester Boserup argued that population growth intensifies agricultural production rather than just shooting past it. In the Soviet Union, which did not share the West's fear of overpopulation and claimed to have produced cabbages three feet across, the agronomist S. I. Volkovitch declared that "any such term as 'limits of growth' almost seems an anachronism." To these experts, there was little reason for worry.[16]

But even if humanity managed to avoid famine and war, some questioned whether such a crowded world would be worth living in. The engineer and physicist Dennis Gabor, later a Nobel Prize winner, expected that "most thinking people will share my horror at the thought of the maximum population living on fish rations in huge tenements so crowded that they cannot all take their exercise at the same time." Others expressed more prosaic concerns, like the newspaper reporter who worried that a growing population would increase demand for tickets at sports stadiums, forcing those of limited means to watch the game at home on television. Why such a large percentage of people was looking forward to such crowding in the first place remained a mystery to Harrison Brown, a geochemist at the California Institute of Technology and a noted futurist. "It is behaving," he wrote in 1954, "as if it were engaged in a contest to test nature's willingness to support humanity and, if it had its way, it would not rest content until the earth is covered completely and to a considerable depth with a writhing mass of human beings."[17]

In the long term, some of the more hopeful agriculturalists expected that chemistry would come to the rescue. Successful research in synthetic foods dated to at least the First World War, when German scientists produced edible fats from petroleum. By the 1920s and 1930s, scientists were also discussing the possibility of manufacturing starches and sugars directly from the cellulose in trees and developing new foods from cottonseeds, animal blood, and yeast derived from liquid wastes. Such ideas reached large numbers of people through newspapers and popular magazines and were endorsed by political leaders at the highest levels. Lord Birkenhead believed that synthetic foods would "finally set at rest those timid minds which prophecy a day when the earth's resources will not feed her children." Like J. B. S. Haldane, one of the most influential biologists of the day, Birkenhead expected synthetic food to become commercially viable by the middle of the twenty-first century.[18]

The chemical revolution after World War II seemed to bring such goals within sight. Building on wartime discoveries and momentum, the postwar chemical industry produced an astounding array of futuristic products: new vaccines and medications to improve health, new fibers to replace traditional ones like cotton, wool, and silk, and new pesticides to control harmful insects on farms and mosquitoes in suburban neighborhoods. New preservatives, paints, dyes, detergents, and building materials appeared, and new plastics changed the face of everything from toys to dishware to cars. Popular symbols of the new chemical era ranged from Disneyland's Monsanto Home of the Future, unveiled in 1957 and made entirely of plastic, to any modern chemical plant. For Victor Cohn, such manufacturing facilities stood for "progress that never stops—progress toward technology and culture that will both demand and be able to offer equality, leisure, comfort and education, widespread health and widespread prosperity." The chemical revolution came so swiftly, and left an imprint so large, that many in the scientific community seemed to swoon over the prospect of a synthetic tomorrow.[19]

In light of such rapid advances, it seemed as if future food systems would be awash in a sea of beneficial chemicals as well. In 1956, Cohn gave his readers a peek at what food production might be like at the end of the century. The farmers of 1999, he wrote from the perspective of the future, "used synthetic fertilizers, soil conditioners, hormones and pesticides; antibiotics, trace minerals, leaf removers, growth regulators. Crops sold in chemically treated soil killed weeds. Chemical spraying conquered diseases such as wheat rust. Farmers gave baby pigs synthetic milk, and fed cows electronically treated sawdust." Cohn's attitude toward chemical farming was relentlessly upbeat, which was in keeping with the theme of his book—*1999: Our Hopeful Future*—as well as the future envisioned by advocates of growth.[20]

Only truly synthetic food, however, would free humankind entirely from the bondage of traditional edible plants. Such dreams could sometimes sound more like alchemy than chemistry. Waldemar Kaempffert, the science editor for the *New York Times,* imagined sawdust and wood pulp transformed into sugary foods, and discarded paper table linens and rayon clothing transmuted into candy. Cohn foresaw parents enjoying "wood steak, planked," and their children pining for an "oil-cream cone," while Isaac Asimov expected "mock-turkey" to be served at the 2014 world's fair. These chemical miracles would take place inside giant food factories that the British scientist Archibald Low considered absolutely essential to feeding the future. "They will make forecasts of 'inevitable' starvation," he predicted, "seem as foolish as those of Malthus."[21]

Some chemists had so much confidence in the benefits of synthetic foods that they argued for their superiority to more natural ones. Jacob Rosin was director of research at Montrose Chemical Company in Newark, New Jersey, when he published his 1953 book *The Road to Abundance* with writer Max

Eastman. Rosin argued that the general preference for the natural over the artificial was wrong-headed, particularly in the case of plant-based foods. According to Rosin, natural foods such as potatoes were neither designed nor meant for human consumption and therefore had no advantages over artificial foods. "For the benefit of the nature worshipers," he wrote, "let us put it this way: our use of nature's products for purposes for which they were not created is *unnatural*. The natural thing is to use synthetics which are especially made for our purposes and therefore meet all our requirements." Rosin saw himself as revealing the true nature of so-called natural foods: "a poorly assorted mixture of chemicals containing a large amount of indigestible materials, and a certain proportion of materials injurious to our health." Synthetic foods, in contrast, would be tailor-made for human beings and therefore healthier to eat.[22]

Two weekly American newspaper comic strips, both first published in 1958 and syndicated internationally, brought similarly optimistic views of synthetic foods to millions of people around the world. The illustrator Arthur Radebaugh devoted *Closer Than We Think* to all things futuristic and frequently discussed the future of food production. One of his strips, titled "Fat Plants and Meat Beets," explained that "there will be less grazing land in tomorrow's crowded world, so beefsteaks may have to be replaced by extracted vegetable proteins flavored with synthetics that taste like real meat." Athelstan Spilhaus, dean of the University of Minnesota Institute of Technology, wrote the comic strip *Our New Age* to teach children about science and used it to speculate about the potential for fossil fuel-based synthetic foods to help feed the growing population. The influence of these two cartoons, which were persistently optimistic, is hard to overestimate. When Spilhaus met President John F. Kennedy in 1962, the president joked that everything he had ever learned about science came from Spilhaus's comic strip.[23]

But chemical miracles could also lead to disaster rather than deliverance, at least in the imaginations of science fiction writers. In 1947, Ward Moore published *Greener Than You Think,* a satirical and now classic book that contemplates the destruction of humankind by genetically enhanced Bermuda grass. In Moore's story, an amateur scientist produces a chemical compound that will produce mutations in any member of the grass family

In November 1965, Athelstan Spilhaus used his popular *Our New Age* comic strip to tout the potential of fossil fuel-based synthetic foods like "Fakin' Bacon," "Petro Pizza," and "Pseudo Crackers" to feed the ever-growing population of the future. This is a detail of the larger strip. (Courtesy of Matt Novak)

so that it will grow in spectacular abundance. Her well-meaning intention is to apply the formula to corn and wheat, which are both grasses. "I want no more backward countries," she insists, "no more famines in India or China; no more dustbowls; no more wars, depressions, hungry children." Pressed for funds, however, she employs a salesman to use the unperfected formula on local crops in order to raise some cash. The salesman, in need of money himself, decides there is more to be made by applying the formula to lawns and uses it on a neighbor's yard instead. The treated grass proves able to nourish itself on absolutely anything at hand and grows to gigantic size. From there, it spreads aggressively across the world, adapting itself to any altitude, climate, and environmental circumstance as it pushes humankind and most other forms of life to the brink of extinction.[24]

## Resource Exhaustion

The other fear contributing to the emerging vision of environmental disaster was resource exhaustion. Writing ten years after the end of World War I, the prominent English journalist Philip Gibbs found widespread concern among scientists that the West would deplete the world's accessible coal and oil deposits before finding replacement forms of energy. "As far as the future is concerned" he wrote, "it seems to be a race between the scientists and the exhaustion of supplies which would lead us back to barbarism and so to death." The prospect of resource exhaustion also attracted science fiction writers, like the British author Olaf Stapledon. In his groundbreaking and influential book *Last and First Men*, published in 1930, Stapledon imagined a future world society that develops alternative energies but fails to completely eliminate its dependence on fossil fuels. When the last of the coal finally runs out, civilization collapses and begins a Spengler-inspired cycle of rise and fall that Stapledon traces across two billion years and eighteen different species of human being.[25]

The search for renewable sources of energy continued between the wars, sometimes generating schemes of Promethean proportions. In the 1930s, the German engineer Hermann Honnef proposed the construction of massive wind towers, each taller than the Empire State Building and equipped with multiple turbines. Another German, the architect Herman Sörgel, lobbied for an even more ambitious project he called Atlantropa that would transform the Mediterranean basin into a massive hydroelectric power project. The plan's centerpiece was the construction of a dam across the Strait of Gibraltar that would cut off the Mediterranean from the Atlantic and use controlled flows to generate enormous amounts of electricity. Sörgel hoped that the resulting power would save Europe from the inevitable exhaustion of fossil fuels and provide the means for making the environment and climate of Africa more conducive to European colonization. He also expected that evaporation would gradually reduce the level of the Mediterranean Sea, creating a quarter million square miles of new living space for Europe's growing population.[26]

After World War II, fears of resource exhaustion rose to a whole new level. One reason was that the war had consumed a staggering amount of

In the 1930s, the German engineer Hermann Honnef proposed the construction of giant, multi-armed turbines to capture the energy of fast-moving winds. This rendering from a contemporary German postcard includes tiny buildings and streets in the foreground to give a sense for the immense size of the towers that Honnef had in mind. (akg-images)

resources as participants scoured the globe for oil, metal, rubber, and wood to feed their war efforts. Germany felled forests in occupied Eastern Europe, Canadian aluminum companies opened new bauxite mines in British Guiana, and the United States subsidized a dramatic expansion of Brazil's rubber industry. The combatants also exploited resources in their own countries with renewed vigor, leaving their nations more dependent on foreign sources after the war. The United States Department of the Interior reported in 1947 that the war effort had used up 60 percent of the country's zinc and copper supplies, 70 percent of its high-grade bauxite, 83 percent of its silver and lead, and 97 percent of its mercury. Other valuable minerals were diminished as well, raising the specter of future shortages. "The supply of some of our most valuable resources is likely to become deficient in one or two decades," reported an American policy think tank that same year, "and will, therefore, present serious problems in the 1950 decade."[27]

Another reason for concern was that the postwar West, led by the United States and Great Britain, had self-consciously begun to put growth at the center of its economic planning. In fact, not just the capitalist West but also the communist East and indeed much of the rest of the world began following the new gospel of growth. The theoretical roots lay in the prewar work of the economist John Maynard Keynes, whose ideas about government-sponsored consumption underpinned the unprecedented economic expansion that followed the war. Economic growth became an object of universal faith, its costs and even its benefits often unquestioned. "We share the belief of the American people in the principle of Growth," wrote the members of a presidential commission on resources in their 1952 report. "Granting that we cannot find any absolute reason for this belief, we admit that to our Western minds it seems preferable to any opposite, which to us implies stagnation and decay." Economic growth quickly became a fundamental economic principle and a basic article of faith around the world.[28]

It was not long before economists were using cost analysis to argue that the earth's resources were not limited in any meaningful sense of the word. Technological innovations, they noted, had actually reduced production costs for agriculture and minerals since the nineteenth century, effectively expanding the size of the resources. But to ecologists, abstract arguments based in economic theory missed the point. "In the Dictionary of Nature," wrote the

Swedish food scientist Georg Borgstrom, "there exists no such concept as limitless." It seemed like plain common sense to the American lawyer and conservationist Samuel Ordway that ever increasing demand would eventually lead to scarcity, higher prices, and lower industrial production, even if it had not done so yet. "That a limit of expansion will be reached," he argued, "is a more plausible belief than that the resources of the earth are inexhaustible regardless of a limitless, expanding consumption."[29]

The heightened focus on growth through consumption led to visions of a future filled with disposable products. In 1950, when the science editor of the *New York Times* envisioned the home of the year 2000, he saw it in the context of a world where mass production had made material possessions so inexpensive that it would be easier and cheaper—and better for the economy—to replace them than to clean or repair them. His families of the future use soluble plastic plates just once and then dissolve them in the sink with superheated water. They toss soiled napkins and tablecloths made from woven paper into the incinerator. They even expect their houses to last only twenty-five years, since "nobody in 2000 sees any sense in building a house that will last a century." Actually getting people to live that way was sometimes more of a challenge than corporations would have liked. "The American public," lamented the leading manufacturer of paper clothing, "is still hamstrung by the idea that waste is bad." But the company remained optimistic that public opinion would eventually change.[30]

By the early 1950s, the environmental consequences of extending such a profligate lifestyle to undeveloped countries and to future generations had caught the interest of science fiction writers. In Philip K. Dick's short story "Survey Team," thirty years of war have devastated the earth's surface and prompted the dispatch of a crew of explorers to the planet Mars in search of a new home for humanity. There they discover the ruins of an advanced civilization that had used up all of the planet's resources six hundred thousand years before, leaving it "one vast scrap-heap" before fleeing to another world. While searching for the location of the escape planet with the hope of joining the Martians there, the crew learns to its horror that the Martians migrated to earth, where they evolved into primitive humans. Robert F. Young's "The Courts of Jamshyd" almost seems to continue Dick's story. It portrays a ruined earth where the few remaining inhabitants, reduced to primitive conditions and slowly dying out, channel their hatred of previous generations into ritual dances where they chant: "Our ancestors were pigs!"[31]

The geochemist and futurist Harrison Brown found other scenarios to be more likely. In his thoughtful book from 1954, *The Challenge of Man's Future,* Brown concluded that industrial civilization faced three possible futures. The most likely outcome was its slow decay or outright collapse due to some combination of war, overpopulation, and resource exhaustion, and a worldwide reversion to agricultural societies. Brown compared the probable decline of machine civilization to that of a biological species whose food supply had diminished or environment had changed. Less likely was the possibility that industrial society would overcome these challenges, but even then the world would stabilize into a collectivized and heavily controlled civilization. "The third possibility confronting mankind," Brown forecast, "is that of the worldwide free industrial society in which human beings can live in reasonable harmony with their environment. It is unlikely that such a pattern can ever exist for long. It certainly will be difficult to achieve, and it clearly will be difficult to maintain once it is established." He rated the possibility of this latter scenario to be "extremely low."[32]

The postwar expansion even reshaped the study of the future by inspiring a more systematic and scientific approach to prediction. The new field of futures studies, wrote the Columbia sociologist Daniel Bell in 1967, "arises from the simple fact that every society today is consciously committed to economic growth, to raising the standard of living of its people, and therefore to the planning, direction, and control of social change." In the United States, policy think tanks like the RAND Corporation and the Hudson Institute emerged, while the American Academy of Arts and Sciences established a Commission on the Year 2000. Bertrand de Jouvenel founded the Futuribles project in France, and the English Social Science Research Council created the Committee on the Next Thirty Years. Some of the new organizations focused explicitly on issues related to natural resources, like Resources for the Future and Buckminster Fuller's World Resources Inventory. In the private sector, corporations established their own research arms and even hired science fiction writers like Frederick Pohl as speakers and consultants. Where particular visions of the future had long informed Western expansion, the speed of that expansion was now making closer scrutiny of the future a top priority.[33]

In fact, popular interest in the world of tomorrow reached new heights in the quarter century after the Second World War. This was particularly true in the prosperous United States, where the present became saturated with the future. Fictional tales set decades or centuries ahead appeared regularly in print and movies and on radio and television. Serious news stories speculating about life in the future became common features in newspapers, magazines, and television documentaries like the series *The Twenty-First Century* narrated by Walter Cronkite. A fascination with the world of tomorrow inspired corporate leaders like Walt Disney, who began constructing his Experimental Prototype Community of Tomorrow (EPCOT) in Florida, and permeated the daily life of small midwestern towns, where women's groups performed plays and hosted dinner events with futuristic themes. "Under the impact of our relentless momentum," wrote the architect Roderick Seidenberg in 1961, "we seem for the first time in history closer to the future than the past, as though the very speed of our transit created a vacuum, a hiatus, between ourselves and our heritage." The postwar West had entered a period of prophetic excess.[34]

## The Promise of Unlimited Energy

Harrison Brown believed that the immediate limitation facing humankind was less the absolute amount of resources available in the earth's crust and more the availability of enough cheap energy to develop them at a reasonable cost. With an unlimited and inexpensive power source, it would be possible to extract coal from the narrowest veins, metals from the lowest grades of ore, and oil from shale and tar sands. It might even be possible to extract more energy than one spent: Brown's team at Caltech calculated that the four grams of uranium present in a ton of granite, once removed, could provide more than enough energy to perpetuate the mining process. Discoveries like that led Victor Cohn to predict "a new Stone Age" by the year 1999 that would see huge machines ceaselessly grinding away at the world's mountains and extracting valuable substances from the rubble. The technology needed to carry out such work did not yet exist, of course. But the knowledge that it was theoretically possible, combined with a faith in progress, enabled advocates of continued growth to argue that the idea of resource scarcity was nonsense.[35]

Scientists, however, expressed considerable doubt that any of the known sources of energy could meet the growing demands of the future, either alone or perhaps even together. The belief that fossil fuels would eventually run out remained widespread. In 1956, that expectation was strengthened even further by the publication of M. King Hubbert's theory of "peak oil," which predicted that oil production in the United States would begin to decline as soon as 1970. In fact, belief in the eventual exhaustion of fossil fuels was so pervasive that, when the citizens of Tulsa, Oklahoma, buried a brand new Plymouth Belvedere in a time capsule in 1957, they also buried ten gallons of gasoline so that those digging up the car fifty years later would be able to drive it. Renewable sources of energy like wind and solar did not seem to provide a way out: engineers continued to make advances in the necessary technologies, but investment lagged and progress remained slow.[36]

In the absence of more promising sources, the English physicist Charles Galton Darwin mused about a distant day when the world's few remaining manufactories might cling to renewable sources of water power, trading with a world that had otherwise returned to agriculture. "Anyone who disagrees with my forecast," he warned, "must try to get beyond a vague optimism, which merely expresses the confidence that 'something will turn up.'"[37]

Partial salvation seemed to arrive in the surprisingly rapid development of atomic power after the war. Scientists had been working toward it for decades, but in just the four years from 1954 to 1957, first the Soviet Union and then Britain, France, and the United States built their first working nuclear power plants. Nigel Calder, a British science writer and editor of the magazine *New Scientist,* considered the quick progress in nuclear technology to be an extraordinary bit of good luck. "Without it," he wrote, "the prospect of conventional fossil fuels becoming exhausted would be terrifying." Dennis Gabor shared that sentiment, writing with perceptible relief that now "humanity need never run out of power." Optimism ran high that atomic plants would quickly become the dominant supplier of the world's energy. Brown and his team estimated in 1957 that atomic power would provide a third of the world's energy by the end of the twentieth century and most of it by the middle of the twenty-first. Some scientists, including members of the U.S. Atomic Energy Commission, believed that by then atomic energy would be too cheap to meter and that governments would give it away for free.[38]

The military applications of the atom conjured a more complex set of futures. On one hand, the dropping of the atomic bombs had introduced the idea of a nuclear apocalypse. Fiction set in the irradiated ruins of civilization multiplied rapidly after 1945, often envisioning a natural world damaged or changed in frightening ways. Radiation sometimes rendered survivors unable to reproduce, plagued them with genetic defects, or gave them unusual powers like mental telepathy. Mutated animals menaced survivors, with giant insects being particularly common. And genetic mutations occasionally produced a superior species of humans that sought to destroy the remnants of its predecessor. While many of these themes had already appeared in literature earlier in the century after scientists had discovered radiation, atomic bombs provided a very real delivery mechanism for the imagined consequences.[39]

On the other hand, some scientists saw potential for using atomic bombs to further human expansion. With government support, they began developing plans to use underground nuclear explosions for the kinds of large-scale environmental projects that many in the West had been dreaming about for generations. Atomic bombs could potentially carve new harbors, dig fresh canals, build earthen dams, reroute rivers, and vaporize icebergs. They held the potential to revolutionize mining by uncovering deep ore bodies, releasing oil from tar sands, and stimulating the production of natural gas, all while leaving industrial-grade diamonds or useful isotopes in their wake. Although the United States and the Soviet Union had the most ambitious plans, other Western countries such as Canada and Australia also considered using nuclear explosions for similar projects. The title of a 1960 article by Edward Teller, the father of the hydrogen bomb, summed up the hopes of those advocating peaceful nuclear explosions: "We're Going to Work Miracles."[40]

Yet, for all its promise, nuclear fission had significant drawbacks. Public concern about radioactivity released through the testing of nuclear bombs increased as time went on, and fission plants had limited lifespans and lots of radioactive byproducts that would have to be stored safely for centuries. "Nobody can be happy," claimed Gabor, despite his sense of relief, "when thinking of a world of the future full of dead power stations surrounded by barbed wire." With such limitations in mind, some in the scientific community framed fission as an intermediate step. The prominent British science fiction writer and futurist Arthur C. Clarke was among them, predicting that energy from fission reactions would play no more than a passing role in human history. "One hopes they will not," he added, "for fission is the dirtiest and most unpleasant method of releasing energy that man has ever discovered." In the long term, an alternative would have to be found.[41]

Clarke and others invested their hopes for a lasting energy solution in fusion. Where fission released energy by breaking heavy atomic nuclei apart, fusion released it by joining lighter ones together. Two things made fusion particularly attractive: first, its fuel was easily extractable from ordinary water, and second, the reaction produced far less radioactive waste with much shorter half-lives than fission. Although the process had never been demonstrated on a large scale, the rapid progress of nuclear technology encouraged almost universal optimism among scientists that fusion was just around the corner. Homi Bhabha, soon to become the father of India's nuclear program, opened the Atoms for Peace conference in Geneva in 1955 with the prediction that controlled fusion would become a reality in the next twenty years. Clarke thought it might take another fifteen beyond that, but he was confident that the seas would provide humanity with unlimited energy long before fossil fuels ran out. "If, as is perfectly possible," he wrote, "we are short of energy two generations from now, it will be through our own incompetence. We will be like Stone Age men freezing to death on top of a coal bed."[42]

Brown was one of the few to acknowledge that humans would still face resource limitations even with an endless supply of energy at their disposal. The earth, after all, was only so big. So in his 1956 book, he calculated how quickly the planet would diminish if the human population continued to grow and acquired the ability to devour the earth's rocky surface at an accelerating pace. "A population of 30 billion persons," he calculated, "would consume rock at a rate of about 1,500 billion tons per year. If we were to assume that all the land areas of the world were available for such processing, then, on the average, man would 'eat' his way downward at a rate of 3.3 millimeters per year or over 3 meters per millennium." Brown's calculation provided an unusual perspective on how large human appetites could grow and the potential environmental costs of satisfying them.[43]

Sixteen years earlier, the science fiction writer Willard Hawkins had anticipated Brown's concern and extrapolated its consequences into the far distant future. His short story "The Dwindling Sphere" begins with the invention of a process that converts any form of matter into "plastoscene," a moldable substance that can be used for any purpose, including food. Future generations embrace the process and repeatedly strip the earth's land and water surfaces to feed the plastoscene machines and provide for the ever growing human population. The process radically changes human culture and the earth itself, which after two hundred thousand years has been reduced to the size of the moon. Nevertheless, people remain just as reluctant to acknowledge environmental limits as they ever were. They dismiss the idea that the earth was once much larger as a myth and find it "impossible . . . to imagine that a time will come when there will be no more Earth for man's conversion."[44]

## The Final Frontiers

Just as concerns about overpopulation and resource exhaustion were raising serious questions about the limits to growth, new technologies opened up the oceans and outer space as potential sites for further human expansion. Before the Second World War, humanity had seen little of what lay beneath the surface of the seas and had yet to travel beyond the earth's atmosphere. But new advances in underwater breathing gear and rocket technology made it possible to visit previously unexplored depths and heights. Some of the research in these areas was motivated by scientific curiosity or a sense of adventure. Most of it, however, was in the interest of increasing the food supply for a hungry world, claiming untapped resources for governments and industries, or creating new living space for a growing population. Soon after the war, it became common to refer to both the oceans and outer space as new frontiers, a metaphor closely tied in Western history to the idea of expansion.[45]

The word "inexhaustible" had long been associated with earth's vast oceans. In 1813, a British commentator claimed that the seas "afford an inexhaustible mine of wealth." In 1883, the great English biologist Thomas Huxley opened the International Fisheries Exhibition by pronouncing all the great fisheries to be "inexhaustible," explaining that "nothing we do seriously affects the number of fish." The idea that ocean resources were literally boundless remained prevalent well into the middle of the twentieth century, even among marine scientists. In 1954, a prominent American oceanographer co-wrote a book titled *The Inexhaustible Sea,* which went through twenty-two editions and was reprinted into the 1960s. "We are already beginning to understand," the authors claimed of the ocean, "that what it has to offer extends beyond the limits of our imagination—that someday men will learn that in its bounty the sea is inexhaustible."[46]

The ever increasing yield from the sea after World War II seemed to confirm this belief. Postwar fishing fleets grew dramatically in size, especially those launched by Japan and the Soviet bloc, and began exploring relatively untapped areas of the oceans. Advances in oceanography supported the expansion, as did the development of new fishing technologies: sonar-based fishfinders made fishing more precise; artificial fibers strengthened fishing nets; and huge factory ships, like those dreamed of generations before, extended the duration and distance of the hunt by processing and freezing fish onboard. As a result, the world's marine catch tripled in the quarter century after the war, suggesting to many that the seas might really be the food source of tomorrow. In its report for 1967, the United States Bureau of Commercial Fisheries estimated that the oceans alone could provide for the annual protein needs of thirty billion people.[47]

The science of oceanography developed as well, with experts working hand-in-hand with governments and corporations to industrialize the seas. In their 1969 plans for an International Decade of Ocean Exploration, oceanographers expressed a clear understanding that their role would be to acquire more knowledge about the sea and its life "for the purpose of more effective utilization of the ocean and its resources." Robert Cowen, the science editor for the *Christian Science Monitor,* had put it more colorfully several years before: "The ocean is like a grab bag stuffed with riches out of which man has been taking only those few packages he can lay hands on easily, often by blindly groping. . . . One of the bright promises of oceanography is that an increase in scientific knowledge of the sea will help man systematically to exploit the resources of the marine grab bag."[48]

In pursuit of that abundance, marine scientists busied themselves imagining new ways for future fishermen to catch ever more fish. They might use new technologies to locate fish from the air, or stun them with electric shocks, or use electric fields to attract or repel them. In 1960, the Oxford oceanographer Sir Alister Hardy suggested that bottom trawling, a largely target-blind process of dragging a net over the seafloor, could be improved by suspending the net between two submarine tractors piloted by frogmen. It might take a century for such a practice to become widespread, he admitted, but a single company could be employing it to great advantage as early as 1984. Fishermen could also harvest previously unexploited species of marine life. Hardy believed that krill, which had provided food for the once abundant whales, could now serve as food for humans. "Can we not save the starving children of the world with krill?" he asked. "I am sure we shall."[49]

Marine scientists calculated that the seas could produce even more food if actively farmed. "Just to catch fish, kill whales, and go after certain dainty invertebrates like lobsters and oysters, simply is not enough," said the leading Soviet marine biologist in 1957. "The whole mass of the marine animal population must be mobilised in human interests."[50] Future farming techniques might include raising young fish in protected areas and then releasing them into the oceans, transplanting fish from overcrowded areas to underutilized ones, fertilizing the seas with phytoplankton, cultivating fish in offshore corrals like cattle, and even herding whales. Plants would do their part as well. Seaweed was already being used for food in Asia and as animal fodder in Europe, and a botanist at Ohio State University was experimenting with protein-rich fungi that could potentially be grown in huge flasks on the seafloor. The 1960s saw a surge of books with titles like *Farming the Sea, Algae and Man,* and *The Sea Against Hunger,* while the RAND Corporation predicted that sea farming would be producing twenty percent of the world's food by the turn of the century.[51]

Many in the scientific community expected the oceans to provide not just food but resources as well. Jacob Rosin and Max Eastman claimed that seawater holds more valuable minerals than all of the world's mines combined. "There are 2.54 pounds of magnesium in a ton of seawater," they explained, "which means that there are 1,800 trillion tons of magnesium in the five oceans. A magnesium shortage in the face of this figure is unthinkable."[52] Since the minerals are suspended in minute concentrations, the trick was to find an economic way to remove them, a challenge that Western countries were already working to meet. A chemical plant in Texas had been extracting magnesium from the Gulf of Mexico since World War II, and a Dutch-Norwegian plant on the North Sea was removing potassium for use in artificial fertilizers.[53] "Sea water, indeed," wrote Rosin and Eastman, "resembles that wonderful table in Grimms's fairy tales which is always covered with food at its master's command. We have only to find out how to take the food from the table." Others looked forward to extracting oil from the seafloor and converting seawater into drinkable water in desalinization plants. The amount of resources hidden in or beneath the oceans seemed endless.[54]

The oceans also came to seem like the next frontier for human colonization. In 1960, Alister Hardy predicted that "quite a large proportion of the population will become sub-aquatic artisans, cultivating the continental shelf and husbanding the stocks of fish." That same year, Edward Link, an inventor and expert in undersea living, foresaw the construction of underwater hostels for skin-diving vacations by the year 1984. Movies like *The Underwater City, City Beneath the Sea,* and *Captain Nemo and the Underwater City* brought detailed images of life beneath the waves to audiences, while scientists began developing actual underwater habitats. Jacques Cousteau's Conshelf I off the coast of Marseille and the U.S. Navy's Sealab I off Bermuda set the pace for numerous efforts to develop the necessary technologies for underwater living, and none too soon: Isaac Asimov predicted that colonization of the continental shelves would be well under way by 2014.[55]

Outer space seemed to hold even more potential for human expansion than the oceans. Before World War II, space flight had been trapped in the realm of futuristic fiction, with scientists and the general public putting little stock in the real-life possibility of leaving the earth. The early pioneers

Conshelf II was a real-life "undersea village" erected on the floor of the
Red Sea in 1964 and led by Jacques Cousteau. This painting of the village by
Pierre Mion includes (clockwise from top left) the residence for the five-man crew,
the diving saucer hangar, the deep cabin, and the diving saucer itself.
(National Geographic Society)

of rocket technology in Germany, the Soviet Union, and the United States—all of them influenced by Jules Verne's stories—did make important advances, and amateur groups that called themselves rocket or interplanetary travel societies conducted their own experimental launches in Europe, the Americas, and Japan. But such efforts all took place on the scientific fringe. As late as 1949, even though fictional characters like Buck Rogers had made the idea of space exploration familiar in the United States, a Gallup poll showed that only fifteen percent of Americans believed humans would reach the moon by the year 2000.[56]

It took an unexpected leap in rocket technology, and the competitive crucible of the Cold War, to turn space into an actual frontier. At the end of World War II, the United States and the Soviet Union captured advanced German rockets and manufacturing facilities along with many of the scientists who had developed them, helping to jump-start their own programs. Almost immediately, space boosters began using the potential of this rocket technology to launch visions of a space-faring tomorrow. In the West, some of the greatest scientists, science writers, and space artists of the day collaborated on award-winning books, articles in major magazines, and even a series of television programs produced by Walt Disney. In a startlingly short time, a culture of astrofuturism developed across the West and the Soviet Union telegraphing the message that humankind would find its manifest destiny in space. As early as 1951, Arthur C. Clarke was claiming that space travel was inevitable, and by 1964 Pan American World Airways was keeping a waiting list for flights to the moon that would eventually grow to over ninety-three thousand people from all over the world.[57]

Space boosters also encouraged the widespread expectation that space colonization would alleviate overpopulation on earth. Arthur Radebaugh published a *Closer Than We Think* comic in 1959 that looked forward to "Space Mayflowers" coming to the rescue of a crowded world. "If the earth should ever become overpopulated," he claimed, "emigration to outer space may become a commonplace. Bands of colonists might settle on distant planets, traveling there at lightning speeds in rockets of unbelievable size." The accompanying illustration showed migrants waiting patiently in line to board a giant spaceship docked on the moon. Television shows like *Lost in Space,* launched in 1965, also reinforced the vision of families happily colonizing the stars to escape an overpopulated earth. With the exception of a small group that included Clarke, the ecologist Garrett Hardin, and the American engineer Dandridge Cole, few were willing to admit that the speed of population growth made this a completely unrealistic solution. But Clarke, at least, saw a silver lining to overly optimistic visions of space colonization: they would help to launch humankind's future in outer space, "even if no more than a millionth of humanity can ever go there."[58]

Scientists further fueled the idea of space migration by speculating about ways to terraform planetary bodies. In the early 1960s, Russian scientists published ideas for making the moon more earth-like by manufacturing oxygen from lunar rocks and increasing its rate of rotation with hydrogen bombs exploded in strategic spots. Meanwhile, the American astronomer Carl Sagan was turning his sights on Venus, which suffered from extreme heat because large amounts of carbon dioxide in its atmosphere produced a greenhouse effect. In an article published in the prestigious journal *Science* in 1961, Sagan proposed seeding the upper atmosphere of Venus with blue-green algae. His hope was that the algae would absorb large amounts of carbon dioxide, thereby cooling the planet sufficiently for water to exist in liquid form on the surface and for the algae to engage in photosynthesis. If successful, the process would form the basis of a new ecological system. At that point, Sagan concluded, scientists could decide "whether to send a paleobotanist, a mineralogist, a petroleum geologist, or a deep-sea diver."[59]

An extreme form of terraforming emerged from the mind of Fritz Zwicky, a renowned astrophysicist at Caltech. Zwicky expected that humans would someday reconstruct the solar system itself to provide themselves with more living space. Nuclear explosions could nudge smaller planets like Mercury and Venus into more favorable orbits, while Mars could be temporarily diverted toward another planet to draw off some of the latter's atmosphere and then returned to its original path. Reducing Jupiter's extremely high gravity would require whittling the planet down with rock melting machines and nuclear explosions, and engineers could use the resulting debris to build up its moons. If existing nuclear power was not sufficient to the task, Zwicky was confident that fusion power was on the near horizon and would undoubtedly do the trick.[60]

Dandridge Cole was unusual among space boosters in that he disapproved of terraforming because it did not recognize natural limits. He believed that population pressure and increasing resource consumption would eventually force earth-based civilization to become a closed-cycle society, one that conserves and recycles all material resources but might apply additional supplies of energy to maintain itself. The same problem would replicate itself on terraformed planets as they approached their own environmental limits, he claimed, so such societies might as well be planned as closed environmental systems from the start. In the case of the moon, Cole recommended building closed-cycle, self-sufficient units in the form of domes, caves, or covered craters designed to house a specific number of inhabitants. Each unit would produce only what it needed and recycle everything. As with Ebenezer Howard's garden cities, more units would be added as needed, although Cole saw much of the moon remaining in a natural state.[61]

Human expansion into space also meant harvesting the untapped resources of the galaxy and bringing them back to earth. In another *Closer Than We Think* comic, this one titled "Mining the Moon," Radebaugh told his millions of readers that the lunar environment "might well be a source of replacement for many of the elements we earthlings are rapidly using up." His illustration showed a massive machine carving a bottomless pit mine into the lunar surface. Many prominent scientists, Edward Teller among them, looked forward to bringing the wealth of the galaxy back to earth from the moon, nearby planets, and asteroids. Such dreams were not new, but they had almost always been the province of futuristic fiction. Now, many in the scientific community actually expected extraterrestrial resources to supplement those of the earth, and quite soon. Arthur C. Clarke predicted that space mining would become a reality by the year 2030.[62]

Clarke was anything but alone in his optimism. Rocket technology had developed at an astonishing pace, evolving in about fifteen years from the first practical ballistic missiles to rockets capable of putting a satellite in orbit. Extrapolating from that rate of progress produced widespread visions of space exploration in the very near term. Wernher von Braun, who played a central role in designing both Germany's V-2 rockets and those of the American space program, believed that spacecraft would be shuttling astronauts back and forth from a permanent moon base by 1985. A study by the RAND Corporation concluded that astronauts would be manufacturing

This painting by Arthur Radebaugh depicts huge machines grinding away at the surface of Mars in search of iron ore. The image first appeared in a 1954 advertisement for mechanical parts.

rocket propellant from lunar mines and would have landed on Mars by 2000. The head of General Dynamics' Aerospace Division anticipated Martian colonies by 2063. And Clarke predicted interstellar flights by the end of the twenty-first century. The landing of *Apollo 11* on the moon in July 1969 confirmed for many that humankind's journey to the stars had begun.[63]

Behind much of the enthusiasm for space travel was the deep belief that human expansion was natural and inevitable. Humans would therefore always need new geographical frontiers, an idea firmly embraced by Clarke. "In all the long history of man," he wrote, "ours is the first age with no new frontiers on land or sea, and many of our troubles stem from this fact." Clarke recognized that there were still unexplored areas of the planet, particularly in the oceans, but believed that the earth would not keep humankind busy for long. That was a problem, he claimed, because humans needed frontiers to provide new resources and living space and also to fulfill spiritual needs, like the quest for adventure and novelty. The pursuit of endless expansion was simply part of being human, which made space travel indispensable. "The road to the stars," Clarke wrote, "has been discovered none too soon. Civilization cannot exist without new frontiers."[64]

## Two Tomorrows

Despite the promise of expansion into the oceans and outer space, concerns about the environmental implications of growth coalesced into a rival vision of the future soon after World War II. As early as 1954, Harrison Brown was drawing a distinction between "Malthusians" and "Technologists." The former, he wrote, warn that accelerating population growth, resource consumption, and abuse of the land will bring disaster. The latter point to the fantastic technological developments of the past as evidence of the still more spectacular ones that lie ahead and look forward to continued expansion into the more thinly populated areas of the earth. Although Brown recognized the truths embedded in both visions, he made no effort to bridge, blend, or reconcile them. He must have realized that the stories they told were just too different, the assumptions on which they relied too contradictory.[65]

Contemporaries often framed the difference between the two visions as a matter of optimism. Such an approach only scratched the surface of what truly underlay these competing narratives, but it did provide some ground for comparison and discussion. As the American zoologist Marston Bates explained in 1963, optimists expected scientific and technological progress to solve future problems, while pessimists feared that human cleverness might not be up to the task. Those looking forward to unending progress and growth were happy to be labeled optimists and considered it an entirely justified and reasonable attitude. Victor Cohn encountered many optimistic scientists who "believe in a cornucopia of science, the ever-flowing horn of plenty." But rather than basing their optimism on blind faith, Cohn claimed, they grounded it in "knowledge of what can be done now, plus what ought to be possible with reasonable gains." Optimism was, for him, a position based on evidence and reason.[66]

But to those who feared the consequences of growth, such optimism was so recklessly unrealistic that it seemed more like hubris. Robert Jungk, a prominent Austrian futurist, singled out the United States for exhibiting a particularly notable lack of humility toward the natural world. "To occupy God's place," he wrote in 1952, "to repeat his deeds, to re-create and organize a man-made cosmos according to man-made laws of reason, foresight and efficiency: that is America's ultimate objective. . . . It destroys whatever is primitive, whatever grows in disordered profusion or evolves through patient mutation. What it cannot observe and measure it subdues indirectly to its power. It says the unsayable. It knows no awe." Cohn, however, found Jungk's position hard to fathom. He described the scientists he met as "sensitive and responsible and generally very humble about the power that is in their hands, despite a certain on-the-surface confident patter that might fool a stranger."[67]

Others feared that the unwavering optimism behind progress and growth was misleading their advocates by distorting the nature of history. In 1959, the American economist Robert Heilbroner argued that adherents of what he called the "philosophy of optimism" failed to recognize that it was the product of a particular historical moment, assuming instead that optimism was a universal principle equally appropriate to any period in history. The philosophy of optimism also assumed that humans had been the prime movers of history, thereby failing to prepare humankind for those periods when that might not be the case. Finally, it made the erroneous assumption that historical forces like technological progress would have the same impact in the future as they had in the past, despite radically changed contexts. Heilbroner was not opposed to the act of being optimistic itself. But he did object to the kind of optimism that ignored historical context and misunderstood the nature of causation in history. It would be more useful and less misleading, he argued, to adopt an optimism more carefully rooted in the past.[68]

No third vision emerged during this period to challenge the narratives of development and disaster, although the appeal of the nineteenth century's pastoral utopia had endured, particularly in the teachings of India's Mohandas Gandhi. From an early point in his career, Gandhi criticized the competitive and acquisitive values of industrial society and its heavy environmental cost, advising his countrymen to reject such a future for India.

"God forbid that India should ever take to industrialism after the manner of the West," he wrote. "If an entire nation of 300 millions took to similar economic exploitation, it would strip the world bare like locusts." Heavily influenced by the thought of John Ruskin, Gandhi wanted to renew India's traditional village culture. He developed a detailed vision of an agricultural nation based on traditional farming and husbandry techniques and handicrafts like weaving. When Gandhi was writing in the first half of the twentieth century, it was still possible to imagine such a path for India.[69]

In contrast, those in the already urbanized and industrialized West who feared the long-term consequences of growth tended to offer little more than vague reflections on what a viable third way might look like. Harrison Brown hoped for adequate food, clothing, and housing for the whole world, but otherwise focused on humanity's spiritual needs rather than its material ones. Brown wanted to see "a reestablishment of organic roots with our natural environment and, related to it, the evolution of ways of life which encourage contemplation and the search for truth and knowledge." He valued the kinds of things that were threatened by human expansion: green grass, vegetable gardens, fireplaces, hilltops with views, and primeval forests packed with a wide variety of living things. "To be sure," he wrote, "they are of no 'practical value' and are seemingly unrelated to man's pressing need for food and living space. But they are as necessary to the preservation of humanism as food is necessary to the preservation of human life." Reflections like Brown's provided glimpses of a possible future based on values other than growth. But by themselves they could not hope to rival the dominant and more fully articulated visions of development and disaster.[70]

By the 1960s, the two tomorrows sat side-by-side in the public imagination. Those who thought seriously about the future often oscillated between them, even when immersed in the Promethean wonders of the 1964–1965 World's Fair in New York City. President Lyndon Johnson delivered a speech at the fair that looked forward to the scientific and technological marvels of the future and simultaneously expressed concern about urban crowding and dwindling resources. Isaac Asimov, while waiting in line to enter the techno-utopian Futurama exhibit, warily eyed the "grim" electric sign at a nearby pavilion that recorded the country's current population in six-foot-high numbers and added another person every eleven seconds. Both were experiencing the severe cognitive dissonance about the environmental future that had come to plague the West.[71]

The rest of the world would have to wrestle with this new vision of the future as well, for the disaster narrative was spreading just as the development narrative had before it. Visions of progress and growth still retained their influence around the globe: the Chinese were lifting images of flying cars directly from the covers of American science magazines to use on their own; Jamaican newspapers carried reports about the great potential of synthetic foods; and Soviet futuristic fiction remained as triumphal as the West's had been before the First World War. But any country with Western-style ambitions would ultimately find itself unable to avoid the vision of a growth-induced environmental catastrophe, for all had become part of a global civilization devoted to relentless expansion on an ever-shrinking planet.[72]

# 5

# A Choice of Bad Endings

FEW UNDERSTOOD THE IDEA of progress better than the great British historian J. B. Bury, who had literally written the book on the subject. In fact, he understood it so well that in 1920 he correctly predicted the circumstances that would lead to its demise. The idea would completely lose its power, he wrote, "if there were any cogent reasons for supposing that the time at the disposal of humanity is likely to reach a limit in the near future. If there were good cause for believing that the earth would be uninhabitable in A.D. 2000 or 2100 the doctrine of Progress would lose its meaning and would automatically disappear." He missed the mark, however, when he reassured his readers that dramatic environmental changes would not occur "for a period which transcends and flouts all efforts of imagination." Only half a century after he wrote those words, many in the West had come to believe that a global environmental disaster was just over the horizon. And just as Bury had predicted, the idea of progress suffered a severe blow from which it has never recovered.[1]

The years around 1970 became a tipping point for how Westerners viewed the future, kicking off a decade that one journalist remembered as being "bathed in a cold Spenglerian apprehension." The reasons went beyond environmental anxiety alone. Writing in 1974, the American economist Robert Heilbroner identified a barrage of events that had shaken the confidence of the West: rapid social change, economic malaise, worsening social problems, and the realization that increasing material wealth had not increased happiness. But behind it all, he wrote, was the "stunning discovery" that endless industrial growth was not environmentally sustainable. That discovery had emerged gradually from the work of scientists, who now found their message amplified by an environmental movement that had burst on to the international stage. Long the primary source of support for visions of growth, science was now undermining the expectations that it had helped to create in the first place.[2]

When the social consensus about the benefits of growth and progress weakened, so did the credibility of the development narrative. Yet the rapid pace of growth continued. Human population and world energy consumption doubled in the half-century after 1970, while the global gross domestic product increased five-fold. Environmental problems worsened in those same years, with climate change emerging as a particularly intractable one. For a time, environmentally conscious fiction writers worked to imagine a radically different future that stepped outside the growth paradigm. But the ecotopian moment faded away with little to show for the effort. By the first decades of the twenty-first century, it was no easier to imagine a future without endless growth than it had been in the 1970s. In fact, it had become a lot harder.

## Environmentalism and the Debate over Limits

The rise of the environmental movement in the late 1960s marked the point when concerns about natural limits finally overwhelmed faith in growth and progress. Environmentalism had deep and complex roots: some went back to nineteenth-century romanticism and early twentieth-century conservation; others emerged from intensifying worries about overpopulation and resource exhaustion; while still others grew from contemporary concerns about pollution, radioactive fallout, and declining green space. As a result, different people came to the movement with different environmental concerns foremost in mind. But for many, all of the issues contributing to the perception of crisis seemed to share a common cause. "The whole environmental problem," wrote *Time* magazine in 1970, "stems from a dedication to infinite growth on a finite planet." The decade saw the West become obsessed with limits and disenchanted with growth, at least for a time, and saw fear of overpopulation and resource exhaustion reach their high points.[3]

Historian Thomas Robertson has called this period a "Malthusian Moment," a time of widespread fear of overpopulation among both experts and the larger public. One of the most urgent and widely heard calls for population control came in 1968 with the publication of *The Population Bomb* by Paul Ehrlich, a Stanford biologist and confirmed "Neo-Malthusian." Ehrlich believed that undeveloped countries had failed to improve their agricultural techniques and productivity fast enough to avoid famine. "The battle to feed all of humanity is over," he declared bluntly in the book's opening sentence. "In the 1970s the world will undergo famines—hundreds of millions of people are going to starve to death in spite of any crash programs embarked upon now." Ehrlich's book became an international best seller and Ehrlich himself a celebrity. He appeared on Johnny Carson's immensely popular *Tonight Show* more than twenty times to talk about the dangers of overpopulation.[4]

Such views had a profound impact on Western visions of the future, even leaving their mark on everyday events like graduation ceremonies. Stephanie Mills was a member of the class of 1969 at a small California college and had been selected to give the commencement address. Steeped in the Neo-Malthusian visions of scientists like Ehrlich, Mills announced to her audience that "our days as a race on this planet are, at this moment, numbered" because "we are breeding ourselves out of existence." She also shared her decision to refrain from having children, which she found the most humane course open to her. Mills's words made headlines across the United States and left the speaker who followed her "quite undone." But it was perfectly in keeping with the newly ascendant disaster narrative, as was the title of her address: "The Future Is a Cruel Hoax."[5]

Fears of resource scarcity also rose to fever pitch, largely due to the oil crisis of 1973. That October, the Arab-dominated oil cartel OPEC announced an oil embargo targeting the United States, Japan, Canada, and a number of countries in Western Europe in response to their support for Israel during the Yom Kippur War. All of the embargoed countries had become dependent to one extent or another on Middle Eastern oil. Although the embargo did not mean that the world was running out of oil any time soon, it under-

No single image did more to reinforce the reality of
environmental limits than "Earthrise," a photograph
taken from lunar orbit by one of the *Apollo 8*
astronauts in 1968. (Courtesy of NASA)

scored the possibility of a resource-poor future by causing gasoline shortages in the short term and economic turmoil for the remainder of the decade. It also reminded the industrialized nations that, with the exception of
nuclear power, economically viable substitutes for fossil fuels still did not
exist. That November, *Newsweek* reported that the list of shortages in the
United States "seems to lengthen every day" and acknowledged "the un-
comfortable vision of abundance-turned-to-scarcity."[6]

Even space exploration, usually more closely associated with positive visions of human expansion, provided a lens for viewing the earth as small,
vulnerable, and finite. In 1968, the astronauts of *Apollo 8* returned from
lunar orbit with the first color photograph ever taken of the earth from outer
space. "Earthrise," as the photo came to be known, brought the limited size
of the earth into sharp focus and went on to become the most influential
image of the early environmental movement. A few years before, environmentally minded economists had begun to refer to the planet as "spaceship
earth." Kenneth Boulding contrasted what he called the "cowboy" economy,

which he considered reckless, exploitative, and based on an assumption of unlimited resources, with the "spaceman" economy "in which the earth has become a single spaceship, without unlimited reservoirs of anything, either for extraction or for pollution." In an unexpected way, the limitless expanse of space seemed to make the limits of a single planet easier to see.[7]

But what really crystallized the debate over the environmental future was a scientific study with a simple but powerful title: *The Limits to Growth*. Prepared by an international research team at the Massachusetts Institute of Technology and published in 1972, the study argued that there are limits to how much pollution the earth can absorb, how much food it can produce, and how many resources it can provide. The researchers came to their conclusions through the use of computer simulations, which were a new tool at the time. They ran scenarios showing how resource availability, food production, industrial output, population growth, and pollution levels would interact under various sets of conditions. The results showed that, if human environmental management did not change, "the most probable result will be a rather sudden and uncontrollable decline in both population and industrial capacity." The study concluded that only population control and the adoption of a steady-state world economy, and in a timely manner, would prevent worldwide collapse.[8]

It is hard to overestimate the impact that *The Limits to Growth* had on public discussions about the environmental future. The book sold tens of millions of copies, was translated into dozens of languages, and was, in the words of one journalist, "the first vision of the apocalypse ever prepared by computer." It also threw advocates of unending growth on the defensive. Perhaps for the first time, they found themselves pressed to articulate and defend the largely unspoken arguments for the growth-oriented vision of the future that had dominated the West for generations. That is not to say that the findings were generally accepted. Some praised *The Limits to Growth* while others denounced it. But the study moved to the center of the debate, where in many ways it remains today.[9]

Herman Kahn, a former RAND employee and nuclear strategist, became one of the study's most vocal critics and responded with a diametrically opposed environmental vision. In 1976, he published a book arguing that in two hundred years virtually all of the world's people would be "numerous, rich and in control of the forces of nature." He acknowledged the reality of contemporary environmental problems and, unlike many other growth advocates, expected that growth would gradually drop to zero over the next several generations on its own in response to declining demand. But he insisted that, in the meantime, a combination of technological innovation and reasonable investment would correct "nearly every measurable environmental blight or hazard." Fusion power would solve energy problems by becoming commercially viable by the 1990s, and growing concerns about an imminent "carbon dioxide catastrophe" would prove to be overstated. For Kahn, the environmental problems that had everyone so worried were simply products of a transitionary period on the path to prosperity for everyone.[10]

The noted futurist Harrison Brown disagreed with Kahn's assessment. Reflecting on the views he had expressed more than twenty years earlier in *The Challenge of Man's Future,* Brown found his least optimistic predictions to have been "surprisingly and depressingly accurate." He did not fault Kahn on his technological optimism and agreed that humans had the ability to develop technologies that could alleviate shortages of energy, resources, and food. But he feared that humans would fail to overcome the social, political, and economic challenges necessary to develop and deploy such technologies. He also believed that environmental limits existed and that growth must therefore eventually stop. "We might argue among ourselves as to exactly where those limits lie," he wrote. "But we must recognize that neither population nor affluence can continue to grow forever. Unless we willfully stop the growth ourselves, nature will stop this growth for us." Brown favored a gradual transition to a global society with a stable population and stable per capita energy and resource use.[11]

In response to widespread fears of a disastrous tomorrow, then president of the United States Jimmy Carter became the first Western leader to devote the full resources of his government to peering into the environmental future. Fourteen government agencies contributed to a study that projected contemporary environmental trends to the end of the twentieth century. Released in 1980, *The Global 2000 Report to the President* foresaw a troubled tomorrow. The continued expansion of humankind and its industrial economies would put enormous pressure on food, water, and energy supplies, decimate forests, deplete agricultural soils, increase the extinction rate, and saturate the atmosphere with carbon dioxide, possibly altering the world's climate as a result. "If present trends continue," the authors concluded, "the world in 2000 will be more crowded, more polluted, less stable ecologically, and more vulnerable to disruption than the world we live in now." The report's projections received intensive media coverage around the world, inspired similar studies in Europe, and sank deep into the public psyche.[12]

The cornucopian counterargument was not long in coming. Kahn and the economist Julian Simon responded to the report in 1984 with an edited volume called *The Resourceful Earth*. Simon summarized the volume's findings by explaining that *Global 2000* was "totally wrong in its specific assertions and its general conclusions." Chapters by twenty-four scholars supported his claim, although almost half of the contributors were economists or employed in related fields. That fact suggested a particular perspective on the natural world: contemporary economists tended to see economies as independent of the environment, making concerns about environmental limits relatively unimportant. Ecologists, in contrast, considered the economy to be a subsystem of the environment, where limits clearly helped to determine whether a species rose or fell. The kinds of environmental assumptions that economists carried into the study with them helped Simon to claim that environmental problems were actually getting better, not worse, and would trouble humankind less and less in the future.[13]

Simon had already become one of the best-known theoreticians of unlimited human expansion. He explained his thinking in 1981 in a book titled *The Ultimate Resource*. For Simon, resources could only be limited in the short term, since rising prices would encourage innovations, and those innovations would help to increase production of the scarce resource or lead to its replacement with something else. Humans had, according to Simon, surmounted one scarcity crisis after another in just this way for centuries. "The term 'finite,'" he concluded, "is not meaningful when applied to resources," particularly since civilization would always have recourse to the "ultimate resource": the immense creativity of human beings. Because of this creativity, Simon argued, the human population should be allowed to grow as large as possible. More people meant more creative solutions to short-term scarcity problems and therefore more resources in the long term. Simon's book gave the development narrative a theoretical foundation that

made it unnecessary to actually measure resources to determine their limits. They were limitless because human ingenuity was limitless.[14]

In 1980, Simon tried to resolve the debate through a public wager with
Paul Ehrlich on the future price of raw materials. Rising prices would jus-
tify Ehrlich's claim that population pressures were making resources scarce,
while falling prices would support Simon's claim that resources were becoming more abundant. Ehrlich accepted the bet, choosing to track copper,
chromium, nickel, tin, and tungsten over a period of ten years. But when
1990 rolled around, all five materials had decreased in cost, and Ehrlich
lost the wager by a wide margin. Advocates of growth celebrated the victory,
although choosing different resources or a different time period would have
handed the win to Ehrlich instead. In the end, the much-publicized bet settled nothing.[15]

As Western economies recovered from the fiscal woes of the 1970s and
the initial fervor of environmentalism receded, many governments largely
abandoned concerns about potential limits to growth. This was especially
true in the United States, where Simon's ideas often provided the intellectual basis for pro-growth positions. President Ronald Reagan, speaking at
a convocation ceremony in 1983, assured his audience that "there are no
such things as limits to growth, because there are no limits on the human
capacity for intelligence, imagination, and wonder." His successor, George
H. W. Bush, pushed the point even harder in a speech at the 1992 Earth
Summit in Rio de Janeiro. "Twenty years ago," Bush said, "some spoke of
limits to growth. Today we realize that growth is the engine of change and
the friend of the environment." Other Western leaders expressed similar
positions. With opposing sets of assumptions lined up against each other,
the question of limits—at least in a theoretical sense—remained unresolv-
able into the twenty-first century.[16]

But the theoretical stalemate did not keep scientists from expanding their
understanding of environmental limits. In 2009, an international team of
researchers proposed a framework of "planetary boundaries" through which
to study the global environment. They set a series of thresholds for nine key
environmental support systems like the atmosphere, fresh water, and the
oceans. If human development pushed atmospheric carbon dioxide levels,
demands on fresh water, and acidification of the oceans, for example, be-

yond those boundaries, the results would threaten the larger earth system. Crucially, the researchers warned that humankind had already moved beyond three of the nine boundaries. Although planetary boundaries are not quite the same as environmental limits, they point in the same direction: toward lines that humankind crosses at its own peril.[17]

## Limits Become Tangible

While the theoretical debate continued, the world began bumping up against actual environmental limits. One of the earliest involved the amount of human-generated pollutants that the atmosphere could absorb and still remain friendly to human life. In the 1970s, chemists discovered that chlorofluorocarbons and other chemicals were rising into the stratosphere and breaking down ozone, which absorbs harmful ultraviolet radiation. Governments responded by signing an international agreement in 1987 that phased out use of the chemicals, although ozone concentrations are not expected to return to 1980 levels until the middle of the twenty-first century.[18]

The next decade demonstrated that the oceans have limits as well. Although marine scientists had long treated the world's wild fisheries as if they were infinitely abundant, by the 1990s there was widespread agreement that they were in critical condition. Overfishing, along with warming and oxygen depletion due to climate change, had taken a tremendous toll on fish populations. In 2016, a United Nations commission found that over thirty percent of fish stocks were overfished, with another sixty percent being fished at maximum sustainable levels. The total size of the wild catch had not increased since the 1980s. Marine scientists were also abandoning their earlier belief that wild fish stocks were infinitely resilient. They now admitted that Atlantic cod levels, which had fallen to one percent of their initial numbers, were unlikely to rebound.[19]

A dramatic increase in the extinction rate provided more evidence that there are limits to how much pressure humans can put on other species. The earth has experienced at least five mass extinction events in the past half billion years, where natural forces caused sharp and rapid decreases in the abundance and diversity of life. By the 1990s, ecologists had begun to argue that the planet was in the midst of a sixth extinction event, this one caused largely by human activity. Estimates of the global extinction rate vary, since scientists disagree about how many species inhabit the earth to begin with and find it difficult to know with certainty whether a species has disappeared entirely or just where they are looking for it. But a widely accepted estimate is that the extinction rate has risen to between one hundred and one thousand times the historically typical rate.[20]

By the twenty-first century, scientists were even arguing that human lifespan and athletic achievement are subject to limits. Improved medicine and nutrition had been extending lifespans for so long that, at least for many in the industrialized world, living longer than the previous generation had come to seem like a birthright. In tales of the future, characters had routinely lived decades or even centuries beyond their predecessors. Yet scientists were once again finding themselves faced with limits. "Our results," wrote the authors of a 2016 study, "strongly suggest that the maximum lifespan of humans is fixed and subject to natural constraints." They considered it unlikely that improved medicine and nutrition alone would move the upper limit of human lifespan beyond one hundred and twenty years. Human athletic achievements were also encountering limits, as the late twentieth century's trail of broken records across the world of sports began to peter out. One writer called it "Peak Olympics," a time when "the steady march of human progress reaches its final, depressing plateau."[21]

But the most frightening limit to emerge at the end of the century was the amount of greenhouse gases that the earth's atmosphere could absorb without producing dramatic alterations in the climate. Scientists had been aware since the 1930s that world temperatures were rising but assumed it was part of a natural fluctuation. It was not until the mid-1950s that they began to seriously entertain the idea that human induced increases in greenhouse gases like carbon dioxide could influence the climate. A decade later, America's National Academy of Sciences reported that scientists were "just now beginning to realize that the atmosphere is not a dump of unlimited capacity." Contemporary science writers and futurists took this research seriously. Even Victor Cohn in the United States and Ritchie Calder in Britain, both deeply committed to a narrative of endless progress and growth, built the possibility of a more disruptive form of climate change into their scenarios of the future.[22]

By the late 1980s, a scientific consensus had emerged that the growth of greenhouse gas emissions was largely responsible for rising world temperatures. From there, it was a matter of gauging the size and speed of the threat. The United Nations' newly formed International Panel on Climate Change began producing periodic reports based on comprehensive reviews of existing scientific literature. The reports, which became the gold standard in climate science, warned of higher temperatures, melting ice sheets, rising seas, extended droughts, more extreme heat waves, and more intense storms, all of which would contribute to water shortages, poor harvests, flooded coasts, lower air quality, and increased rates of species extinction. The effects were already visible and measurable around the world and would likely last for centuries, even if carbon dioxide emissions were reduced in the near term.[23]

The world had hit a clear and global environmental limit with potentially catastrophic results. As such, climate change presented an unprecedented challenge to the development narrative. A vision of endless growth under a fossil fuel energy regime had always depended on the assumption that the atmosphere could absorb an unlimited amount of carbon dioxide. But now solid scientific evidence showed otherwise. In fact, the evidence suggested that the environmental damage caused by pumping more carbon dioxide into the atmosphere would threaten not only the nonhuman natural world, which had always been the cost of doing business in the development narrative, but also industrial civilization and perhaps even human existence. The implications of climate change were so profound that they inspired a new term for the current geological epoch: the Anthropocene, or the age of humans.

In fact, climate change presented such an overwhelming challenge to the concept of unlimited human expansion that those most invested in growth, like advocates of free markets and economic expansion, felt compelled to dismiss climate science as wrongheaded or even a hoax. Supporters of minimum government regulation could not recognize climate change as a threat of global proportions without admitting that the problem would require major governmental action to manage it. Promoters of economic growth could not embrace a call for decreasing carbon emissions without conceding that it might be necessary to slow or even halt growth, at least until cleaner energies could be brought online. As a result, many corporations and governments—especially in countries with strong frontier traditions like the United States and Australia—simply rejected climate science altogether despite the overwhelming scientific consensus supporting it.[24]

## Technological Disappointment

At the same time that the West found itself bumping up against environmental limits, technological innovation in key areas began to slow. Without question, the industrialized world still experienced astonishing advances after the 1960s, especially in computers, robotics, the medical sciences, and communication technologies. New fossil fuel extraction techniques postponed the arrival of peak oil, and engineered seeds boosted crop yields in troubled areas like Mexico and India, avoiding the widespread famines that many had predicted. These were not insignificant advances. But in the words of economist Tyler Cowen, by about 1970 the industrialized world had finished picking the "low-hanging fruit." After that, further innovation on the life-changing scale of electric lights, automobiles, airplanes, telephones, televisions, phonographs, and mass production proved harder to come by. "Apart from the seemingly magical internet," Cowen wrote in 2011, "life in broad material terms isn't so different from what it was in 1953."[25]

The pace of change had not matched expectations, resulting in a certain amount of disillusionment. Science writer Mark Hanlon has labeled the period from 1945 to 1970 the "Golden Quarter" to differentiate it from the baser era that followed, while the economist Paul Krugman has called the period after 1970 "an era of technological disappointment." Even the Silicon Valley entrepreneur and techno-futurist Peter Thiel lamented, "we wanted flying cars, instead we got 140 characters." By 2012, *Popular Mechanics*—a champion of futuristic transportation technologies for more than a century—had begun an online series titled "Why Don't We Have?" that explained why highly anticipated technologies like super-high-speed-rail and personal jetpacks would probably never see the light of day. In many ways, the world of *The Jetsons* seemed even farther away than it had in 1962.[26]

The most consequential disappointments came in the area of energy technologies, where more than a century of effort had left humankind still overwhelmingly dependent on fossil fuels. Nuclear fission, on which the world had pinned so many of its hopes, turned out to be a particularly large letdown. Engineers found it extremely difficult to scale down the size and weight of reactors, upending dreams of atomic powered airplanes, cars, and smaller devices; radioactive waste continued to be a challenge to store; and many feared that the spread of nuclear power promoted the spread of nuclear weapons. Perhaps most important, the industry never fully convinced the public that the technology was safe. A number of serious accidents, from Windscale in the United Kingdom to Three Mile Island in the United States and Chernobyl in the Soviet Union, garnered international headlines and drained public confidence. After the meltdowns and release of radioactive material at Japan's Fukushima plant in 2011, a number of industrialized countries began scaling back their use of fission. Back in 1956, Disney's popular book *Our Friend the Atom* had portrayed atomic power as a genie that would grant humankind all of its wishes. Just half a century later, many countries found themselves trying to stuff the genie back into its bottle.[27]

Compounding the setbacks of fission was the failure of fusion, once widely seen as commercially feasible by the 1990s. Fusion continues to suffer from two fundamental problems. First, it requires fantastically high temperatures that reach levels more than six times hotter than the sun. That takes an enormous amount of energy to generate. The other problem is developing a material that can withstand that kind of heat. Since 2013, a consortium of six countries and the European Union have been busy in southern France constructing the International Thermonuclear Experimental Reactor, a huge and immensely complex fusion experiment designed to overcome these challenges. But even if the reactor is successful, which is anything but guaranteed, much more work would still be needed to produce power on an industrial scale. Fusion remains one of those technologies that always seems to be fifty years away.[28]

Also disappointing was the lack of progress in manned space exploration, which neither the United States nor the Soviet Union ever managed to make cost-effective. Despite popular memory to the contrary, support for the space program in the United States had always been tepid, with surveys showing that most Americans preferred spending the money in other ways. In the

1970s, a time of straitened financial conditions worldwide and cooling tensions between the Cold War giants, space budgets declined and program
goals transitioned from manned space flight to robotic exploration and the
cooperative effort of the international space station. Although the new emphasis yielded vast troves of data on planetary bodies near and far, it did little
to further the far costlier goals of populating and mining them. Even today,
engineers have yet to bring a more powerful rocket to operational status
than the one that took American astronauts to the moon in 1969. Colonizing the oceans proved to be too difficult and expensive as well. Within the
span of a decade, it began to seem as if there would be no more new resource frontiers after all.[29]

Transportation, long a favorite topic of futurists, also failed to make the
predicted progress. One of the more conspicuous disappointments was
commercial supersonic air travel. Based on the technology used in faster-
than-sound fighter jets, supersonic transportation promised unprecedented
speeds and embodied the future of flight in the second half of the twentieth
century. Yet its commercial run lasted only twenty-seven years. The British-
and French-made *Concorde* began service in 1976, making it possible to fly
from London to Washington, D.C., in under four hours, less than half the
time of an ordinary jet. But the planes were plagued by concerns about their
noise levels, impact on the ozone layer, and incredible expense. They were
permanently grounded in 2003.[30]

Weather control made even fewer advances, even after generations of
corporate and government research. In 1954, the chair of the United States
Advisory Committee on Weather Control had looked at the rapid progress
under way in nuclear weaponry and jet propulsion and forecast a similar
rate of advance in the human ability to manipulate the weather. He predicted in a cover article for *Collier's* that, within forty years, science would
"influence all our weather to a degree that staggers the imagination." Most
of his dreams, however, have not come to pass. Attempts to dissipate hurri-
canes by dispersing chemicals into them have been unsuccessful, and efforts to create rain by seeding clouds with silver iodide, a technique still used
today, remain unproven in their effectiveness. Controlling the weather, even
on a small and local scale, continues to be well beyond human abilities.[31]

By the first decades of the twenty-first century, scientists had become

The *Concorde,* flown by Air France and British Airways until 2003, traveled
at more than twice the speed of sound and was widely regarded as
the airliner of the future. (Courtesy of the National Archives)

more willing to admit that the human ability to master nature might have
limits. Researchers acknowledged that trying to predict the weather with
any certainty more than a week or two in advance is an impossible task due
to the infinite number of ever-changing variables that need to be taken into
account. The larger planetary climate system proved to be just as difficult
to understand, with the physicist and historian Spencer Weart calling it
"so irreducibly complicated that we will never grasp it completely." All the
while, scientific advances were coming at an ever steeper cost that seemed
unsustainable in the long term. Investment in research had grown dramatically since the 1930s, but the returns on that investment had been steadily
diminishing as good ideas became harder to find. In 2020, a group of economists at Stanford University and MIT found that the United States needed
to double its research capacity every thirteen years just to maintain its usual

economic growth. Some scientists even began to admit that humans simply have a limited capacity for understanding the universe, suggesting that knowledge itself has limits.[32]

Adding to the sense of disappointment was the fact that many of the technological advances that did take place were not as problem-free as advertised. Toxic pollution from the chemical revolution became a major public concern as early as 1962 with the publication of Rachel Carson's *Silent Spring*. A marine biologist and accomplished writer, Carson explained in careful and engaging prose how the kinds of chemicals championed in books like Jacob Rosin's *The Road to Abundance* were working their way through the food chain and poisoning people and environments. Carson's book, which built on earlier chemical scares and ongoing fears of radiation, attracted enormous international attention and was instrumental in the launching of the environmental movement. Had she lived another twenty years, Carson would have been unsurprised to learn that the site around the chemical factory where Jacob Rosin served as director of research had become so heavily contaminated that the federal government had to assume control of its cleanup.[33]

The list of futuristic accomplishments with discouraging or at best mixed outcomes was actually quite a long one. Nutritionists remained unconvinced that synthetic foods were as healthy as their less-processed counterparts. Industrial robots did not ease workers into more leisure-oriented lives but instead pushed them into unskilled and less well paying jobs. The city of the future, embodied in modernist architecture throughout the West, was sterile and unpleasant to work and live in. Pesticides kept unwanted insects under control but also contributed to their evolution into newly resistant "superbugs." And global warming, long dreamed of in the colder West, made the weather more volatile rather than universally pleasant. The future had not turned out the way it was supposed to.

Yet the development narrative had the capacity to absorb such failures. In the story it told, disappointing results were simply temporary setbacks on the road to more of everything. Given enough time and funding, humankind would unquestionably be able to perfect fusion power, build Martian colonies, extend human life indefinitely, and so on. Slow progress in these areas did not represent permanent scientific and technological limits so much as transitory ones, often blamable on a failure of political or economic will. They simply remained challenges to overcome.

Even climate change, at least when viewed through the lens of the development narrative, became just another environmental problem to solve so that growth could continue. Beginning in the first years of the twenty-first century, scientists began to speak more publicly about finding ways to slow warming through climate engineering. Some researchers considered ways to absorb carbon emissions, such as adding iron or lime to the seas or building immense air purifiers to cleanse the atmosphere. Others studied ways to repel sunlight, either by spraying a sulphate aerosol into the upper atmosphere to mimic the effect of a volcanic eruption or by pumping sea salt into clouds to promote condensation and increase reflectivity. Still others proposed massive underwater walls a thousand feet high designed to redirect warm water away from melting glaciers, unaware that similar projects had been proposed in the nineteenth century to guide warm currents *toward* the poles to warm the planet. Measures like these found an increasingly receptive audience among environmentally minded scientists, who saw them as a way to buy time while engineers continued to work on alternative energy sources.[34]

But decades of doubt and disillusionment, and the sense that humankind was living in the midst of a slowly unfolding environmental calamity of its own making, had taken its toll on faith in progress. So had other cultural transformations since the 1960s. Many in the West had simultaneously lost faith in the triumphal narrative of the Western past, the Christian faith as the exclusive path to salvation, the superiority of Western culture, and the belief that scientific and technological advancement was always for the good. By the 1990s, climate change denial had even undermined the legitimacy of Western science itself. Nothing, however, posed as large a threat to long-held expectations about the material future as the idea that environmental limits were real and that humans might not prove clever enough to find a way around them.[35]

## Come the Apocalypse

With the environmental future looking grim, and science and technology failing to provide the promised utopia, the disaster narrative gradually became the more commonly encountered vision of the environmental future. Science fiction had gained considerable respect and a sizable audience over the course of the twentieth century and played a large role in spreading it. As fears of environmental crisis emanated from the scientific community, the creators of science fiction books, films, and television shows translated them into compelling images and stories, often incorporating technological dystopias as well. Popular culture, however, had come to a parting of the ways with political culture. Even though the former increasingly embraced a vision of growth-induced disaster, the latter remained committed to growth at any cost.[36]

In the 1970s, the idea that the world was headed toward a severe ecological crisis became the default setting in works of near-future science fiction. Pollution joined overpopulation and resource exhaustion as a major theme, with writers imagining a world so poisoned by the byproducts of human overproduction, overconsumption, and technological mismanagement that people sicken and civilization buckles under the weight of its own waste. Even some old utopian visions were reinterpreted through a new dystopian lens. The utopian dream of billions of humans living perfect, technologically advanced lives in cities built deep underground or high in the air, all so that every available inch of the earth's surface could be devoted to feeding them, morphed into a dystopian backdrop instead. Visions of a bleak environmental future became so common that publishers released entire anthologies with titles like *The Ruins of Earth, The Wounded Planet,* and *Nightmare Age.*[37]

The trend continued through the 1980s and 1990s and into the new millennium. From William Gibson's pathbreaking *Neuromancer* to Margaret Atwood's Maddaddam trilogy to Kim Stanley Robinson's multi-award-winning work, writers set their stories in environmentally impoverished futures. Stories tended to reflect the particular environmental concerns of the day, such as nuclear winter or overdevelopment. As the real earth heated up, stories set in a world destroyed by climate change became increasingly common, eventually coalescing into a powerful new subgenre known as climate fiction, or cli-fi for short. Even when the major theme of a work was not environmental, or the author foresaw the continued advancement of science and technology to ever-loftier heights, the tale was likely to be set in a future defined by some kind of environmental catastrophe. Stories of environmental ruin had become more believable than any alternative.[38]

Movies often reached even larger audiences and helped the public to visualize an environmentally calamitous future. One cluster of memorable movies appeared in the 1970s in response to fears of overpopulation, resource exhaustion, and nuclear mishaps. *Soylent Green* takes place in the year 2022, when overpopulation has led to urban crowding, the rationing of synthetic food to the largely destitute population, and increasingly violent police actions to keep society from complete collapse. *Logan's Run* is set in 2274 in a domed dystopia, where the inhabitants remain ignorant of the ruined world outside and manage their population through the ritual killing of anyone who reaches the age of thirty. The Road Warrior movies, beginning with *Mad Max,* explore the social breakdown that follows the depletion of oil reserves around the world. And *The China Syndrome* presents a corporate cover-up of safety problems in a nuclear power plant. All became important icons in popular culture.[39]

Heightened concern about climate change in the early twenty-first century brought another wave of movies portraying ecological catastrophes. Among the most popular were *The Day After Tomorrow* and *Wall-E.* Released in 2004, *The Day After Tomorrow* depicts the disruption of the North Atlantic current by climate change. The result is a series of superstorms, portrayed through an impressive array of special effects, that throw the entire northern hemisphere into a new ice age. Despite being criticized for its scientific inaccuracies—in particular the fantastically abrupt onset of global cooling—the movie was commercially successful and attracted international scholarly study of its impact on attitudes toward climate change. *Wall-E,* released in 2008 by the Disney studios, combines the disaster narrative with the dystopian branch of the development narrative. It is set in the distant year of 2805, when humans have long since abandoned a hopelessly polluted earth for giant spaceships where they devote their lives to meaningless leisure and consumption.[40]

The turn of the century also saw an explosion of young adult novels premised on visions of environmental ruin, many paired with technological dystopias. Perhaps the best known was Suzanne Collins's enormously popular Hunger Games trilogy, which is set in a world transformed by rising sea levels and beset with chronic shortages of food. Veronica Roth's Divergent series is built on a past history of wars brought on by the disastrous efforts of the United States government to genetically improve its population. And the works of Paolo Bacigalupi take place in settings that have been radically altered by everything from drought to rising sea levels to peak oil to genetic engineering gone wrong. Such books, several made into popular movies, played an important role in spreading a vision of impending environmental catastrophe among young people.[41]

But by the twenty-first century, one did not have to be a fan of science fiction or dystopian literature to be immersed in the imagery of environmental disaster. It was everywhere. Scientists, journalists, and government officials broadcast an unending stream of sobering projections as the world watched islands sink, lakes dry up, temperatures reach new highs, and superstorms devastate major cities. Many still refused to believe that human actions were changing the climate, or that the climate was changing at all. But even they could not possibly block out the drumbeat of apocalypse. It had become easier to imagine the end of the world than a human society that could live in balance with the global environment.

## The Future Is Not What It Used to Be

In contrast, the utopian strand of the development narrative, which had guided Western ambitions for almost two centuries, lost much of its hold over the public imagination after the 1960s. New understandings of the past would no longer support it. A small number of particularly enthusiastic scientists, engineers, and journalists did continue to promise flying cars, floating cities, dramatically longer lives, and unlimited abundance for everyone. And by the end of the century, advances in computers, genetic engineering, and the internet became the basis for new visions of uploaded brains, designer children, and bodies so transformed by technology that they would no longer be human but "transhuman." Some even found a creative way to incorporate the environmental crisis into their visions: they reimagined climate change as an exciting opportunity that would force humankind to push itself to greater heights. Godhood, it seemed, was still just around the corner. But these Promethean dreamers no longer held the same level of public confidence that they once had.[42]

Science fiction writers also abandoned the growth-oriented utopia of glittering technologies, with the important exception of the Star Trek universe. The original *Star Trek* television series ran from 1966 to 1969 and was set three centuries into the future, when earth plays a leading role in the enlightened and expansionist United Federation of Planets. *Star Trek* was a classic technological utopia where science, technology, and the new frontiers offered by space travel have encouraged social and moral progress and ushered in a period of abundance and peace (although there are still plenty of evil aliens to fight). Since then, the Star Trek franchise has spun off additional television series and numerous movies, all set in the same narrative universe. It continues to be a major force in popular culture and an influential vision of tomorrow.[43]

One of the main reasons that Star Trek has retained its popularity in an age of limits is that most of the action takes place on the leading edge of an endless frontier. Unlimited human expansion across the galaxy is not only an assumed good but the central premise. The focus of its television episodes and movies has generally been on the discovery of new worlds, the development of their resources, and the spread of humankind and allied alien species. Environmental concerns have remained muted because it is difficult to imagine meaningful environmental damage in the infinitude of space. For every world devoted to industry and resource extraction, another might be reserved as a pastoral paradise. In short, Star Trek provides a space where viewers can still immerse themselves in the old dream of endless growth without having to worry about the environmental consequences.[44]

For much the same reason, real-life space exploration has remained closely tied to the utopian strain of the development narrative. Prompted by the debate over environmental limits, the physicist Gerard O'Neill became a particularly prominent advocate of space migration, publishing *The High Frontier: Future Colonies in Space* in 1976 and founding the Space Studies Institute at Princeton University. Although interest in space colonization waned for a time, mounting environmental worries in the first years of the twenty-first century led to its revival. This time, profit-driven corporations

In the mid-1970s, NASA asked several artists to illustrate possible designs
for space colonies. This painting by Rick Guidice shows a cutaway
view of a ring-shaped colony that rotates to create its own gravity.
(Courtesy of NASA Ames Research Center)

like Planetary Resources, SpaceX, and Blue Origin promoted visions of mining the moon, settling Mars, and constructing rotating space cylinders like
those designed by O'Neill. "We get to choose," said Jeff Bezos, founder of
Blue Origin and the online retailer Amazon. "Do we want stasis and rationing, or do we want dynamism and growth?" Proposals like these received
a good deal of media attention, but they failed to revive the once widespread
expectation that outer space was poised to become the next frontier.[45]

In the meantime, many environmentalists had come to regard space colonies in a less favorable light. Writing in 1977, the author Wendell Berry saw
in them a "rebirth of the idea of Progress with all its old lust for unrestrained

expansion." Space would simply become a new frontier to abuse, since "humans are destructive in proportion to their supposition of abundance; if they are faced with an infinite abundance, then they will become infinitely destructive." He also believed that space colonization would likely enrich corporations, impoverish taxpayers, and simply transfer the worst characteristics of human society into outer space. Those characteristics would have to change first, and that would only come with an acceptance of limits. "Good character," he concluded, "requires the discipline of finitude."[46]

The surest sign that the utopian vision of progress and growth had become a less credible guide to the future was that it receded behind the mist of nostalgia that began to envelop Western culture in the late 1960s. From Germany to Britain to the United States, people turned to the past in the music they listened to, the movies and television shows they watched, and the fashions they wore. The shift was particularly noticeable among younger people. "Instead of reading Jules Verne or watching Buck Rogers or musing about the future like their parents and grandparents did," lamented a journalist for the *Chicago Tribune* in 1970, "young people seem to be regressing." Businesses were quick to commercialize the new trend, helping it to become the staple of popular culture that it remains today.[47]

The futurist Alvin Toffler saw this unprecedented wave of nostalgia as a direct result of what he called "future shock." The pace of change, he believed, had become so unsettling that people were turning to the past in a desperate search for stability. They were craving the old and familiar in a world they no longer recognized. But Toffler was only partly right. Rapid social and technological change had been constants in the West for generations but had never before sparked a turn to the past quite like this one. What was different by the end of the 1960s was that the future—on a planetary scale—no longer looked so promising. Or, as the journalist Lance Morrow put it a few years later, people "tutored in the gospels of progress began for the first time to peer at the future as a possible enemy."[48]

The utopian version of the development narrative quickly assumed a prominent place in the culture of nostalgia. In the 1970s, the creators of the *Star Wars* movies looked backward to the *Flash Gordon* serials of the 1930s for artistic and narrative inspiration. By the 1980s, entire literary and artistic movements were emerging that recycled the future visions of earlier generations. Steampunk took its look from the work of Jules Verne and Albert Robida, setting stories in worlds that evoke the Victorian era and imagining technologies that use lots of brass, gears, and steam. Dieselpunk drew on mid-twentieth-century diesel technology, while atompunk harkened back to the styles and machinery of the postwar period. The phenomena extended to Russia as well, which has experienced considerable nostalgia for the mid-twentieth-century space program of the former Soviet Union.[49]

These "retrofutures" retained not only their recognizability into the twenty-first century but their marketability as well. Companies and government agencies, particularly those related to technology industries, self-consciously used retro styles to advertise their much more up-to-date products and plans. NASA's Jet Propulsion Laboratory created a series of posters titled "Visions of the Future" inspired by artwork from the 1930s, while both NASA and SpaceX promoted a human future on Mars through posters that evoked the height of the Space Age. In 2016, a company that develops lightweight metals for the technology industry produced a popular video ad that updated the introduction to *The Jetsons* with twenty-first-century technologies. Even Disney's theme park Tomorrowlands, intended by Walt Disney to provide "a living blueprint of our future," now evoke past futures instead, with the park in Paris giving particular prominence to the world of tomorrow as imagined by Jules Verne. Visitors are eager to surround themselves with the kind of absolute faith in progress and growth that has become difficult to find outside the park gates. They are homesick for a world that never was and never will be.[50]

## The Ecotopian Moment

For a brief period from the 1960s through the 1980s, the sense of environmental crisis opened up a creative and hopeful space for imagining possible futures without growth. The fictional "ecotopias" that emerged were very much products of their time, reflecting the concerns of the contemporary civil rights and women's movements and responding to events like the Vietnam War. But their fundamental environmental approaches were remarkably similar to those of the pastoral utopias that had appeared at the end of the nineteenth century. In general, they portrayed small, self-sufficient

# FARMERS WANTED

NASA produced this poster in 2009 to generate support for the colonization of Mars. The poster taps into nostalgia for past futures by using an artistic style that conjures earlier and more optimistic periods of space exploration. (Courtesy of NASA/KSC)

communities with steady-state economies that focused production on the needs of the community. They encouraged simpler material lifestyles, lower levels of consumption, and closer relationships with natural surroundings. All were premised on a fundamental change in human attitudes toward growth and the environment.[51]

In 1962, the same year that Rachel Carson's *Silent Spring* ignited the environmental movement, Aldous Huxley published *Island* as the utopian answer to his dystopian *Brave New World*. Set on a remote island, Huxley's society educates children in ecology from a very young age to instill the understanding that all living things exist in relationship with each other. This early emphasis on connection becomes the foundation for a "do unto others" code of ethics that the inhabitants apply to both human and non-human nature. The result is a society that emphasizes spiritual and intellectual pursuits over material gain and selectively adopts new technologies. They have "no heavy industries to be made more competitive, no armaments to be made more diabolical, not the faintest desire to land on the backside of the moon." They also minimize their numbers and their appetites. "Not being overpopulated," explains one resident, "we have plenty. But, although we have plenty, we've managed to resist the temptation that the West has now succumbed to—the temptation to overconsume."[52]

The British science writer Nigel Calder took a different approach to restructuring human values. In his book *The Environment Game*, published in 1967, Calder argued that social institutions since the advent of agriculture had functioned as a kind of game, with the prizes being wealth and power. "Only with a radical alteration of the rules of the game," he wrote, "to make the enjoyment of a pleasing environment as coveted as money and material goods are today, is there any hope at all that two or three times as many people can live on this planet without defacing it irretrievably." Calder imagined a worldwide civilization in which environmental rewards—such as the right to enjoy the countryside, go hunting, participate in governing the environment, or live in a house with a beautiful view—would be coveted and earned. Human society would go out of its way to have the lowest possible impact on the nonhuman natural world: people would live in small towns or platforms at sea, rely on nuclear or solar power, and abandon their farms, eating only synthetic foods. Most of the earth would return to a wild state, although Calder imagined that humans would play a large role in tending it like a garden.[53]

Among the most iconic contributions to the ecotopian vision of tomorrow was Ernest Callenbach's 1975 book *Ecotopia*, which coined the term. In Callenbach's twenty-first-century future, northern California, Oregon, and Washington have broken away from the United States to pursue a different environmental path. The new country is founded on the principle that humans were meant not to maximize production but "to take their modest place in a seamless, stable-state web of living organisms, disturbing that web as little as possible. . . . People were to be happy not to the extent they dominated their fellow creatures on the earth, but to the extent they lived in balance with them." The people of Ecotopia reject traditional ideas of growth and progress, embracing instead a self-sufficient, steady-state economy, a smaller population, renewable energy, simpler material lives, and the recycling of everything. All government policies encourage a single goal: maintaining a low-impact and sustainable relationship with the natural environment.[54]

In 1976, Marge Piercy fused the ecotopia with the feminist utopia in *Woman on the Edge of Time*. When her protagonist travels telepathically to the year 2137, she expects to see "rocket ships, skyscrapers into the stratosphere, an underground mole world miles deep, glass domes over everything." Instead, she finds herself in a modest-looking village of six hundred people with complete gender equality and limited but advanced technology. The village draws its power from solar panels and windmills and is largely able to feed itself. Piercy's protagonist also briefly visits this future society's dystopian counterpart: a hopelessly polluted police state where technology is used as a weapon of oppression and the rich have abandoned the surface of the earth for space platforms. The implication is that both societies represent possible futures.[55]

Ursula Le Guin took a deeply anthropological approach to the ecotopian future in *Always Coming Home*, published in 1985. The novel explores the life and culture of a small village with few memories of our current civilization, which collapsed long before in an apocalypse of its own making. A member of the Kesh people narrates the first part of the book, but the second takes the form of ethnographic field notes prepared by an outside ob-

server. This format allows Le Guin to develop her fictional culture in unusual depth, revealing its language, legends, rituals, music, poetry, recipes,
and more. The picture that emerges is of a cooperative society that never
takes more than it needs from the natural world. The economy consists of
hunting, gathering, farming, and small-scale industry, and social norms
keep the birthrate low. Le Guin contrasts the Kesh with the Condor, a nearby
people who are more urban, technological, hierarchical, competitive, and
warlike. By the end of the book, the Condor have managed to destroy themselves.[56]

As in these earlier works, Kim Stanley Robinson founded the fictional
ecotopia in his 1990 book *Pacific Edge* on a radical change in human values.
The second quarter of the twenty-first century sees American society down-
size corporations, nationalize resources, and limit development. A green
party becomes a powerful and respected force in politics. The story takes
place a generation later in Orange County, California, where the main character works to retrofit existing houses to make them more environmentally
friendly. Robinson does not naively assume, however, that the urge to expand will entirely disappear. The primary struggle at the center of the story
is over the proposed development of the last wild area in the main character's hometown. Robinson also explored two alternate futures for Orange
County in earlier volumes of what became a three-book series, one set in a
world devastated by nuclear war and the other in a landscape of endless
sprawl and development.[57]

Although most of these works were widely influential and remain classics
of utopian literature and science fiction today, few fully imagined fictional
ecotopias appeared after *Pacific Edge*. The gradual absorption of environmental ideas into mainstream thought blunted their radicalism, and—perhaps
more important—the immanence of climate change overwhelmed their vision of hope. People around the world had begun to feel the negative effects
of global warming; governments remained unable or unwilling to cut emissions; and scientists warned that it was already too late to avoid many of the
catastrophic consequences. As a result, it became harder to imagine that
humankind could have a real impact on shaping the future, since it seemed
like the future was already written. Green utopian thought did not disappear
entirely. But in the words of sociologist Lisa Garforth, it became "less ex-

plicit and powerful, more fugitive and fleeting, often framed by narratives of loss and mourning."[58]

## Sustainable Development

As ecotopian visions faded in the late 1980s, a seemingly new vision of the environmental future coalesced around the concept of "sustainability." The most frequently referenced definition appeared in an influential report by the United Nations World Commission on Environment and Development. Published in 1987 and titled *Our Common Future,* the report defined sustainable development as "development that meets the needs of the present without compromising the ability of future generations to meet their own needs." The report embraced economic growth and sidestepped the debate over limits, helping the concept of sustainable development to achieve broad appeal and provide a new framework for international conversations about environmental problems.[59]

Although sustainability has been applied to everything from agriculture to resource extraction, its main contribution to images of the future has been the "sustainable city." This has been partly due to the constantly growing percentage of the world's population that lives in urban areas. In 2008, for the first time in human history, more people lived in cities than outside of them. Demographers have predicted that seventy-five percent of the world's population will be urban by 2050. The second reason was that urbanists began to reject the conventional wisdom that cities are the source of most environmental problems. Instead, they began to argue the opposite, noting that individual city dwellers tend to consume less water, energy, and space than their rural counterparts, and produce less trash as well. Cities had, of course, long held a prominent place in visions of tomorrow. But this shift in thought suggested that an urban future might also be a more environmentally responsible one, especially if cities were redesigned along more sustainable lines.[60]

Architects, urban planners, and technologists led the way in creating a popular image of the sustainable city of tomorrow. Energy will come from wind turbines, rooftop solar panels, or photovoltaic sheets that cover the south-facing sides of buildings. Transportation will focus on electrically powered light rail and bicycles rather than cars. Food will be imported short distances from local farms or grown right in the city, either on rooftop gardens or in multi-story vertical farms that rise above the surrounding cityscape to catch the sunlight. Water and waste will be managed closely and recycled for reuse. Overall, the image of the sustainable city that spread through popular culture was of a place that is denser and greener and uses advanced technologies to more efficiently manage environmental inputs and outputs. It is often portrayed in images as a modern and high-tech development with lots of green vegetation.[61]

In the first decades of the twenty-first century, plans to build entirely new cities designed around sustainable principles attracted significant public attention. The City of San Francisco created a public authority to redevelop Treasure Island, an artificial landmass in the bay, as an example of environmentally responsible growth. In the English countryside, a consortium of developers began constructing the new eco-friendly town of Sherford, and the United Arab Emirates set to work building Masdar City, a clean-tech hub that uses wind towers and closely built buildings to cool the hot desert air. The Chinese announced plans to build a whole series of sustainable cities, the first of which was projected to be Dongtan on an island near Shanghai. The designers and builders of these cities often viewed them as experiments in developing more environmentally sustainable ways of housing the human population.[62]

In practice, however, the sustainable city and sustainable development in general are not as new and transformative as they might appear. In the minds of those who consider environmental limits an essential component of sustainability, the vision of a sustainable tomorrow does break free of the growth paradigm. But in the hands of the policy makers and business leaders who actually set the world's economic agenda, it simply offers a greener way to grow, similar to what one finds among so-called ecopragmatists like Steven Pinker. Social practices, cultural beliefs, economic systems, political structures, and consumer lifestyles all remain largely the same, even in the new sustainable cities currently under construction. Growth and expansion continue apace, and the resulting future looks almost exactly like the present, except more environmentally efficient. Despite the many successes that the sustainability movement can claim, the sustainable vision of the future embraced by governments, businesses, and much of the wider public is simply the newest manifestation of the utopian development narrative.[63]

The truth is that neither of the industrialized world's two most influential visions of tomorrow offers much inspiration for action or even hope. One vision is a narrative of disaster, a story of a growth-induced ecological catastrophe no less inevitable than Grainville's early vision of apocalypse, and already taking place. Any part of society that survives the disaster will either return to a primitive state or become an oppressive technological dystopia. Whichever the case, it will struggle to persist in a ruined world. The other is a story of development but also of sameness and resignation: humankind will continue to expand, tweaking its existing social and economic systems to make them a bit more sustainable while accepting that human activities will continue to make the planet less friendly to life. Both of these visions are stories of growth and its consequences, for it seems impossible to imagine a world without it. And both are visions of disaster of one kind or another that offer no real future for anyone.

# Epilogue: Changing the Dream

If we do not learn from history, we shall be compelled to relive it. True. But if we do not change the future, we shall be compelled to endure it. And that could be worse.

Alvin Toffler, *The Futurists* (1972)

THIS BOOK DOES NOT TRY TO PREDICT which imagined future is most likely. Although historians have useful perspectives to offer about how history might unfold, they remain famously reluctant to make predictions because they tend to be wrong just as often as everyone else. Occasionally, however, some student of history does hit the nail on the head. Writing in the 1970s, William Catton warned that the West's growth-oriented culture was overshooting the planet's environmental capacity and that humans would have to reduce their dominance over the natural world. "The changes this will entail," he predicted, "are so revolutionary that we will be almost overwhelmingly tempted instead to prolong and augment our dominance at all costs. And, as we shall see, the costs will be prodigious. We are likely to do many things that will make a bad situation worse."[1]

Of the hundreds of prophecies strung throughout this book, that one hits home the hardest because it speaks so directly to the present moment. Rather than acting to curb human expansion and ease pressure on global ecosystems, human beings have not only doubled down on growth since Catton wrote those words but have also spent the subsequent decades denying limits and attacking the scientific consensus around climate change. The delay in action has, to use Catton's words, made a bad situation worse and has perhaps even dulled our prophetic imaginations. "It seems," writes the science fiction author Ursula Le Guin, "that the utopian imagination is trapped, like capitalism and industrialism and the human population, in a one-way future consisting only of growth." The world has now been stuck in that trap for so long that it has become hard to imagine that alternatives even exist.[2]

The stakes in the world's mounting environmental crisis are even higher than most people realize. It has become common knowledge that, with sufficient atmospheric warming, life could become extraordinarily difficult for human beings and impossible for many other forms of life. But there is another risk as well: if the world's industrial base were to collapse, or if the industrialized world were to lose a key part of its technological know-how, civilization would be unlikely to climb the industrial ladder again because all of the easy-to-reach resources are gone. The remaining deposits of coal, oil, copper, zinc, and other essential mineral resources are so low-grade that a less technologically advanced society will be unable to use them. Olaf Stapledon recognized this in the 1920s, when his *Last and First Men* portrayed post-collapse humans as "hampered by living in a used planet." Harrison Brown's team at the California Institute of Technology came to the same conclusion in the 1950s. Such a possibility is little discussed today but remains a very real risk. The human race will likely get one shot at building a civilization with highly advanced technology, and this is it.[3]

Fortunately, the world has more choices for its future than to be stuck in an endless and ever deteriorating present or to welcome a seemingly inevitable apocalypse. Back in 1956, at one of the first interdisciplinary conferences convened to assess the human impact on the earth, the urbanist Lewis Mumford emphasized the sheer variety of futures open to humankind. "To assume," he said, "that there is only one possibility left, that represented by our now-dominant technological civilization, is an act of religious faith, committed by those who believe in the civilization, and in no sense an objective scientific judgment." New ideas would come not from science and technology, he argued, but instead from the arts, the humanities, and religious and ethical thought. Mumford believed that, "within the limits of earth's resources and of man's biological nature, there are as many different possible futures as there are ideals, systems of values, goals and plans, and social, political, educational, and religious organizations for bringing about their realization." Humankind, in other words, does not need to settle for a future with no future.[4]

But it will make little real progress toward solving global environmental problems until it does as the Achuar have asked: change the dream of the modern world, at the heart of which is the paradoxical expectation of unlimited human expansion on a finite planet. This expectation has been a powerful motivating force, so powerful that the centuries-old stories of development and disaster have both been realized in broad outline: growth has provided an unprecedentedly abundant and technology-driven lifestyle, at least for the world's wealthiest inhabitants, and it has also brought environmental disaster to the doorstep, in this case for everyone.[5] That dream has now spread from the West to the rest of the world and has become an expectation shared by most of our species. Its dominance has made it difficult to imagine a path forward that would lead to a more desirable world, leaving us stuck with visions of the future that most people would not want. All of our dreams seem to have become nightmares from which we stubbornly refuse to awake.

Tweaking the existing growth-oriented visions will not do the trick, for they are incapable of embodying anything that resembles a healthy relationship with the natural world, at least for as long as humankind remains confined to a single planet. Neither the development nor the disaster narrative, for example, contains space for animals to enjoy a wild existence. They end up in zoos at best, at worst extinct. That is why animal activists today still have to argue for the practical usefulness of the animals they want to save: they are always battling the assumption that the natural world must make room for further human expansion. Narratives premised on unlimited growth also contain no room for humans to have everyday access to natural surroundings. "It seems inconceivable," notes the historian Rosalind Williams, "that future humanity could dwell in a natural environment—not a primitive one, to be sure, but one where experiences such as seeing the starry sky, picking berries, and walking by an unlittered brook are commonplace. Such an environment is imaginable only if catastrophe, conceived of as an outside force, makes us change direction." Visions with such large and obvious deficiencies are poor guides to a livable future.[6]

Nor can the modern world simply manufacture new dreams. They cannot be designed, cut from whole cloth, and then marketed to consumers, at least not with any realistic expectation of broad acceptance. Instead, images of the future develop through a more organic process. Their roots are in social memory, in shared understandings of the past built on shared values. That is not to say that the seeds of future dreams cannot be intentionally planted. The pastoral utopias of the nineteenth century and the ecotopias of the twentieth remain important sources of inspiration today, and efforts to create new narratives about climate change or to envision solarpunk societies help to generate new questions, ideas, and perspectives about how humans might form a healthier relationship with the natural world. They also have the power to change minds. But without enough common ground in which to grow, observes the French futurist Jacques Ellul, "no invented concept of the future could possibly be implemented. None would possess the power to put the social body into motion, to give it meaning and direction."[7]

In other words, to reimagine the future one needs first to reimagine the past, and in a way that does not celebrate growth in human history as an unqualified triumph. That is the real challenge, and it is a large one. Although an unquestioned belief in the benefits of expansion originally emerged in the West, it has since achieved mythological status in much of the rest of the world as well. The society that must come to a new and shared understanding of its past is now a global one where countries cannot agree on much of anything—except perhaps the need for more growth. Some progress has been made: historians have been busy since the 1970s rewriting the world's environmental history in light of what scientists now know about ecological limits. But while historians can reshape written history, they cannot rewrite social memory, which still clings to obsolete stories about growth with what is beginning to look like a death grip.[8]

Those looking for solutions often paint the world's environmental dilemma as a crisis of culture, and rightly so. Depending on who one asks, its resolution requires a transformation of consciousness, worldview, spirituality, character, perspective, or values that will revolutionize human relationships with the natural world. But that cultural transformation will not support new visions of tomorrow until it first reshapes our understanding of yesterday. Only by embracing new stories about the past can the world develop new stories about the future that can serve as maps to a truly sustainable civilization. We cannot, of course, expect those fresh visions of tomorrow to solve our environmental dilemma by themselves. But we cannot solve it without them.[9]

# ACKNOWLEDGMENTS

I OWE PARTICULAR THANKS TO David Troyansky, Christian Warren, and Christopher Wells for reading the entire manuscript. Their comments were invaluable, as were those of the anonymous reviewers chosen by the press. Some of my students, Francisco Manitas, Erik Wallenberg, and Stephen Zimmer, provided research assistance, and Brian Horrigan and Matt Novak helped me to track down elusive images that I was not willing to do without. Thanks also go to my colleagues in the Brooklyn College History Department—I cannot image a more supportive and collegial group of teacher scholars—and the undergraduate students in my History of the Future course, who have served as sounding boards for much of the material in this book. The members of the Workshop on Modern American History at Princeton University offered insightful comments on an early draft of the introduction, and Adina Berk, Phillip King, and Ashley Lago at Yale University Press brought an enormous amount of energy and expertise to the production process.

My research benefited from the assistance of an Ethyle R. Wolfe Institute for the Humanities Fellowship, a Brooklyn College School of Humanities and Social Sciences Grant, a CUNY Book Completion Award, and the generosity of the PSC-CUNY Research Award program, which remains an essential source of support for scholars at the City University of New York.

I owe special gratitude to my wife Lisa, who read the entire manuscript and provided essential advice on prose, images, and everything else, and to my good friend Tiberius for his untiring support.

Finally, a thank you to all of those who have tried to steer the world toward a better future by sharing their visions of tomorrow through books, articles, artwork, movies, and countless other means. Caring about what life will be like for generations that we will never meet is one of the most profoundly human acts that I can imagine.

# NOTES

## Prologue: Dreaming the Environmental Future

1. This is a foundational story for the Pachamama Alliance (see www.pachamama
.org/about/origin).
2. The term "pattern of expectation" comes from I. F. Clarke, *The Pattern of Expectation, 1644–2001* (New York: Basic, 1979).
3. The literature on past futures spans a large variety of historical works on world's fairs, advertising, science fiction, industrial design, utopias, and other topics. The standard overviews include Clarke, *Pattern of Expectation;* Joseph J. Corn and Brian Horrigan, *Yesterday's Tomorrows: Past Visions of the American Future* (New York: Summit, 1984); and Robert Heilbroner, *Visions of the Future: The Distant Past, Yesterday, Today, and Tomorrow* (New York: Oxford University Press, 1995). For a selection of more recent historical scholarship, see the forum "Histories of the Future" in *American Historical Review* 117, no. 5 (December 2012): 1402–1485. The imagined future is examined through the lenses of literary criticism, anthropology, and sociology, respectively, in Alan Sandison and Robert Dingley, eds., *Histories of the Future: Studies in Fact, Fantasy and Science Fiction* (New York: Palgrave, 2000); Daniel Rosenberg and Susan Harding, eds., *Histories of the Future* (Durham: Duke University Press, 2005); and Nik Brown, Brian Rappert, and Andrew Webster, eds., *Contested Futures: A Sociology of Prospective Techno-Science* (Burlington, Vt.: Ashgate, 2000). Although futurists often draw distinctions between terms like prophecy, forecast, prediction, and projection, there is no general agreement about their respective meanings. I will use them more or less interchangeably based on the context. For a discussion of their use, see Wendell Bell, *Foundations of Futures Studies* (New Brunswick: Transaction, 1997), 1:97–99. The existing literature on the history of the future largely ignores environmental themes in favor of scientific and technological ones, although exceptions are becoming

more common. See Warren Belasco, *Meals to Come: A History of the Future of Food* (Berkeley: University of California Press, 2006); W. Patrick McCray, *The Visioneers: How a Group of Elite Scientists Pursued Space Colonies, Nanotechnologies, and a Limitless Future* (Princeton: Princeton University Press, 2013); chapter 10 of Peter J. Bowler, *A History of the Future: Prophets of Progress from H. G. Wells to Isaac Asimov* (New York: Cambridge University Press, 2017); and Eva Horn, *The Future as Catastrophe: Imagining Disaster in the Modern Age*, trans. Valentine Pakis (New York: Columbia University Press, 2018).

4. For the idea of growth in world history, see in particular Donald Worster, *Shrinking the Earth: The Rise and Decline of Natural Abundance* (New York: Oxford University Press, 2016); Christophe Bonneuil and Jean-Baptiste Fressoz, *The Shock of the Anthropocene: The Earth, History and Us*, trans. David Fernbach (New York: Verso, 2016); Jeremy L. Caradonna, *Sustainability: A History* (New York: Oxford University Press, 2014); Kerryn Higgs, *Collision Course: Endless Growth on a Finite Planet* (Cambridge: MIT Press, 2014); and Fredrik Albritton Jonsson, "The Origins of Cornucopianism: A Preliminary Genealogy," *Critical Historical Studies* 1, no. 1 (Spring 2014): 151–168.

5. William Cronon, "A Place for Stories: Nature, History, and Narrative," *The Journal of American History* 78, no. 4 (March 1992): 1375. The historian Donald Worster and the sociologist William Catton have both argued that the voyages of discovery, particularly the encounter with the Americas, ushered in what Catton has called an "Age of Exuberance" focused on growth and expansion. Worster, *Shrinking the Earth;* and William R. Catton, Jr., *Overshoot: The Ecological Basis of Revolutionary Change* (Urbana: University of Illinois Press, 1980). For European reactions to New World abundance, see William Cronon, *Changes in the Land: Indians, Colonists, and the Ecology of New England* (New York: Hill and Wang, 1983), chapter 2; and David M. Potter, *People of Plenty: Economic Abundance and the American Character* (Chicago: University of Chicago Press, 1953), particularly 78–79.

6. For environmental narratives, see David E. Nye, *America as Second Creation: Technology and Narratives of New Beginnings* (Cambridge: MIT Press, 2003); and Maarten A. Hajer, *The Politics of Environmental Discourse: Ecological Modernization and the Policy Process* (New York: Oxford University Press, 1995). Scholars in the field of futures studies have tended to favor the term "images" of the future over "narratives" and have made the causes and consequences of these images a central concern. For theoretical and historical discussions, see Fred Polak, *The Image of the Future*, trans. Elise Boulding (New York: Elsevier Scientific, 1973); Wendell Bell and James A. Mau, "Images of the Future: Theory and Research Strategies," in Bell and Mau, *The Sociology of the Future: Theory, Cases, and Annotated Bibliography* (New York: Russell Sage, 1971); Robert Bundy, ed., *Images of the Future: The Twenty-First Century and Beyond* (Buffalo: Prometheus, 1976); and Elise Boulding, "The Dynamics of Imaging Futures," *World Future Society Bulletin* 12, no. 5 (September–October 1978): 1–8. For studies that effectively use past visions of the future as historical sources, see Roxanne Panchasi, *Future Tense: The Culture*

*of Anticipation in France Between the Wars* (Ithaca: Cornell University Press, 2009); and Jason Philips, *Looming Civil War: How Nineteenth-Century Americans Imagined the Future* (New York: Oxford University Press, 2019). The foundational work on social memory is Maurice Halbwachs, *On Collective Memory*, trans. Lewis A. Coser (Chicago: University of Chicago Press, 1992).

7. For theoretical and historical explorations of the relationship between past, present, and future, see E. H. Carr, *What Is History?* (New York: Vintage, 1961), especially chapter 5, "History as Progress"; Eric Hobsbawm, "Looking Forward: History and the Future," chapter 4 in *On History* (New York: New Press, 1997); Reinhart Koselleck, *Futures Past: On the Semantics of Historical Time*, trans. Keith Tribe (New York: Columbia University Press, 2004); Francois Hartog, *Regimes of Historicity: Presentism and Experiences of Time,* trans. Saskia Brown (New York: Columbia University Press, 2015); and Thomas F. Green, "Stories and Images of the Future," in Bundy, *Images of the Future*, 35–44. Scientists have also pondered the relationship between past, present, and future. See, for example, Huw Price, *Time's Arrow and Archimedes' Point: New Directions for the Physics of Time* (New York: Oxford University Press, 1996); and Richard A. Muller, *Now: The Physics of Time* (New York: W. W. Norton, 2016).

8. J. B. Bury, *The Idea of Progress: An Inquiry Into Its Origins and Growth*, introduction by Charles A. Beard (1920; New York: Dover, 1932), 5. For the idea of progress, see especially Robert Nisbet, *History of the Idea of Progress* (New York: Basic, 1980); Christopher Lasch, *The True and Only Heaven: Progress and Its Critics* (New York: W. W. Norton, 1991); and Ronald Wright, *A Short History of Progress* (New York: Carroll and Graf, 2004).

9. For a discussion of the "discourse of limits," see John S. Dryzek, *The Politics of the Earth: Environmental Discourses*, 3rd ed. (New York: Oxford University Press, 2013), chapter 2. Robert Nisbet considered economic growth to be one of the five central premises informing the idea of progress. See Nisbet, *History of the Idea of Progress*, 317 and 334–340.

10. Kim Stanley Robinson, *Future Primitive: The New Ecotopias* (New York: Tor, 1994), 9. The development narrative is related to David Nye's "narrative of abundance," one of four energy narratives he discusses in David E. Nye, *Narratives and Spaces: Technology and the Construction of American Culture* (New York: Columbia University Press, 1997), chapter 5. It is also related to what James C. Scott has called "high modernism." See Scott, *Seeing Like a State: How Certain Schemes to Improve the Human Condition Have Failed* (New Haven: Yale University Press, 1998).

11. "Prometheanism" and "cornucopianism" are related but not identical terms, although they are often used interchangeably. See William B. Meyer, *The Progressive Environmental Prometheans: Left-Wing Heralds of a "Good Anthropocene"* (New York: Palgrave Macmillan, 2016); Dryzek, *The Politics of the Earth*, chapter 3; and Paul Wapner, *Living Through the End of Nature: The Future of American Environmentalism* (Cambridge: MIT Press, 2010), which uses the term "dream of mastery" instead of Prometheanism. For the technological utopia, see Howard P. Segal, *Tech-*

*nological Utopianism in American Culture* (Syracuse: Syracuse University Press, 1985).

12. The disaster narrative is related to two of David Nye's energy narratives: the narrative of apocalypse and narrative of existential limits. See Nye, *Narratives and Spaces*, chapter 5.

13. Evan Osnos, "Doomsday Prep for the Super-Rich," *New Yorker* (January 30, 2017). For the various ways of labeling these groups, see for example Marston Bates, *Expanding Population in a Shrinking World* (New York: American Library Association, 1963), 19 (optimists and pessimists); Samuel H. Ordway, Jr., *Resources and the American Dream, Including a Theory of the Limit of Growth* (New York: Ronald Press, 1953) (conservationists and cornucopians); and Harrison Brown, *The Challenge of Man's Future* (New York: Viking, 1954), 6–7 (Malthusians and technologists). Boomsters and doomsters is widely used. The groups have also been labeled "wizards" and "prophets" in Charles C. Mann, *The Wizard and the Prophet: Two Remarkable Scientists and Their Dueling Visions to Shape Tomorrow's World* (New York: Alfred E. Knopf, 2018).

14. Scholars disagree about the extent to which this vision constitutes a coherent and unbroken tradition. See Marius de Geus, *Ecological Utopias: Envisioning the Sustainable Society*, trans. Paul Schwartzman (Utrecht: International, 1999), 20–22; and Lisa Garforth, *Green Utopias: Environmental Hope Before and After Nature* (Medford, Mass.: Polity, 2018), 16–17.

15. Martin E. P. Seligman, Peter Railton, Roy F. Baumeister, and Chandra Sripada, *Homo Prospectus* (New York: Oxford University Press, 2016); and Elise Boulding and Kenneth E. Boulding, *The Future: Images and Processes* (Thousand Oaks, Calif.: Sage, 1994), 1. For some of the many scientists whose careers have been influenced by speculative fiction, see Clarke, *Pattern of Expectation*, 201–202; Edward Cornish, *Futuring: The Exploration of the Future* (Bethesda: World Future Society, 2004), 176; and Wendell Bell, *Memories of the Future* (New Brunswick, N.J.: Transaction, 2012). Whether people speak and think in futured or futureless languages also affects their behavior. See M. Keith Chen, "The Effect of Language on Economic Behavior: Evidence from Savings Rates, Health Behaviors, and Retirement Assets," *American Economic Review* 103, no. 2 (April 2013): 690–731. For the causative role that stories have played in the history of environmental interactions, see Cronon, "A Place for Stories."

16. Wendell Bell, "Futuristics and Social Behavior," in Bundy, *Images of the Future*, 58. Polak, *Image of the Future*. For accessible orientations to the field of futures studies, see Wendell Bell, *Foundations of Futures Studies*, 2 v. (New Brunswick: Transaction, 1997); and Cornish, *Futuring*. For prediction in the realm of technology in particular, see David E. Nye, "Technological Prediction: A Promethean Problem," in *Technological Visions: The Hopes and Fears that Shape New Technologies*, ed. Marita Sturken, Douglas Thomas, and Sandra J. Ball-Rokeach (Philadelphia: Temple University Press, 2004), 159–176. The sociologist Gabriel Tarde made one of the earliest claims for the historical influence of stories about the

future when he wrote: "The action of the future, which is not yet, on the present, seems to me neither more nor less conceivable than the action of the past, which is no more." Gabriel Tarde, "L'Action des Fait Futurs," *Revue de Métaphysique et de Morale* 9, no. 2 (March 1901): 119–137 (quote on p. 121).

17. C. Vann Woodward, "The Future of the Past," *American Historical Review* 75, no. 3 (February 1970), 726; and Carr, *What Is History?* 143. For an argument that historians are particularly suited to write future scenarios, see David J. Staley, "A History of the Future," *History and Theory* 41, no. 4 (December 2002): 72–89.

18. For an overview of the history of environmentalism from a global perspective, see Ramachandra Guha, *Environmentalism: A Global History* (New York: Longman, 2000). For sustainability and the Anthropocene, see Caradonna, *Sustainability*; and Bonneuil and Fressoz, *The Shock of the Anthropocene*.

19. For histories that explore the values behind developmentalist thought, see in particular Donald Worster, *Dust Bowl: The Southern Plains in the 1930s* (New York: Oxford University Press, 1979); and Meyer, *Progressive Environmental Prometheans*.

20. For an introduction to the environmental literature on economic growth, see Herman E. Daly, *Beyond Growth: The Economics of Sustainable Development* (Boston: Beacon, 1996); Donella Meadows, Jorgen Randers, and Dennis Meadows, *The Limits to Growth: The 30-Year Update* (White River Junction, Vt.: Chelsea Green, 2004); Bill McKibben, *Deep Economy: The Wealth of Communities and the Durable Future* (New York: Henry Holt, 2007); Tim Jackson, *Prosperity Without Growth: Foundations for the Economy of Tomorrow* (New York: Earthscan, 2009); and Rob Dietz and Dan O'Neill, *Enough Is Enough: Building a Sustainable Economy in a World of Finite Resources* (San Francisco: Berrett-Koehler, 2013).

21. The Indian author Amitav Ghosh writes: "Let us make no mistake: the climate crisis is also a crisis of culture, and thus of the imagination." Ghosh, *The Great Derangement: Climate Change and the Unthinkable* (Chicago: University of Chicago Press, 2016), 9.

## Chapter 1. A Story of Progress and Growth

1. Rogerii Baconis, *Epistola de Secretis Operibus Artis et Naturae, et de Nullitate Magiae* (Hamburgi: Frobeniano, 1618), 36–38 (chapter 4). The translations are from Roger Bacon, *Letter on Secret Works of Art and of Nature and on the Invalidity of Magic*, trans. Michael S. Mahoney, accessed June 15, 2020, https://www.princeton.edu/~hos/h392/bacon.html.

2. For the development of a culture of economic growth during the Early Modern period, see Joel Mokyr, *A Culture of Growth: The Origins of the Modern Economy* (Princeton: Princeton University Press, 2016). For the widening of Western perspectives on the future in the seventeenth and eighteenth centuries, see Andrea Brady and Emily Butterworth, eds., *The Uses of the Future in Early Modern Europe* (New York: Routledge, 2010).

3. To gain a sense for the European reaction to New World abundance, see William

Cronon, *Changes in the Land: Indians, Colonists, and the Ecology of New England* (New York: Hill and Wang, 1983), chapter 2. Also see John F. Richards, *The Unending Frontier: An Environmental History of the Early Modern World* (Berkeley: University of California Press, 2003).

4. Michael Rawson, "Discovering the Final Frontier: The Seventeenth-Century Encounter with the Lunar Environment," *Environmental History* 20, no. 2 (April 2015): 194–216.

5. The literature on the Scientific Revolution is vast, and historians continue to debate whether it was as scientific or as revolutionary as we sometimes like to think. For an overview, see Steven Shapin, *The Scientific Revolution* (Chicago: University of Chicago Press, 1996).

6. René Descartes, "Discourse on Method," in *Discourse on Method and Other Writings*, trans. with an intro. by Arthur Wollaston (1637; New York: Penguin, 1960), 84 (Part 6).

7. Francis Bacon, "Novum Organum" (1620), Aphorisms II, no. 52, in *The Works of Francis Bacon*, v. 4, bk. 2, ed. James Spedding, Robert Leslie Ellis, and Douglas Denon Heath (London: Longman, 1858), 247–248.

8. Paul Slack, *The Invention of Improvement: Information and Material Progress in Seventeenth-Century England* (New York: Oxford University Press, 2015). Also see David Alff, *The Wreckage of Intentions: Projects in British Culture, 1660–1730* (Philadelphia: University of Pennsylvania Press, 2017). John Wilkins, *Mathematical Magick: or, the Wonders that May Be Performed by Mechanichal Geometry* (1648; London: Golden Ball in St. Pauls Church-yard, 1680); Marquis of Worcester, *Century of Inventions*, ed. Charles F. Partington (1663; London: John Murray, 1825), nos. 77 and 100 (originally written in 1655); and Joseph Glanvill, *Scepsis Scientifica: or, Confest Ignorence, the Way to Science; in an Essay of the Vanity of Dogmatizing, and Confident Opinion*, ed. John Owen (1665; London: Kegan Paul, Trench, 1885), 156–157.

9. Jonathan Sawday, *Engines of the Imagination: Renaissance Culture and the Rise of the Machine* (New York: Routledge, 2007). Also see Carolyn Merchant, *Reinventing Eden: The Fate of Nature in Western Culture*, 2nd ed. (New York: Routledge, 2013).

10. Wilkins, *Mathematical Magick*, 190; Worcester, *Century of Inventions*, 100; Glanvill, *Scepsis Scientifica*, 157.

11. Jacqueline Hecht, "L'Avenir Était Leur Affaire: De Quelques Essais de Prévision Démographique au XVIIIème Siècle," *European Journal of Population* 6, no. 3 (September 1990): 285–322.

12. Genesis 1:28; and John Edwards, *Polpoikilos Sophia, a Complete History or Survey of All the Dispensations and Methods of Religion* (London: Printed for Daniel Brown, Jonath. Robinson, Andrew Bell, John Wyatt, and E. Harris, 1699), 615. For the debate over the influence of Christianity on Western attitudes toward the environment, see David and Eileen Spring, eds., *Ecology and Religion in History* (New York: Harper & Row, 1974).

13. There were other seventeenth-century utopias that touched on scientific themes

but did not embed their societies as deeply in natural knowledge as the three I explore here. See Nell Eurich, *Science in Utopia: A Mighty Design* (Cambridge: Harvard University Press, 1967). For the history of utopia generally, see Krishan Kumar, *Utopia and Anti-Utopia in Modern Times* (Cambridge: Basil Blackwell, 1987). The first fictional forays into the future were a British political tract published in 1644 and a French romance published in 1659. Neither developed its future setting in a very sophisticated way or gave a large role to science, and their poor literary merit guaranteed their obscurity. Clarke, *Pattern of Expectation*, 15–16. For other changes in ideas about nature during this period, see Keith Thomas, *Man and the Natural World: Changing Attitudes in England, 1500–1800* (New York: Oxford University Press, 1983).

14. Tommaso Campanella, *The City of the Sun: A Poetic Dialogue*, trans. with introduction and notes by Daniel J. Donno (Berkeley: University of California Press, 1981). The walls are described on pp. 33–37. Slightly different details appear in the later Latin edition. Campanella's book circulated in manuscript form until its publication in 1623. For Campanella's thoughts about science and nature more broadly, see Germana Ernst, *Tommaso Campanella: The Book and the Body of Nature*, trans. by David L. Marshall (New York: Springer, 2010); and John M. Headley, *Tommaso Campanella and the Transformation of the World* (Princeton, N.J.: Princeton University Press, 1997).

15. Campanella, *City of the Sun*, 113.

16. Johann Valentin Andreae, *Christianopolis*, introduced and translated by Edward H. Thompson (Dordrecht, The Netherlands: Kluwer Academic, 1999). For Andreae's thought more generally, see especially John Warwick Montgomery, *Cross and Crucible: Johann Valentin Andreae (1586–1654), Phoenix of the Theologians*, 2 vol. (The Hague: Martinus Nijhoff, 1973). Andreae also figures prominently in the literatures on alchemy and the Rosicrucian phenomenon.

17. Andreae, *Christianopolis*, 219 (ch. 52).

18. Andreae, *Christianopolis*, 175 (ch. 16).

19. Francis Bacon, *New Atlantis*, in *Famous Utopias: Being the Complete Text of Rousseau's Social Contract, More's Utopia, Bacon's New Atlantis, and Campanella's City of the Sun*, ed. Charles M. Andrews (New York: Tudor, 1901); and H. G. Wells, "Utopia" (1939), *Science-Fiction Studies* 9, no. 2 (July 1982), 120.

20. Quotes appear in Bacon, *New Atlantis*, 252, 244, 252, and 271. For knowledge as power, see Bacon, "Novum Organum," Aphorisms I, no. 3, 47.

21. Bacon, *New Atlantis*, 263–270. For the imitation of nature, see J. Peter Zetterberg, "Echoes of Nature in Salomon's House," *Journal of the History of Ideas* 43, no. 2 (April–June, 1982): 179–193.

22. Bacon, *New Atlantis*, 263–267.

23. Bacon, *New Atlantis*, 263.

24. Bacon, *New Atlantis*, 254–257. On growth in these utopias, see Kumar, *Utopia and Anti-Utopia*, 36.

25. Samuel Grott, *Nova Solyma: The Ideal City; or Jerusalem Regained*, trans. Walter

Begley (1648; New York: Charles Scribner's Sons, 1902), 171 (vol. 1, book 2, ch. 1); and Eurich, *Science in Utopia*, 81–86.

26. Bacon, "Novum Organum," Aphorisms I, no. 129, 115. For Bacon's thoughts on the dangers of science, see Heidi D. Studer, "Francis Bacon on the Political Dangers of Scientific Progress," in *Canadian Journal of Political Science* 31, no. 2 (June, 1998): 219–234.

27. Robert Nisbet, *History of the Idea of Progress* (New Brunswick, N.J.: Transaction, 2009), particularly Part II: introduction and chapter 6; and Nathaniel Wolloch, *History and Nature in the Enlightenment: Praise of the Mastery of Nature in Eighteenth-Century Historical Literature* (New York: Routledge, 2011). For the Enlightenment more generally, see Anthony Pagden, *The Enlightenment: And Why It Still Matters* (New York: Random House, 2013).

28. Richards, *Unending Frontier.*

29. Clarke, *Pattern of Expectations,* 29–34.

30. Anne-Robert-Jacques Turgot, "A Philosophical Review of the Successive Advances of the Human Mind," in *The Turgot Collection: Writings, Speeches, and Letters of Anne Robert Jacques Turgot, Baron de Laune,* ed. David Gordon (1750; Auburn, Ala.: Ludwig von Mises Institute, 2011), 339.

31. Nicolas de Condorcet, "Sketch for a Historical Picture of the Progress of the Human Mind: Tenth Epoch," trans. Keith Michael Baker, *Daedalus* 133, no. 3 (Summer 2004): 65–82.

32. William Godwin, *Enquiries Concerning Political Justice, and Its Influence on Morals and Happiness,* 2nd ed. (London: Printed for G. G. and J. Robinson, Paternoster-Row, 1796), 1:451; and 3rd ed. (1798), 2:527 and 528.

33. Nisbet, *History of the Idea of Progress,* Part II: introduction and chapter 6; Joel Barlow, *The Columbiad: A Poem* (Philadelphia: Fry and Kammerer, 1807), 364, 366–367 (Book X, lines 239, 287–302).

34. William Thomson, *Mammuth; or, Human Nature Displayed on a Grand Scale: In a Tour with the Tinkers, into the Inland Parts of Africa. By the Man in the Moon* (London: J. Murray, 1789), 1:226.

35. Frank E. Manuel and Fritzie P. Manuel, *Utopian Thought in the Western World* (Cambridge: Belknap Press of Harvard University, 1979), chapter 18; and Reinhart Koselleck, *Futures Past: On the Semantics of Historical Time* (New York: Columbia University Press, 2004), chapter 1.

36. Michael Williams, *Deforesting the Earth: From Prehistory to Global Crisis* (Chicago: University of Chicago Press, 2002); Richard H. Grove, *Green Imperialism: Colonial Expansion, Tropical Island Edens and the Origins of Environmentalism, 1600–1860* (New York: Cambridge University Press, 1995); and Clarence Glacken, *Traces on the Rhodian Shore: Nature and Culture in Western Thought from Ancient Times to the End of the Eighteenth Century* (Berkeley: University of California Press, 1967), chapter 13.

37. Robert Wallace, *Various Prospects of Mankind, Nature, and Providence* (London: Printed for A. Millar, 1761), 122.

38. Wallace, *Various Prospects*, 116, 117, and 120. Also see Robert B. Luehrs, "Population and Utopia in the Thought of Robert Wallace," *Eighteenth-Century Studies* 20, no. 3 (Spring 1987): 313–335.

39. For Malthus's ideas in the context of Western ideas about nature, see Glacken, *Traces on the Rhodian Shore*, chapter 13; for his ideas in the context of the history of the idea of progress, see Nisbet, 216–220; for reactions to Malthus's thought through the centuries, see Robert J. Mayhew, *Malthus: The Life and Legacies of an Untimely Prophet* (Cambridge: Belknap Press of Harvard University, 2014).

40. Thomas Malthus, *An Essay on the Principle of Population, as It Affects the Future Improvement of Society, with Remarks on the Speculations of Mr. Godwin, M. Condorcet, and Other Writers* (London: J. Johnson, 1798), 16–17 and 167.

41. Malthus, *Essay*, 162 and 16.

42. Genesis 1:28; and Thomas Malthus, *Principles of Political Economy, Considered with a View to Their Practical Application* (London: John Murray, 1820), 228.

43. William Godwin, *Of Population: An Enquiry Concerning the Powers of Increase in the Numbers of Mankind* (London: Longman, Hurst, Rees, Orme, and Brown, 1820), 450–451. Malthus framed his vision as the destiny of a single country bent on producing the maximum amount of food, but it can logically be extrapolated to a more global vision. Thomas Malthus, *An Essay on the Principle of Population; or, a View of Its Present and Past Effects on Human Happiness*, 6th ed. (London: John Murray, 1826), 2:88–89.

44. The literary implications of Mercier's book are explored in Paul K. Alkon, *Origins of Futuristic Fiction* (Athens: University of Georgia Press, 1987). Also see Robert Darnton, *The Forbidden Best-Sellers of Pre-Revolutionary France* (New York: W. W. Norton, 1995).

45. Louis-Sébastien Mercier, *Memoirs of the Year Two Thousand Five Hundred*, trans. W. Hooper (Philadelphia: Thomas Dobson, 1795), 223. The institute, called the "King's Cabinet," is described in chapter 31.

46. Mercier, *Memoirs*, 311–315.

47. For the impact of the printing press and science, see Mercier, *Memoirs*, 155–156 and 330, respectively.

48. For the population of France, London, and Russia, see Mercier, *Memoirs*, 40, 349, and 342, respectively; for canals, see 132–133.

49. See Louis-Sébastien Mercier, *L'An Deux Mille Quatre Cent Quarante. Reve S'Il En Fut Jamais; Suivi de L'Homme de Fer, Songe*, New Edition (Paris: 1786), vol. 2, chapter 56 for commerce and chapter 59 for colonies. Mercier had come to the conclusion that colonies were vital to the future of France. See Laure Marcellesi, "Louis-Sébastien Mercier: Prophet, Abolitionist, Colonialist," *Studies in Eighteenth Century Culture* 40, no. 1 (January 2011): 247–273.

50. Mercier, *L'An Deux Mille Quatre Cent Quarante*, 3:173 and 174–175. For Mercier's attitude toward unutilized natural areas, see vol. 2, chapter 50, "Uncultivated Lands," particularly p. 280, note b.

51. Mercier, *L'An Deux Mille Quatre Cent Quarante*, 2:304 and 306.

52. Jean-Baptiste Francois Xavier Cousin de Grainville, *The Last Man,* trans. I. F. and M. Clarke (1805; Middletown, Conn.: Wesleyan University Press, 2002); and Morton D. Paley, "*Le Dernier Homme:* The French Revolution as the Failure of Typology," *Mosaic: An Interdisciplinary Critical Journal* 24, no. 1 (Winter 1991): 67–76.

53. The history of earth's decline related in this and the following paragraph appears in Grainville, *Last Man,* Canto III. For the senescence of nature, see Glacken, *Traces on the Rhodian Shore,* passim.

54. Grainville, *Last Man,* 27, 62, and 46–47.

55. Grainville, *Last Man,* 31.

56. Grainville, *Last Man,* 133.

57. Grainville, *Last Man,* xxxi–xli. The larger context for end-of-the-world stories is explored in W. Warren Wagar, *Terminal Visions: The Literature of Last Things* (Bloomington: Indiana University Press, 1982).

58. For a discussion of the many editions and translations of the books during Mercier's lifetime (he died in 1814), see Everett C. Wilkie, Jr., "Mercier's L'An 2440: Its Publishing History During the Author's Lifetime," *Harvard Library Bulletin* 32, no. 1 (Winter 1984): 5–35, and Wilkie, "Mercier's L'An 2440: Its Publishing History During the Author's Lifetime, Part II: Bibliography," *Harvard Library Bulletin* 32, no. 4 (Fall 1984): 348–400.

## Chapter 2. Industrializing the Plot

1. Jane Webb, *The Mummy! A Tale of the Twenty-Second Century,* 2nd ed. (London: Henry Colburn, 1828), 1:189.

2. For the relationship between the industrial revolution and economic growth, see Joel Mokyr, *The Enlightened Economy: An Economic History of Britain, 1700–1850* (New Haven: Yale University Press, 2010).

3. The quote is from John Stuart Mill, "M. de Tocqueville on Democracy in America" (1840), in Mill, *Dissertations and Discussions: Political, Philosophical, and Historical* (London: John W. Parker and Son, 1859), 2:70. For the emergence of future fiction as a genre, see I. F. Clarke, *The Pattern of Expectation: 1644–2001* (New York: Basic, 1979), 57.

4. See, for example, Julius Von Voss, *Ini: Ein Roman aus dem Ein Und Zwanzigsten Jahrhundert* (Berlin: Karl Friedrich Amelang, 1810), 233–235; Edgar Allan Poe, "Mellonta Tauta" (1849), in *Collected Works of Edgar Allan Poe: Volume 3: Tales and Sketches, 1843–1849,* ed. Thomas Ollive Mabbott (Cambridge: Belknap Press of Harvard University Press, 1978), 1289–1309, especially 1298; *A Hundred Years Hence; or the Memoirs of Charles, Lord Moresby, Written by Himself* (London: Longman, Rees, Orme, Brown, and Green, 1828), 123; and Webb, *The Mummy!* For Webb's description of how she and Loudon met, see Jane Webb Loudon, "An Account of the Life and Writings of John Claudius Loudon," in J. C. Loudon,

*Self-Instruction for Young Gardeners, Foresters, Bailiffs, Land-Stewards, and Farmers*
(London: Longman, Brown, Green, and Longmans, 1845), xxxv.

5. Webb, *The Mummy!* 13.

6. Dominique Francois Arago, *Historical Eloge of James Watt,* trans. James Patrick
Muirhead (London: John Murray, 1839), 149–152. Arago delivered the address in
1834.

7. Webb, *The Mummy!* 67–68; J. J. Grandville, *Un Autre Monde* (Paris: H. Fournier,
1844), 22; and *Mrs. Maberly; or, the World as It Will Be* (London: J. Macrone, 1836),
3:128–130.

8. See Henry Alken's series "The Progress of Steam, Alken's Illustration of Modern
Prophecy" (1828), which includes "A View in White Chapel Road 1830" and "A
View in Regent's Park, 1831"; William Heath, "March of Intellect" and "March of
Intellect No. 2" (1828); Robert Seymour, "Locomotion" and "Locomotion, Plate 2"
(c. 1830); and Charles Jameson Grant, "The Century of Invention, Anno Domini
2000, or the March of Aerostation, Steam, Rail Roads, Moveable Houses, and
Perpetual Motion" (c. 1834).

9. Poe is quoted in Jeffrey Meyers, *Edgar Allan Poe: His Life and Legacy* (New York:
Cooper Square, 2000), 154. The quote originally appeared in Edgar Allan Poe,
"Doings of Gotham: Letter II," *The Columbia Spy* (Columbia, Pa.), May 25, 1844,
3. For mid-century speculations about the future of flight, see "Flying Machines
in the Future," *Scientific American,* September 8, 1860, 165.

10. J. A. Etzler, *The Paradise Within Reach of All Men, Without Labor, by Powers of Nature and Machinery. An Address to All Intelligent Men. In Two Parts.* (Pittsburgh:
Etzler and Reinhold, 1833), reprinted in Etzler, *The Collected Works of John Adolphus Etzler,* intro. Joel Nydahl (Delmar, N.Y.: Scholars' Facsimiles and Reprints,
1977), part 2, 16–17. For the role of useful knowledge in the industrial revolution,
see Joel Mokyr, *The Gifts of Athena: Historical Origins of the Knowledge Economy*
(Princeton: Princeton University Press, 2002).

11. Robert Owen, *The Book of the New Moral World* (London: Effingham Wilson, 1836),
xxi; and Etienne Cabet, *Travels in Icaria,* trans. Leslie J. Roberts, intro. Robert Sut-
ton (1840; Syracuse, N.Y.: Syracuse University Press, 2003), lviii. For a general
orientation, see Gregory Claeys, "Socialism and Utopia," in *Utopia: The Search for
the Ideal Society in the Western World,* eds. Roland Schaer, Gregory Claeys, and
Lyman Tower Sargent (New York: Oxford University Press, 2000).

12. Scholars have only recently rediscovered the environmental thought of Marx and
Engels. See John Bellamy Foster, "Marx and the Environment," in *Marx Today:
Selected Works and Recent Debates,* ed. John F. Sitton (New York: Palgrave Mac-
Millan, 2010), 229–239. For a more critical view of Marx and Engels, see Peter
Coates, *Nature: Western Attitudes Since Ancient Times* (Berkeley: University of Cal-
ifornia Press, 1998), 146–152.

13. Charles Fourier, *Théorie de l'Unité Universelle,* in *The Utopian Vision of Charles Fourier: Selected Texts on Work, Love, and Passionate Attraction,* ed. and trans. Jonathan

Beecher and Richard Bienvenu (Boston: Beacon, 1970), 288. For an analysis of Fourier's environmental values, see Joan Roelofs, "Charles Fourier: Proto-Red Green," *Capitalism, Nature, Socialism* 4, no. 3 (September 1993): 69–88. For a contemporary story that pokes fun at the enormous potential size of future consumption levels, see Anti-Humbug, "Phrenology a Detector of Murder; A Tale of the Fortieth Century," *The London Magazine, Charibari, and Courrier des Dames,* February 1840, 27–33, and April 1840, 200–205.

14. Michael Angelo Garvey, *The Silent Revolution; or the Future Effects of Steam and Electricity upon the Condition of Mankind* (London: William and Frederick G. Cash, 1852), 161. For human needs as unlimited, see Gregory Claeys, *Machinery, Money, and the Millennium: From Moral Economy to Socialism, 1815–1860* (Princeton: Princeton University Press, 1987), xxviii. For the movement from utopias of sufficiency to utopias of abundance, see Krishan Kumar, *Utopia and Anti-Utopia in Modern Times* (Cambridge, Mass.: Basil Blackwell, 1987), 46–47.

15. For Fourier's estimates, see Charles Fourier, *The Theory of the Four Movements,* ed. Gareth Stedman Jones and Ian Patterson (New York: Cambridge University Press, 1996), 47, and Fourier, *Théorie de l'Unité Universelle,* 290; Etzler, *The Paradise Within Reach of All Men,* part 1, 97–98. Speculation about future population was quite common at the time. See, for example, "Future Population of the United States," *Christian Reflector,* September 7, 1842, 2; and "Population of the United States—Past and Future," *Liberator,* October 1, 1852, 159.

16. Cabet, *Travels in Icaria,* 99; Duc de Lévis, *Les Voyages de Kang-hi* (1810), as described in Clarke, *Pattern of Expectation,* 52; and "Specimen of a Prospective Newsletter: The North American Luminary, 1st July, 4796," *New Monthly Magazine and Literary Journal* 2 (London: Henry Colburn, 1821): 129–135.

17. Cabet, *Travels in Icaria,* chapter 36; *A Hundred Years Hence; or the Memoirs of Charles, Lord Moresby,* 126; John Banim, *Revelations of the Dead-Alive* (London: W. Simpkin and R. Marshall, 1824) (for the growth of London); Vladimir Fedorovich Odoevsky, *The Year 4338. Letters from Petersburg* (1838–1840), in *Pre-Revolutionary Russian Science Fiction: An Anthology,* ed. and trans. Leland Fetzer (Ann Arbor: Arbis, 1982) (for the growth of Moscow and St. Petersburg), quote on p. 40.

18. Faddei Bulgarin, "Plausible Fantasies; or a Journey in the Twenty-Ninth Century" (1824), in Fetzer, ed. and trans., *Pre-Revolutionary Russian Science Fiction,* 15; and Garvey, *The Silent Revolution,* 170–171.

19. Von Voss, *Ini,* illustration opposite title page; Emile Souvestre, *The World As It Shall Be,* ed. I. F. Clarke, trans. M. Clarke (1846; Middletown, Conn.: Wesleyan University Press, 2004), 70–71; Etzler, *The Paradise Within Reach of All Men,* part 1, 25–26, 46, quote on 95. Jules Verne later wrote his own book about a floating city. See Verne, *The Self-Propelled Island,* trans. Marie-Thérèse Noiset (1895; Lincoln: University of Nebraska Press, 2015). For a twenty-first-century vision of floating cities, see the advocacy of the Seasteading Institute, founded in 2008.

20. Fourier, *Theory of Four Movements,* 328; Webb, *The Mummy!* 3 (quote) and 281.

21. Louis-Sébastien Mercier, *Memoirs of the Year Two Thousand Five Hundred,* trans. W. Hooper (Philadelphia: Thomas Dobson, 1795), 224; Cabet, *Travels in Icaria,* 231 and 132 (quote on 122).

22. Von Voss, *Ini,* 175–177; Fourier, *Theory of Four Movements,* 52; Félix Bodin, *The Novel of the Future,* adapted by Brian Stableford (1834; Encino, Calif.: Black Coat, 2008), 49.

23. *Conversations of Goethe with Eckermann and Soret,* trans. John Oxenford (London: Smith, Elder, 1850), 1:365. Humboldt outlines his research in Alexander de Humboldt, *Political Essay on the Kingdom of New Spain,* trans. John Black (London: Printed for Longman, Hurst, Rees, Orme, and Brown, 1811), vol. 1, chapter 2. Also see Andrea Wulf, *The Invention of Nature: Alexander Von Humboldt's New World* (New York: Knopf, 2015).

24. A. K. Ruh, *Guirlanden um die Urnen der Zukunft* (Leipzig: Polti, 1800), 57–58; Bulgarin, "Plausible Fantasies," 9; and Théophile Gautier, "Future Paris" (1851), in *Investigations of the Future: Seven Proto-Science Fiction Tales,* ed. Brian Stableford (Tarzana, Calif.: Black Coat, 2012), 29. A warmer Spain grows figs and coconuts in Von Voss, *Ini,* 289–290. Etzler, in contrast, simply expected northern peoples to migrate to the south. Etzler, *The Paradise Within Reach of All Men,* 80. Predictions of day-to-day control of the weather also appeared at this time but were less common. See "Specimen of a Prospective Newsletter," 129; and Webb, *The Mummy!* 28. For the United States, see Jan Golinski, *British Weather and the Climate of Enlightenment* (Chicago: University of Chicago Press, 2007), 192–202. Also see Anya Zilberstein, *A Temperate Empire: Making Climate Change in Early America* (New York: Oxford University Press, 2016); and James Rodger Fleming, *Historical Perspectives on Climate Change* (New York: Oxford University Press, 1998).

25. Fourier, *Theory of Four Movements,* 47–50.

26. Gautier, "Future Paris," 29; Vladimir Fedorovich Odoevsky, *The Year 4338. Letters from Petersburg* (1838–1840), in Fetzer, ed., *Pre-Revolutionary Russian Science Fiction,* 40.

27. Cabet, *Travels in Icaria,* 132; Odoevsky, *Year 4338,* 48; Charles Fourier, *Théorie des Quatre Mouvements et des Destinées Générales,* in Beecher and Bienvenu, *The Utopian Vision of Charles Fourier,* 404–406.

28. Mark V. Barrow, Jr., *Nature's Ghosts: Confronting Extinction from the Age of Jefferson to the Age of Ecology* (Chicago: University of Chicago Press, 2009); Fourier, *Theory of Four Movements,* 50; and Cabet, *Travels in Icaria,* 130–131.

29. Quote is from Odoevsky, *Year 4338,* 42. For humorous treatments of horse extinction, see Charles Jameson Grant, *The Century of Invention, Anno Domini 2000,* in *Every Body's Album, & Caricature Magazine,* no. 3, 1834, republished in Norman Brosterman, *Out of Time: Designs for the Twentieth-Century Future* (New York: Harry N. Abrams, 2000), p. 46; Cruikshank, "Horses 'Going to the Dogs'" (1829); and W. H. Freeman, *Three Hundred Years to Come: A New Comic Song* (London: George and Manby, c. 1835). Horses are also either extinct or almost extinct in Anti-Humbug, "Phrenology a Detector of Murder," 32; and Mary Griffith, *Three*

*Hundred Years Hence,* in Griffith, *Camperdown; or, News from "Our Neighbourhood"* (Philadelphia: Carey, Lea & Blanchard, 1836), 31.

30. Bulgarin, "Plausible Fantasies," 10.

31. E. A. Wrigley, *Energy and the English Industrial Revolution* (New York: Cambridge University Press, 2010). For statistics, see p. 37.

32. Arago, *Historical Eloge of James Watt,* 151; Ralph Waldo Emerson, "Wealth," in *The Conduct of Life,* The Complete Works of Ralph Waldo Emerson (Boston: Houghton Mifflin, 1883), 6:86–87; and Lewis Mumford, *Technics and Civilization* (New York: Harcourt, Brace, 1934), 169.

33. John Williams, *The Natural History of the Mineral Kingdom* (Edinburgh: Thomas Ruddiman, 1789), 1:172–173; and John Ramsay McCullough, *A Statistical Account of the British Empire: Exhibiting Its Extent, Physical Capacities, Population, Industry, and Civil and Religious Institutions* (London: Charles Knight, 1837), 1:89. The debate over the extent of Britain's coal deposits is discussed in Rolfe Peter Sieferle, *The Subterranean Forest: Energy Systems and the Industrial Revolution,* 2nd ed. (Cambridge: White Horse, 2001), 184–191. For concerns about coal's possible exhaustion, see Nuno Luis Madureira, "The Anxiety of Abundance: William Stanley Jevons and Coal Scarcity in the Nineteenth Century," *Environment and History* 18, no. 3 (2012): 395–421; and Fredrik Albritton Johnsson, *Enlightenment's Frontier: The Scottish Highlands and the Origins of Environmentalism* (New Haven: Yale University Press, 2013), chapter 7.

34. See John Adolphus Etzler, *The Collected Works of John Adolphus Etzler,* intro. Joel Nydahl (Delmar, N.Y.: Scholars' Facsimiles and Reprints, 1977); and Gregory Claeys, "John Adolphus Etzler, Technological Utopianism, and British Socialism: The Tropics Emigration Society's Venezuelan Mission and Its Social Context, 1833–1848," *The English Historical Review* 101, no. 399 (April 1986): 351–375.

35. Cabet, *Travels in Icaria,* 15; Bulgarin, "Plausible Fantasies," 12; Mary Griffith, *Three Hundred Years Hence,* 47; and William Stanley Jevons, *The Coal Question: An Inquiry Concerning the Progress of the Nation, and the Probable Exhaustion of our Coal-Mines* (London: Macmillan, 1865), 144.

36. Jevons, *The Coal Question,* 349.

37. For an overview of economic thought at this time, see Thomas Sowell, *On Classical Economics* (New Haven: Yale University Press, 2006); and Robert L. Heilbroner, *The Worldly Philosophers: The Lives, Times, and Ideas of the Great Economic Thinkers,* 7th ed. (New York: Simon and Schuster, 1999).

38. Adam Smith, *An Inquiry into the Nature and Causes of the Wealth of Nations* (London: Printed for W. Straham and T. Cadell, 1776), 1:87 (chapter 8). For a detailed, if technical, exploration of Ricardo's thought, see Mark Blaug, *Economic Theory in Retrospect,* 4th ed. (New York: Cambridge University Press, 1985), chapter 4.

39. Smith, *Wealth of Nations,* 87–88 (quotes are from p. 99).

40. John Stuart Mill, *Principles of Political Economy, with Some of Their Applications to Social Philosophy* (Boston: Charles C. Little and James Brown, 1848), 2:311–317 (book 4, chapter 2).

41. Mill, *Principles of Political Economy*, 315 and 314.

42. Mill, *Principles of Political Economy*, 317.

43. Mill, *Principles of Political Economy*, 316.

44. Mill, *Principles of Political Economy*, 317.

45. Mill, *Principles of Political Economy*, 317. Mill is often credited with being the first to use the term "dystopia." See *Hansard's Parliamentary Debates, Third Series: Commencing with the Accession of William IV* (London: Cornelius Buck, 1868), 1517.

46. Mill to the Secretary of the Commons Preservation Society, January 22, 1866, in John Stuart Mill, *The Letters of John Stuart Mill*, ed. Hugh S. R. Elliot (New York: Longmans, Green, 1910), 2:56.

47. Mill, *Principles of Political Economy*, 316.

48. Romanticism informed some of these critiques, although the divide between romanticism and science was never as sharp as sometimes painted by historians. Many early nineteenth-century technologies inhabited a middle ground between romanticism and mechanism, and natural philosophers wrote poetry while poets dabbled in science. See John Tresch, *The Romantic Machine: Utopian Science and Technology After Napoleon* (Chicago: University of Chicago Press, 2012); and Richard Holmes, *The Age of Wonder: How the Romantic Generation Discovered the Beauty and Terror of Science* (New York: Pantheon, 2008).

49. Owen, *Book of the New Moral World*, xxii. Owen describes his community in Robert Owen, "Report to the Committee of the Association for the Relief of the Manufacturing and Labouring Poor" (1817), in Owen, *A Supplementary Appendix to the First Volume of the Life of Robert Owen* (London: Effingham Wilson, 1858), Vol. I.A, Appendix I, No. 1; and Owen, *A Developement of the Principles and Plans on which to Establish Self-Supporting Home Colonies* (London: Home Colonization Society, 1841), 37–40. For a fictional visit to a future Owenite community, see Robert Cooper, "A Contrast Between the New Moral World and the Old Immoral World; a Lecture Delivered in the Social Institution, Salford" (1838), in *Owenite Socialism: Pamphlets and Correspondence, 1838–1839*, ed. Gregory Claeys (New York: Routledge, 2005), 29–42. For Fourier, see Charles Fourier, *Théorie de l'Unité Universelle*, 240–242, and for a fictionalized version, Nikolai Chernyshevski, "Vera Pavlovna's Fourth Dream" (1863), in Fetzer, ed., *Pre-Revolutionary Russian Science Fiction*, 58–68. Some of the utopian socialists, like Cabet, embraced cities but hoped to make them cleaner and greener. See Cabet, *Travels in Icaria*, 19–22.

50. Henry David Thoreau, "Paradise (To Be) Regained," *United States Magazine, and Democratic Review*, November 1843, 452.

51. Bodin, *Novel of the Future*.

52. Bodin, *Novel of the Future*, 148–150. Bodin almost seems to anticipate C. P. Snow's 1959 claim that the West had split into "two cultures," the sciences and the humanities, that often seemed incapable of understanding each other. See C. P. Snow, *The Two Cultures and the Scientific Revolution* (New York: Cambridge University Press, 1959).

53. Bodin, *Novel of the Future*, 145–147 (quote is on p. 147).

54. Bodin, *Novel of the Future,* 145 and 146.
55. The landscapes that tended to attract the most attention from preservationists, however, were landscapes connected to the kind of national identity that Bodin expected to wither in the future. See Charles-François Mathis, "Nation and Nature Preservation in France and England in the Nineteenth Century," *Environment and History* 20, no. 1 (February 2014): 9–39.
56. Souvestre, *The World As It Shall Be,* 37.
57. Souvestre, *The World As It Shall Be,* 75 and 76.
58. Souvestre, *The World As It Shall Be,* 126. The French caricaturist and writer J. J. Grandville imagined that science, in time, would produce some odd animal hybrids like turtle elephants and rabbit snails and some new animal combinations as well. See J. J. Grandville, *Un Autre Monde* (Paris: H. Fournier), 116–118.
59. Souvestre, *The World As It Shall Be,* 118.
60. C. F. Volney, *Volney's Ruins, or Meditation on the Revolutions of Empires* (Paris: Bossange Fréres, 1820), 17. The classic overview of this motif remains Rose Macaulay, *Pleasure of Ruins* (New York: Walker, 1953). Also see Christopher Woodward, *In Ruins* (New York: Pantheon, 2001), especially chapter 9.
61. For examples of this genre, see "Specimen of a Prospective Newsletter: The North American Luminary, 1st July, 4796," *New Monthly Magazine and Literary Journal* (London: Henry Colburn, 1821), 2:129–135; Edgar Allan Poe, "Mellonta Tauta" (1849), in *Collected Works of Edgar Allan Poe: Volume 3: Tales and Sketches, 1843–1849,* ed. Thomas Ollive Mabbott (Cambridge: Belknap Press of Harvard University Press, 1978), 1289–1309; Robert William, *Eureka: A Prophecy of the Future,* 3 vol. (London: Longman, Rees, Orme, Brown, Green and Longmans, 1837); Hans Christian Andersen, "In a Thousand Years' Time" (1852), in *Tales and Stories of Hans Christian Anderson,* trans. Patricial L. Conroy and Sven H. Rossel (Seattle: University of Washington Press, 1980), 178–181; Alfred Bonnardot, "Archeopolis" (1857), in *Nemoville: Twelve Proto-Science Fiction Tales,* ed. Brian Stableford (Tarzana, Calif.: Black Coat, 2012); and Souvestre, *The World As It Shall Be,* 10.
62. Alan P. Wallach "Cole, Byron, and the Course of Empire," *The Art Bulletin* 50, no. 4 (December 1968): 375–379. The quote is from Byron's *Childe Harold,* canto IV, stanza 108.
63. Bodin, *Novel of the Future,* 141.

## Chapter 3. An Evolutionary Tale

1. H. G. Wells, *Seven Famous Novels* (New York: Alfred A. Knopf, 1934), ix; Wells, *The Food of the Gods and How It Came to Earth* (1904; Mineola, N.Y.: Dover, 2006), 192. For Wells as a prophet, see Patrick Parrinder, *Shadows of the Future: H. G. Wells, Science Fiction, and Prophecy* (Syracuse, N.Y.: Syracuse University Press, 1995).
2. For the increasing popularity and influence of future literature during this period, see I. F. Clarke, *The Pattern of Expectation, 1644–2001* (New York: Basic, 1979),

133–142. Technological advances during this period were even changing Western conceptions of time and space. See Stephen Kern, *The Culture of Time and Space: 1880–1918* (Cambridge: Harvard University Press, 1983). For literary utopias in the second half of the nineteenth century, see Kenneth M. Roemer, *The Obsolete Necessity: America in Utopian Writings, 1888–1900* (Kent, Ohio: Kent State University Press, 1976); and Darko Suvin, *Victorian Science Fiction in the UK: The Discourse of Knowledge and of Power* (Boston: G. K. Hall, 1983).

3. "The Promise of Science: A Symposium of Eminent Scientists," *The Strand Magazine* (December 1904), 668. H. G. Wells, who had academic training in science and experience as a teacher, set the standard for nonfiction forecasts with his widely read *Anticipations of the Reaction of Mechanical and Scientific Progress Upon Human Life and Thought* (London: Chapman & Hall, 1901). Some writers combined fiction and nonfiction prophecy. See Herbert Gubbins, *The Elixir of Life; or, 2903: A Novel of the Far Future* (London: Henry J. Drane, 1914); and William Wonder, *Reciprocity (Social and Economic) in the Thirtieth Century: The Coming Cooperative Age: A Forecast of the World's Future* (New York: Cochrane, 1909).

4. Jean Brunhes, *Les Limites de Notre Cage* (Fribourg: Imprimerie de L'Oeuvre de Saint-Paul, 1911), 35. For the anxiety produced by a shrinking world, see Rosalind Williams, *The Triumph of Human Empire: Verne, Morris, and Stevenson at the End of the World* (Chicago: University of Chicago Press, 2013).

5. Ernst Haeckel, *The History of Creation*, trans. E. Ray Lankester (1868; New York: D. Appleton, 1880), 2:367; and H. G. Wells, *A Modern Utopia* (1905; Lincoln: University of Nebraska Press, 1967), 5. For the history of evolutionary theory, see Peter J. Bowler, *Evolution: The History of an Idea* (Berkeley: University of California Press, 2009).

6. Quote is from Nunsowe Green, *A Thousand Years Hence. Being Personal Experiences* (London: Sampson Low, Searle, and Rivington, 1882), 82–83. The Eskimo appears in Julian Hawthorne, "June, 1993," *Cosmopolitan Magazine*, February 1893, 456. For racial evolution, also see Albert Adams Merrill, *The Great Awakening; The Story of the Twenty-Second Century* (Boston: George, 1899), 338; Camille Flammarion, *Omega: The Last Days of the World* (New York: Cosmopolitan, 1894), 199–200; and William Delisle Hay, *Three Hundred Years Hence; or, a Voice from Posterity* (London: Newman, 1881), 102 and chapter 6. In John Jacob Astor's future, Americans of Spanish and Portuguese descent "show a constant tendency to die out." Astor, *A Journey in Other Worlds: A Romance of the Future* (New York: D. Appleton, 1894), 74. For a rare effort to turn such racial triumphalism on its head, see T. Shirby Hodge, *The White Man's Burden: A Satirical Forecast* (Boston: Gorham, 1915).

7. Hay, *Three Hundred Years Hence*, 242 and 271.

8. Charles Richet, *Dans Cent Ans*, 2nd ed. (Paris: Paul Ollendorff, 1892), 152; Souvestre, *The World As It Shall Be*, 126. For ideas about extinction at this time, see Mark V. Barrow, Jr., *Nature's Ghosts: Confronting Extinction from the Age of Jefferson to the Age of Ecology* (Chicago: University of Chicago Press, 2009).

9. "One Hundred Years Hence," *The Times and Democrat*, March 2, 1911, 3. Animal extinction appears in many places. See, for example, Astor, *A Journey in Other Worlds*, 44–45; Flammarion, *Omega*, 201; Hay, *Three Hundred Years Hence*, 293; Wonder, *Reciprocity*, 69–70; Chauncey Thomas, *The Crystal Button; or, Adventures of Paul Prognosis in the Forty-Ninth Century* (Boston: Houghton, Mifflin, 1891), 100–102; Paul Devinne, *The Day of Prosperity: A Vision of the Century to Come* (New York: G. W. Dillingham, 1902), 77; Charlotte Perkins Gilman, *Moving the Mountain* (New York: Charlton, 1911), 146–151; and H. G. Wells, *The Time Machine*, in *The Definitive Time Machine: A Critical Edition of H. G. Wells's Scientific Romance with Introduction and Notes*, ed. Harry M. Geduld (1895; Bloomington: Indiana University Press, 1987), 47.

10. Hay, *Three Hundred Years Hence*, 293; Charles Lyell, *Principles of Geology*, 11th ed. (London: John Murray, 1872), 2:464–465; Wonder, *Reciprocity*, 69.

11. Cabet, *Travels in Icaria*, 99. For dystopian stories that set eugenics and Christianity in opposition, see Robert Buchanan, *The Rev. Annabel Lee. A Tale of To-morrow* (London: C. Arthur Pearson, 1898); and Mary Bramston, "The Island of Progress," in *The Wild Lass of Estmere and Other Stories* (London: Seeley, 1893).

12. Edward Bulwer-Lytton, *The Coming Race* (1871; Middletown, Conn.: Wesleyan University Press, 2005).

13. Samuel Butler, "Darwin Among the Machines," in *The Note-Books of Samuel Butler*, ed. Henry Festing Jones (New York: E. P. Dutton, 1917), 44, originally published in *The Press*, June 13, 1863; Samuel Butler, *Erewhon, or Over the Range*, ed. Hans-Peter Breuer and Daniel F. Howard (1872; Newark: University of Delaware Press, 1981), 190.

14. W. Grove, *The Wreck of a World* (London: Digby and Long, 1889), 18. Other stories that feature machine revolts tend to emphasize human creation of sentient machines rather than their development through an evolutionary process. See, for example, Didier de Chousy, *Ignis: The Central Fire*, adapted by Brian Stableford (1883; Encino, Calif.: Black Coat, 2009); and Émile Goudeau, "The Revolt of the Machines" (1891), in *Scientific Romance: An International Anthology of Pioneering Science Fiction*, ed. Brian Stableford (Mineola, N.Y.: Dover, 2017), 164–171, which links the events of its story to Darwinism only at the very end.

15. Wells, *Time Machine*, 50.

16. See A. Garland Mears, *Mercia, the Astronomer Royal: A Romance* (London: Simpkin, Marshall, Hamilton, Kent, 1895), 10, for moral suasion; Merrill, *Great Awakening*, 336, for birth control and wealth; Edward A. Caswell, *Toil and Self* (New York: Rand, McNally, 1900), 135–136, for sex selection; and Adolphe Alhaiza, *Cybele: An Extraordinary Voyage into the Future*, trans. Brian Stableford (1891; Tarzana, Calif.: Black Coat, 2013), 135, for naturally lowered desire to procreate. Quote is from Hay, *Three Hundred Years Hence*, 368.

17. Quotes are from Andrew Blair, *Annals of the Twenty-Ninth Century; or, the Autobiography of the Tenth President of the World-Republic* (London: Samuel Tinsley, 1874), 35; and Richet, *Dans Cent Ans*, 156. For floating factories, see William Ford

Stanley, *The Case of The. Fox, being his Prophecies under Hypnosis of the Period Ending A.D. 1950: A Political Utopia* (London: Truslove and Hanson, 1903), 157–158. For sea farming and underground agriculture, see Hay, *Three Hundred Years Hence,* 149–150 and 195, respectively. For a less optimistic and therefore more unusual view of future population growth, see "Population Close to 'Standing Room Only,'" *Chicago Tribune,* April 30, 1899, 1.

18. For a city explicitly built with tall buildings in order to free up every inch of land for grain production and "avoid famine," see Kurd Lasswitz, "To the Absolute Zero of Existence: A Story from 2371" (1878), in *The Black Mirror and Other Stories: An Anthology of Science Fiction from Germany and Austria,* ed. Franz Rottensteiner, trans. Michael Mitchell (Middletown, Conn.: Wesleyan University Press, 2008), 5. The literature on nineteenth-century urbanization is large. For an analysis of the economic factors involved in urban growth, see Paul Bairoch and Gary Goertz, "Factors of Urbanisation in the Nineteenth Century Developed Countries: A Descriptive and Econometric Analysis," *Urban Studies* 23, no. 4 (August 1986): 285–305.

19. Hudson Maxim, "Man's Machine-Made Millennium," *Cosmopolitan Magazine,* November 1908, 576, which includes an illustration by William Robinson Leigh. For similar illustrations, see "New York City as It Will Be in 1999," *The New York World,* December 30, 1900, supplement foldout; *King's Views of New York, 1908–1909* (New York: Moses King, 1908), cover; and *New-York Tribune,* January 16, 1910, 1. For cities of the future more generally, see Howard Mansfield, *Cosmopolis: Yesterday's Cities of the Future* (New Brunswick, N.J.: Center for Urban Policy Research, 1990).

20. The literature on urban pollution during this period is large. See, for example, Martin V. Melosi, *The Sanitary City: Environmental Services in Urban America from Colonial Times to the Present* (Pittsburgh: University of Pittsburg Press, 2008); Joel A. Tarr, *The Search for the Ultimate Sink: Urban Pollution in Historical Perspective* (Akron, Ohio: University of Akron Press, 1996); and Peter Thorsheim, *Inventing Pollution: Coal, Smoke, and Culture in Britain Since 1800* (Athens, Ohio: Ohio University Press, 2006).

21. Edward Bellamy, *Equality* (New York: D. Appleton, 1897), 294 (for Boston); A Capitalist [Alonzo van Deusen], *Rational Communism: The Present and the Future Republic of North America* (New York: Truth Seeker, 1885), 21–29 (for Manhattan); Emile Calvet, *In a Thousand Years,* trans. Brian Stableford (1883; Tarzana, Calif.: Black Coat, 2013), 101 (for Paris); and Merrill, *Great Awakening,* 330–331 (for New York City). For other examples of this process, see Hawthorne, "June, 1993," 451–453; John Macnie, *The Diothas; or, a Far Look Ahead* (New York: G. P. Putnam's Sons, 1883), 7; "One Hundred Years Hence"; and H. G. Wells, *Anticipations,* chapter 2. The garden suburb in utopian thought is explored in Nathaniel Robert Walker, "Architecture and Urban Visions in Nineteenth-Century Utopian Literature," Ph.D. diss., Brown University, 2014.

22. Jules Verne, *The Begum's Fortune* (Philadelphia: J. B. Lippincott, 1879), 152. Verne

took many of his ideas for a hygienic utopia from Benjamin Ward Richardson's *Hygeia: A City of Health* (London: Macmillan, 1876).

23. Quote is from Devinne, *Day of Prosperity*, 207. See Calvet, *In a Thousand Years*, 100; and Thomas, *The Crystal Button*, 51–52. For examples of roof gardens, see Lasswitz, "To the Absolute Zero of Existence," 5; Henry Hartshorne, *1931: A Glance at the Twentieth Century* (Philadelphia: E. Claxton, 1881), 30; MacNie, *The Diothas*, 31–32, 56; and Hay, *Three Hundred Years Hence*, 311. For an earlier vision of roof gardens, see Louis-Sébastien Mercier, *Memoirs of the Year Two Thousand Five Hundred*, trans. W. Hooper (Philadelphia: Thomas Dobson, 1795), 34.

24. Edward Bellamy, *Looking Backward: 2000–1887* (Boston: Houghton Mifflin, 1888).

25. H. G. Wells, "A Story of the Days To Come," in *Tales of Space and Time* (London: Harper and Brothers, 1899), 264. Also see Wells, "When the Sleeper Wakes" (1899), in *The Collector's Book of Science Fiction by H. G. Wells*, ed. Alan K. Russell (Secaucus, N.J.: Castle, 1978).

26. Wells, "Days to Come," 222 and 228. Despite a positive reference to Morris and Hudson's books in *When the Sleeper Wakes* (see Wells, *Sleeper Wakes*, 420), Wells would later poke fun at those who advocated living more in tune with nature by limiting development, wearing clothes made from natural products, and adopting a vegetarian diet (see Wells, *Modern Utopia*, 116–117).

27. Albert Robida, *Electric Life*, trans. Brian Stableford (1892; Tarzana, Calif.: Black Coat, 2013); and "The Electric City of the Future," *Galveston Daily News*, June 27, 1909. The literature on the cultural impact of electrification during this period is large. See, for example, David E. Nye, *American Technological Sublime* (Cambridge: MIT Press, 1994); John A. Jakle, *City Lights: Illuminating the American Night* (Baltimore: Johns Hopkins University Press, 2001); and Linda Simon, *Dark Light: Electricity and Anxiety from the Telegraph to the X-Ray* (New York: Harcourt, 2004).

28. "Future Sources of Energy," *The Electrical Age*, February 1, 1905, 131. For a contemporary assessment of the various natural sources of power by a well-respected electrical engineer, see Dr. Louis Bell, "Natural Sources of Energy: the Probable Extensive Development of Solar Power," *Electrical Age*, May 1905, 334–337. Fiction writers also favored made-up forces that supposedly extended the power of electricity, such as "apergy" in Astor, *Journey in Other Worlds*, 29; "Basilicity" in Hay, *Three Hundred Years Hence*, 139–148; and the "cross-electric force" in Green, *A Thousand Years Hence*, 264.

29. Antonio Stoppani, *Corso di Geologia* (Milano: G. Bernadoni e G. Brigola, 1873), 2:740; and Joseph Le Conte, *Elements of Geology* (New York: D. Appleton, 1879), 558.

30. Blair, *Annals of the Twenty-Ninth Century*, 50–56, 105–108; Ira S. Bunker, *A Thousand Years Hence or Startling Events in the year A.D. 3000. A Trip to Mars. Incidents by the Way* (Portland, Ore.: Ira S. Bunker, 1903), 8; Thomas, *The Crystal Button*, 104; N. S. Shaler, "How to Change the North American Climate," *The Atlantic Monthly*, December 1877, 724–730; and Robida, *Electric Life*, 11–12. For more context on the history of climate science at the time, see James Rodger Fleming, *Historical Perspectives on Climate Change* (New York: Oxford University Press, 1998).

31. Captain Roudaire, "Survey for an Inland Sea in Algeria," *Minutes of Proceedings of the Institution of Civil Engineers* 49 (London: Institution of Civil Engineers, 1877): 339–342, originally published in *Revue des Deux Mondes* (May 1874); Donald Mackenzie, *The Flooding of the Sahara* (London: Sampson Low, Marton, Searle, and Rivington, 1877); and G. A. Thompson, "Plan for Converting the Sahara into a Sea," *Scientific American*, August 10, 1912, 114, 124–125. For fictional interpretations, see Jules Verne, *Invasion of the Sea*, trans. Edward Baxter (1905; Middletown, Conn.: Wesleyan University Press, 2001); Edward Maitland, *By and By: An Historical Romance of the Future*, v. 3 (London: Richard Bentley and Son, 1873); and Louis Tracy, *An American Emperor: The Story of the Fourth Empire of France* (New York: G. W. Dillingham, 1897).

32. Hay, *Three Hundred Years Hence*, 287–288; Blair, *Annals of the Twenty-Ninth Century*, 218 (the work is largely described in chapter 7). For a brief reference to the removal of the Rocky Mountains to secure the materials to build a giant climate-altering barrier, see Bunker, *A Thousand Years Hence*, 8.

33. Albert Robida, *The Twentieth Century*, trans. Philippe Willems (1882; Middletown, Conn.: Wesleyan University Press, 2004), 350–354; Green, *A Thousand Years Hence*, 53.

34. Alexander Kuprin, "A Toast" (1906), in *Pre-Revolutionary Russian Science Fiction: An Anthology*, ed. and trans. Leland Fetzer (Ann Arbor: Arbis, 1982), 182–184 (quotes on pp. 182 and 183).

35. Green, *A Thousand Years Hence*, 385; R. W. Cole, *The Struggle for Empire: A Story of the Year 2236* (London: Elliot Stock, 1900), 19, quoted in Clarke, 151. Also see Blair, chapter 18. For a fictional attempt to draw the moon closer to the earth so that it can be mined, see André Laurie, *The Conquest of the Moon: A Story of the Bayouda* (London: Sampson Low, Marston, Searle, and Rivington, 1889). For a rare contemporary illustration of what mining operations on the moon might look like, see Fred Jane, "Guesses at Futurity. No. 7. Interplanetary Communication. Gold Mining in the Mountains of the Moon," *The Pall Mall Magazine*, April 1895, between pages 618 and 619.

36. Jules Verne, *The Purchase of the North Pole: A Sequel to "From the Earth to the Moon"* (1889; London: Sampson Low, Marston, Searle, and Rivington, 1891).

37. Verne, *Purchase of the North Pole*, 182.

38. Astor, *Journey in Other Worlds*, 30; and Carroll Livingston Riker, *Power and Control of the Gulf Stream* (New York: Baker and Taylor, 1912), chapter 12. Riker, an American engineer and pioneer of refrigeration, saw the further tilting of the earth's axis as a side benefit of his plan for improving the climate of North America by blocking the Labrador Current. For other fictional attempts to straighten the earth's axis during this period, see William Hawley Smith, *The Promoters: A Novel Without a Woman* (Chicago: Rand McNally, 1904); George Griffith, *The Great Weather Syndicate* (London: F. V. White, 1906); and William Wallace Cook, "Tales of Twenty Hundred," *Blue Book*, December 1911–May 1912.

39. For a discussion of the relationship between environment and the idea of civiliza-

tion, see the introduction to Felipe Fernández-Armesto, *Civilizations: Culture, Ambition, and the Transformation of Nature* (New York: Simon and Schuster, 2001).

40. Macnie, *The Diothas*, 85–86; "One Hundred Years Hence." Also see, for example, Green, *A Thousand Years Hence*, 66; and Maurice Spronck, "Year 330 of the Republic" (1894), in *Investigations of the Future: Seven Proto-Science Fiction Tales*, ed. Brian Stableford (Tarzana, Calif.: Black Coat, 2012), 98. For the future of food during this period more generally, see Warren Belasco, *Meals to Come: A History of the Future of Food* (Berkeley: University of California Press, 2006), chapter 4.

41. Quote is from Mary E. Bradley, *Mizora: A Prophecy* (New York: G. W. Dillingham, 1890), 44–45. Also see Macnie, *The Diothas*, 86; Jules Verne, *Paris in the Twentieth Century* (New York: Ballantine, 1997), 197–198; Gabriel de Tarde, *Underground Man* (1896; London: Duckworth, 1905), 81–82; and Philip Norton, *Sub Sole: or, Under the Sun. Missionary Adventures in the Great Sahara. By the Right Reverend Artegall Smith, D.D.* (London: James Nisbet, 1890), 135–136.

42. "What People Will Eat a Century Hence," *Scientific American*, February 23, 1895, 122; "Foods of the Future, *Current Literature* 18, no. 5 (November 1895), 369; and W. O. Atwater, "The Food-Supply of the Future," *Century Illustrated Magazine*, November 1891, 110 and 112. In contrast, the British chemist and physicist Sir William Cooke called chemical food "one of the platitudes of pseudo-science." See "The Promise of Science," 671. For the history of the food pill, see Warren Belasco, "Future Notes: The Meal-in-a-Pill," *Food and Foodways* 8, no. 4 (2000): 253–271.

43. Lasswitz, "To the Absolute Zero of Existence," 13; and Anna Bowman Dodd, *The Republic of the Future; or, Socialism a Reality* (New York: Cassell, 1887), 30. For other examples, see Stanley, *The Case of The. Fox*, 155; Blair, *Annals of the Twenty-Ninth Century*, 31; Flammarion, *Omega*, 198; Hartshorne, *1931*, 31; and Arthur Bird, *Looking Forward: A Dream of the United States of the Americas in 1999* (Utica: L. C. Childs and Son, 1899), 184.

44. H. G. Wells, "Of a Book Unwritten," *The English Illustrated Magazine*, October 1901–March 1902, 383–384, originally published as "The Man of the Year Million," *Pall Mall Budget*, November 16, 1893, 1796–1797. For other examples of future humans with larger heads and smaller bodies, see Gubbins, *The Elixir of Life*, 74; Flammarion, *Omega*, 199; Robida, *Electric Life*, 157; Kenneth Folingsby, *Meda: A Tale of the Future* (Glasgow: Aird and Cogshill, 1891), 31–32; and Louis Boussenard, *Ten Thousand Years in a Block of Ice* (1889; New York: F. Tennyson Neely, 1898). For a future in which intelligence devolves instead because most jobs require no more than tending machines, see Stanley, *The Case of The. Fox*, 102–103, 185–186, and 188. Twenty-first-century scientists and science writers have revisited Wells's thought experiment in Damien Broderick, ed., *Year Million: Science at the Far Edge of Knowledge* (New York: Atlas, 2008).

45. Green, *A Thousand Years Hence*, 60 and 61. Also see Hay, *Three Hundred Years Hence*, 184–191. For the underground in the Western imagination during this

period, see Rosalind Williams, *Notes on the Underground: An Essay on Technology, Society, and the Imagination* (Cambridge: MIT Press, 2008).

46. E. M. Forster, "The Machine Stops," *Oxford and Cambridge Review* 8 (November 1909): 83–122.

47. Forster, "The Machine Stops," 100 and 114.

48. Gabriel de Tarde, *Underground Man* (1896; London: Duckworth, 1905). The original French title was *Fragment d'Histoire Future.*

49. Tarde, *Underground Man,* 87 and 135.

50. Tarde, *Underground Man,* 180–181. For an alternative environmental reading of Tarde, *Underground Man,* see Williams, *Notes on the Underground,* 135–139.

51. Tarde, *Underground Man,* 169–170, 187, and 188. Much later, Ursula K. Le Guin used the isolation of a space station to make a similar point. See Le Guin, "Newton's Sleep," in *A Fisherman of the Inland Sea: Science Fiction Stories* (1991; New York: HarperPrism, 1994), 23–55.

52. George P. Marsh, *Man and Nature; or, Physical Geography as Modified by Human Action* (New York: Charles Scribner, 1865), 44.

53. Media coverage included, for example, Herbert C. Fyfe, "How Will the World End?" *Pearson's Magazine,* July 1900, 4–5; and "Destroying Oxygen," *New Castle News,* October 9, 1901, 6. For metered air in fiction, see William Wallace Cook, *A Round Trip to the Year 2000; or, a Flight through Time* (New York: Street and Smith, 1908), 50.

54. W. Warren Wagar, "The Rebellion of Nature," in *The End of the World,* ed. Eric S. Rabkin, Martin H. Greenberg, and Joseph D. Olander (Carbondale: Southern Illinois University Press, 1983), 141.

55. Alexander Bogdanov, *Red Star,* ed. Loren R. Graham and Richard Stites (1908; Bloomington: Indiana University Press, 1984), 79 and 80. For human history as a struggle against nature, also see Jules Verne, "The Eternal Adam," in *Yesterday and Tomorrow,* ed. I. O. Evans (New York: Ace, 1965), 13. For Mars and environmental thought, see Robert Markley, *Dying Planet: Mars in Science and the Imagination* (Durham: Duke University Press, 2005).

56. Eugène Mouton, "The End of the World" (1872), in *The Supreme Progress and Other French Scientific Romances,* ed. Brian Stableford (Tarzana, Calif.: Black Coat, 2012). The future society in Green's *A Thousand Years Hence* also inadvertently disrupts the climate, although technology comes to the rescue in the form of glass roofing that somehow evens out the temperature. Green, 252.

57. Louis Pope Gratacap, *The Evacuation of England: The Twist in the Gulf Stream* (New York: Brentano's, 1908); and H. C. M. Watson, *The Decline and Fall of the British Empire; or, the Witch's Cavern* (London: Trischler and Company, 1890). Also see E. A. Robinson and G. A. Wall, *The Disk: A Prophetic Reflection* (Boston: Cupples Upham, 1884).

58. John Mills, "The Aerial Brickfield," *The Windsor Magazine,* June 1897: 64–71; and Robert Barr, "Within an Ace of the End of the World," *McClure's Magazine,* April 1900, 545–554.

59. Thomas J. Vivian and Grena J. Bennett, "The Tilting Island," *Everybody's Magazine* 21, September 1909, 380–389 (quotes are from 385 and 389). For a similar prediction containing an illustration of the aftermath, see Winsor McCay, "The Last Day of Manhattan," *New York Herald*, Magazine Section, February 26, 1905, 6.

60. A. L. Green, *The End of an Epoch. Being the Personal Narrative of Adam Godwin, the Survivor* (London: William Blackwood and Sons, 1901) (designer plague); and W. D. Hay, *The Doom of the Great City, Being the Narrative of a Survivor, Written A.D. 1942* (London: Newman, 1880) (industrial fog). Outside of fictional circles, there seems to have been some concern that the excessive extraction of oil might lead to the collapse of the earth's crust. See Fyfe, "How Will the World End?" 10 and 11.

61. Jules Verne, *Underground City; or, the Child of the Caverns*, trans. W. H. G. Kingston (1877; Philadelphia: Porter and Coates, n.d.), 34.

62. Northrop Frye, "Varieties of Literary Utopias," *Daedalus* 94, no. 2 (Spring 1965): 323–347. Edward Bellamy's *Equality* (1897), his sequel to *Looking Backward*, has at least one foot in the pastoral tradition since he traded his industrial city for rural villages. For a comparison between the two settings, see John R. Mullin, "Edward Bellamy's Ambivalence: Can Utopia Be Urban?" *Utopian Studies* 11, no. 1 (2000): 51–65.

63. W. H. Hudson, *A Crystal Age* (London: T. Fisher Unwin, 1887).

64. William Dean Howells, *A Traveler from Altruria*, ed. David W. Levy (1894; Boston: Bedford Books of St. Martin's Press, 1996). The history and description of Altruria appear in the final two chapters. Howells later described a visit to Altruria itself in a sequel: *Through the Eye of the Needle* (1907). William Meyer argues that Altruria also has some Promethean characteristics. See Meyer, *The Progressive Environmental Prometheans: Left-Wing Heralds of a "Good Anthropocene"* (New York: Palgrave Macmillan, 2016), 145–146.

65. Quote is from William Morris, "How I Became a Socialist," *Justice*, July 16, 1894, republished in Morris, *News from Nowhere and Other Writings*, ed. Clive Wilmer (New York: Penguin, 2004), 382. For Morris's environmental views, see Margaret S. Kennedy, "Ecotopian London: Morris's Geography of Conservation," in *Environments in Science Fiction: Essays on Alternative Spaces*, ed. Susan M. Bernardo (Jefferson, N.C.: McFarland, 2014), 101–117.

66. Morris, *News from Nowhere*, 105. Morris's vision of the future has parallels with the thought of his friend Peter Kropotkin. See in particular Kropotkin's *Fields, Factories and Workshops; or, Industry Combined with Agriculture and Brain Work with Manual Work* (New York: G. P. Putnam's Sons, 1898).

67. Morris, *News from Nowhere*, 158 and 200.

68. Algernon Petworth, *The Little Wicket Gate: An Experience Ex Nihilo* (London: A. C. Fifield, 1913), 56.

69. Petworth, *Little Wicket Gate*, 57. One also finds wilderness parks preserved in Alhaiza, *Cybele*, 147.

70. Vicky Albritton and Fredrik Albritton Jonsson, *Green Victorians: The Simple Life in*

*John Ruskin's Lake District* (Chicago: University of Chicago Press, 2016). The Lake District was also the site of one of the period's first environmental battles. See Harriet Ritvo, *The Dawn of Green: Manchester, Thirlmere, and Modern Environmentalism* (Chicago: University of Chicago Press, 2009).

71. The environmental problems are laid out in Robida, *Electric Life*, 157–160.

72. Robida, *Electric Life*, 88.

73. John Davidson, "The Salvation of Nature," in Davidson, *The Great Men and a Practical Novelist* (London: Ward and Downey, 1891), 140; Robida, *The Twentieth Century*, 262–265.

74. Robida, *Electric Life*, 89.

75. H. G. Wells, *The Discovery of the Future* (1902; New York: B. W. Huebsch, 1913), 59. For a discussion of the spread of future fiction internationally, see Clarke, 167. For fictional representations of future wars, see I. F. Clarke, *Voices Prophesying War: Future Wars 1763–3749*, 2nd ed. (New York: Oxford University Press, 1992).

## Chapter 4. Narrating the Apocalypse

1. J. P. Lockhart-Mummery, *After Us; or, the World as It Might Be* (London: Stanley Paul, 1936), 22; and Bertrand Russell, *Icarus; or, the Future of Science* (New York: E. P. Dutton, 1925), 57. Although futurists had often described humans as superior beings climbing toward godhood, some began favoring a less complimentary metaphor: children playing with dangerous toys. See, for example, Lockhart-Mummery, 22.

2. Victor Cohn, *1999: Our Hopeful Future* (New York: Bobbs-Merrill, 1956), 19. Cohn's book provides a good representation of the development narrative as it appeared in the middle of the twentieth century. This was the period defined by what James C. Scott has called "high-modernist ideology." See James C. Scott, *Seeing Like a State: How Certain Schemes to Improve the Human Condition Have Failed* (New Haven: Yale University Press, 1998).

3. *Official Guide Book of the Fair, 1933* (Chicago: A Century of Progress, 1933), 11. For the theme of science in word's fairs during this period, see Folke T. Kihlstedt, "Utopia Realized: The World's Fairs of the 1930s," in *Imagining Tomorrow: History, Technology, and the American Future*, ed. Joseph Corn (Cambridge: MIT Press, 1986), 97–118; and Robert W. Rydell, *World of Fairs: The Century-of-Progress Expositions* (Chicago: University of Chicago Press, 1993). A visit to the Chicago fair directly inspired the distinguished chemical engineer C. C. Furnas to speculate about the future. See Furnas, *The Next Hundred Years: The Unfinished Business of Science* (New York: Reynal and Hitchcock, 1936). For the development of science fiction between the wars, see Brian Stableford, *Scientific Romance in Britain, 1890–1950* (New York: Palgrave Macmillan, 1985).

4. Edward Alden Jewell, "'Machines, Machines!' the Futurist's Cry," *New York Times*, December 11, 1927, SM13; "To Find Some Use for Every Wild Animal," *Galveston Daily News*, November 11, 1926, 6; and Wells, *Men Like Gods: A Novel* (New York:

Macmillan, 1923). For other mentions of animal extinction, see Lockhart-Mummery, *After Us*, 81–82; and Philip Wylie, "Your Leisure," in "You and Your World in 2000 A.D.," *Redbook*, January 1950, 33.

5. On the city of the future during this period, see Howard Mansfield, *Cosmopolis: Yesterday's Cities of the Future* (New Brunswick, N.J.: Center for Urban Policy and Research, 1990); Carl Abbott, *Imagining Urban Futures: Cities in Science Fiction and What We Might Learn from Them* (Middletown: Wesleyan University Press, 2016); and Carol Willis, "Skyscraper Utopias: Visionary Urbanism in the 1920s," in Corn, ed., *Imagining Tomorrow*, 164–187.

6. For descriptions of Futurama, see The Queens Museum, *Remembering the Future: The New York World's Fair from 1939 to 1964* (New York: Rizzoli, 1989); and Lawrence R. Samuel, *The End of the Innocence: The 1964–1965 New York World's Fair* (Syracuse, N.Y.: Syracuse University Press, 2007), 184–186.

7. For an orientation to *The Jetsons*, see Matt Novak, "50 Years of *The Jetsons*: Why the Show Still Matters," *Smithsonian Magazine*, September 19, 2012, http://www.smithsonianmag.com/history/50-years-of-the-jetsons-why-the-show-still-matters-43459669/.

8. Oswald Spengler, *The Decline of the West*, 2 vols. (1918; New York: Alfred A. Knopf, 1926). Fear of decline had already become a part of Western culture. See Arthur Herman, *The Idea of Decline in Western History* (New York: Free Press, 1997). For the influence of the postwar sense of foreboding on visions of tomorrow, see for example Philip Gibbs, *The Day After To-Morrow: What Is Going To Happen To the World?* (New York: Doubleday, Doran, 1928), 119–120 and 193; and Nathan Israeli, "Attitudes to the Decline of the West," *Journal of Social Psychology* 4 (February 1933): 92–101.

9. Aldous Huxley, *Brave New World* (1932; New York: Harper Perennial, 2006).

10. Karel Čapek, *R.U.R.*, trans. Claudia Novak-Jones (1921; New York: Penguin, 2004); Yevgeny Zamyatin, *We*, trans. Clarence Brown (1924; New York: Penguin, 1993). For Döblin, see Evan Torner, "A Future-History Out of Time: The Historical Context of Döblin's Expressionist Dystopian Experiment, *Berge Meere und Giganten*," in *Detectives, Dystopias, and Poplit: Studies in Modern German Genre Fiction*, ed. Bruce B. Campbell, Alison Guenther-Pal, and Vibeke Rützou Petersen (Rochester: Camden House, 2014), 49–66. At this writing, there is no published English translation of Döblin's book. For German futuristic fiction between the wars generally, see Peter S. Fisher, *Fantasy and Politics: Visions of the Future in the Weimar Republic* (Madison: University of Wisconsin Press, 1991).

11. Lewis Mumford, *Technics and Civilization* (New York: Harcourt, Brace, 1934), 298–299; Earl of Birkenhead, *The World in 2030 A.D.* (New York: Brewer and Warren, 1930), 49; Nikola Tesla, as told to George Sylvester Viereck, "A Machine to End War," *Liberty*, February 9, 1935, 7.

12. For the connections drawn between overpopulation and the causes of World War I, see Robert J. Mayhew, *Malthus: The Life and Legacies of an Untimely Profit* (Cambridge: Belknap Press of Harvard University, 2014), 188–189.

13. Edward M. East, *Mankind at the Crossroads* (New York: Charles Scribner's Sons, 1923), 299; Gibbs, *Day After To-Morrow*, 99. Also see Thomas Robertson, *The Malthusian Moment: Global Population Growth and the Birth of American Environmentalism* (New Brunswick: Rutgers University Press, 2012), chapter 1; and Alison Bashford, *Global Population: History, Geopolitics, and Life on Earth* (New York: Columbia University Press, 2014).

14. Fairfield Osborn, *Our Plundered Planet* (Boston: Little, Brown, 1948); William Vogt, *Road to Survival* (New York: William Sloane, 1948), 288; and "Eat Hearty," *Time*, November 18, 1948, 29. Also see Lizzie Collingham, *The Taste of War: World War II and the Battle for Food* (New York: Penguin, 2012); Robertson, *Malthusian Moment*, chapter 2; and Thomas Jundt, "Dueling Visions for the Postwar World: The UN and UNESCO Conferences on Resources and Nature, and the Origins of Environmentalism," *Journal of American History"* 101, no. 1 (June 2014): 44–70.

15. See, for example, Frederick Pohl and C. M. Kornbluth, *The Space Merchants* (1953); Isaac Asimov, *The Caves of Steel* (1954); Frederik Pohl, "The Census Takers" (1956); Robert Silverberg, *Master of Life and Death* (1957); C. M. Kornbluth, "Reap the Dark Tide" (1958) (reprinted as "Shark Ship"); J. T. McIntosh, "The Million Cities" (1958); Anthony Burgess, *The Wanting Seed* (1962); Harry Harrison, *Make Room! Make Room!* (1966), later made into the movie *Soylent Green* (1973); and *Star Trek*, season 3, episode 16, "The Mark of Gideon," aired January 17, 1969.

16. Possible approaches for increasing the food supply are discussed in Harrison Brown, James Bonner, and John Weir, *The Next Hundred Years: A Discussion Prepared for Leaders of American Industry* (New York: Viking, 1957), 70–81; and A. M. Low, *What's the World Coming To? Science Looks at the Future* (Philadelphia: J. B. Lippincott, 1951), chapter 7. For Clark, see "The Futurists," *Time*, February 25, 1966, 28–29. For Boserup, see Robert J. Mayhew, *Malthus: The Life and Legacies of an Untimely Prophet* (Cambridge: Harvard University Press, 2014), 202–205. Volkovitch is quoted in Mikhail Vassiliev and Sergei Gouschev, eds., *Life in the Twenty-First Century: The Fantastic World of the Immediate Future as Predicted by 29 of Russia's Leading Scientists*, trans. R. J. Wason and H. E. Crowcroft (London: Souvenir, 1960), 95.

17. Dennis Gabor, *Inventing the Future* (New York: Alfred A. Knopf, 1964), 141–142; "Hard Times Facing Joe Fan," in *Progress-Index* (Petersburg, Va.), August 20, 1967, 22; and Harrison Brown, *The Challenge of Man's Future* (New York: Viking, 1954), 221.

18. Birkenhead, *The World in 2030 A.D.*, 20. For speculations about synthetic food during the interwar years, see, for example, Gregory Benford, *The Wonderful World of the Future that Never Was* (New York: Hearst, 2010), 67 and 70; Eric Hodgins, "What Shall We Eat Tomorrow?" *The Youth's Companion*, November 1928, 562–563, 569; Lockhart-Mummery, *After Us*, 69–82; and Olga Hartley and Mrs. C. F. Leyel, *Lucullus; or, The Food of the Future* (London: K. Paul, Trench, Trubner, 1926). Haldane's prediction appears in J. B. S. Haldane, *Daedalus; or, Science and the Future* (New York: E. P. Dutton, 1923), 38.

19. Cohn, 1999: Our Hopeful Future, 28. For the synthetic revolution, see Roger Adams, "Man's Synthetic Future," Science 115, no. 2981 (February 15, 1952): 157–163; and Edward D. Melillo, "Global Entomologies: Insects, Empires, and the 'Synthetic Age' in World History," Past and Present 223, no. 1 (May 2014): 233–270.

20. Cohn, 1999: Our Hopeful Future, 123.

21. Waldemar Kaempffert, "Miracles You'll See in the Next Fifty Years," Popular Mechanics, February 1950, 116–117; Cohn, 1999: Our Hopeful Future, 130; Isaac Asimov, "Visit to the World's Fair of 2014," New York Times, August 16, 1964; and Low, What's the World Coming To? 154. Charles Galton Darwin, an English physicist and grandson of Charles Darwin, believed that such factories would always remain a fantasy. See Charles Galton Darwin, The Next Million Years (New York: Doubleday, 1953), 176. Despite the continued popular belief that future food would come in pill form, some scientists knew better. See John Yudkin, "Beware the Malnutrition of Affluence," in The World in 1984: The Complete New Scientist Series, ed. Nigel Calder (Baltimore: Penguin, 1965), 1:66–67.

22. Jacob Rosin and Max Eastman, The Road to Abundance (New York: McGraw-Hill, 1953), 18–19 and 36. The prominent science writer Nigel Calder argued that the world should move away from agriculture, which he considered unnatural, and toward synthetic foods in order to feed the growing human population and to limit environmental damage. See Nigel Calder, The Environment Game (London: Secker and Warburg, 1967).

23. Arthur Radebaugh, "Closer Than We Think: Fat Plants and Meat Beets," Chicago Tribune, September 28, 1958; Athelstan Spilhaus, "Our New Age," Boston Sunday Globe, November 14, 1965; Matt Novak, "Sunday Funnies Blast Off Into the Space Age," Smithsonian Magazine, January 27, 2012, http://www.smithsonianmag.com /history/sunday-funnies-blast-off-into-the-space-age-81559551/?no-ist.

24. Ward Moore, Greener Than You Think (1947; New York: Crown, 1985), 5.

25. Gibbs, Day After To-Morrow, 18–19; and Olaf Stapledon, Last and First Men: A Story of the Near and Far Future (London: Methuen, 1930). For debates about resource exhaustion during the interwar period, see for example Lockhart-Mummery, After Us, 194–204; R. Austin Freeman, Social Decay and Regeneration (London: Constable, 1921), 90–96 and 288–293; and Gibbs, Day After To-Morrow, 15–21, 108–119. For an early effort to assess the full resources of a modern state with an eye to the future, see Research Committee on Social Trends, Recent Social Trends in the United States, vol. 1 (New York: McGraw-Hill, 1933). In fiction, themes of waste and resource exhaustion also appeared in Laurence Manning, "The Man Who Awoke" (1933); and Nat Schachner, "Sterile Planet" (1937). In one of Albert Robida's stories, excessive sub-surface resource extraction causes extensive land subsidence, although the narrator remains optimistic that humans will resurface the planet. Robida, Chalet in the Sky, trans. Brian Stableford (1925; Encino, Calif.: Black Coat, 2011), 141–142.

26. "Giant Wind Turbines," Everyday Science and Mechanics, June 1932, 613 and 683; Philipp Nicolas Lehmann, "Infinite Power to Change the World: Hydroelectricity

and Engineered Climate Change in the Atlantropa Project," *American Historical Review* 121, no. 1 (February 2016): 70–100. Sörgel also expected the new land links between Europe and Africa to facilitate European colonization and later devised plans to engineer three artificial lakes in Africa that he hoped would temper the continent's climate. For a work of fiction inspired by Atlantropa, see Georg Güntsche, *Panropa* (Cologne: Gilde-Verlag, 1930).

27. Jacob Darwin Hamblin, "Environmental Dimensions of World War II," in *A Companion to World War II*, ed. Thomas W. Zeiler and Daniel M. DuBois (Malden, Mass.: Wiley-Blackwell, 2013), 698–716; and Rosin and Eastman, *Road to Abundance*, 63–64. Quote is from Frederick J. Dewhurst and Associates, *America's Needs and Resources: A Twentieth Century Fund Survey* (New York: Twentieth Century Fund, 1947), 574. Also see Harold Barnett, *Energy Uses and Supplies, 1939, 1947, 1965*, U.S. Bureau of Mines Pamphlet No. 7582, December 1948.

28. President's Materials Policy Commission, *Resources for Freedom: Volume 1: Foundation for Growth and Security* (Washington, D.C.: U.S. Government Printing Office, 1952), 3. For the role of growth in environmental history, see Robertson, *Malthusian Moment*, 29–35; and Donald Worster, *Shrinking the Earth: The Rise and Decline of Natural Abundance* (New York: Oxford University Press, 2016). For an early articulation of the idea that growth has its limits, see Samuel H. Ordway, Jr., *Resources and the American Dream: Including a Theory of the Limit of Growth* (New York: Ronald Press, 1953). Also see J. R. McNeill and Peter Engelke, *The Great Acceleration: An Environmental History of the Anthropocene Since 1945* (Cambridge: Belknap Press of Harvard University Press, 2016). McNeill writes elsewhere that "the overarching priority of economic growth was easily the most important idea of the twentieth century." J. R. McNeill, *Something New Under the Sun: An Environmental History of the Twentieth-Century World* (New York: W. W. Norton, 2000), 336.

29. Harold J. Barnett and Chandler Morse, *Scarcity and Growth: The Economics of Natural Resource Availability* (Baltimore: Johns Hopkins University Press, 1962); Georg Borgstrom, *The Hungry Planet: The Modern World at the Edge of Famine*, 2nd rev. ed. (1965; New York: Macmillan, 1972), 524; and Ordway, *Resources and the American Dream*, 30. Also see the work of Dennis Gabor, particularly "Material Development," 162, and *Inventing the Future*, post-script between pages 214 and 215.

30. Kaempffert, "Miracles You'll See in the Next Fifty Years," 115; and "Disposable Clothes Seen Just Around the Corner," *Evening Capital* (Annapolis, Md.), October 12, 1961.

31. Philip K. Dick, "Survey Team," *Fantastic Universe*, May 1954, 84–94 (quote on p. 89); and Robert F. Young, "The Courts of Jamshyd" (1957), in *The Worlds of Robert F. Young* (New York: Simon and Schuster, 1965), 163–169 (quote on p. 169). The theme of resource exhaustion became common in televised science fiction as well. See, for example, *The Outer Limits*, season 1, episode 4, "The Man with the Power," aired October 7, 1963.

32. Brown, *Challenge of Man's Future*, 264–265. Also see pp. 226–227. Brown makes the comparison to a biological species in Harrison Brown, "Technological Denudation," in *Man's Role in Changing the Face of the Earth*, ed. William L. Thomas, Jr. (Chicago: University of Chicago Press, 1956), 1030. Aldous Huxley agreed, as did many others, that war, overpopulation, and resource exhaustion were the three main threats to humanity's future. See Huxley, "Your Work," in "You and Your World in 2000 A.D.," *Redbook*, January 1950.

33. Bell, "Introduction," in Herman Kahn and Anthony J. Wiener, *The Year 2000: A Framework for Speculation on the Next Thirty-Three Years* (New York: Macmillan, 1967), xxv. For Poul, see "The Futurists."

34. Roderick Seidenberg, *Anatomy of the Future* (Chapel Hill: University of North Carolina Press, 1961), 1. For local newspaper features, see, for example, "You and the Year 2000," *Southland Magazine*, November 4, 1956. For women's groups, see "A Glimpse Into 2056 for AWC," *Ames Daily Tribune* (Ames, Iowa), March 10, 1956, 3; and *Maryville Daily Forum* (Maryville, Mo.), January 26, 1944, 3.

35. Brown, "Technological Denudation," 1029; and Cohn, *1999: Our Hopeful Future*, 84.

36. M. King Hubbert, "Nuclear Energy and the Fossil Fuels," Publication No. 95 (Houston, Tex.: Shell Development Company, 1956); and Cate Doty, "A 50-Year-Old Time Capsule Sees Daylight, but Will It Start?" *New York Times*, June 16, 2007, A9.

37. Darwin, *The Next Million Years*, 205.

38. Calder, *The Environment Game*, 114; Dennis Gabor, "Material Development," in *Mankind 2000*, ed. Robert Jungk and Johan Galtung (London: Allen and Unwin, 1969), 159; and Brown, Bonner, and Weir, *The Next Hundred Years*, 108–110. For the high expectations the scientific community had for nuclear power, see Steven L. Del Sesto, "Wasn't the Future of Nuclear Engineering Wonderful?" in Corn, ed., *Imagining Tomorrow*, 58–76.

39. Paul Brians, *Nuclear Holocausts: Atomic War in Fiction, 1895–1984* (Kent, Ohio: Kent State University Press, 1987), particularly chapter 4; and Paul Boyer, *By the Bomb's Early Light: American Thought and Culture at the Dawn of the Atomic Age* (New York: Pantheon, 1985), chapter 21.

40. Edward Teller, "We're Going to Work Miracles," *Popular Mechanics*, March 1960, 97. For the U.S. program, see Scott Kaufman, *Project Plowshare: The Peaceful Use of Nuclear Explosives in Cold War America* (Ithaca: Cornell University Press, 2012). For research into environmental warfare during the Cold War, see Jacob Darwin Hamblin, *Arming Mother Nature: The Birth of Catastrophic Environmentalism* (New York: Oxford University Press, 2013).

41. Gabor, *Inventing the Future*, 99; and Arthur C. Clarke, *Profiles of the Future* (New York: Harper and Row, 1962), 142.

42. For Homi Bhabha's prediction, see Ralph E. Lapp, "Limitless Power Out of the Seas," *Life*, October 8, 1956, 176–190; and Clarke, *Profiles of the Future*, 146. One can gain a sense for the scientific consensus at the time from Olaf Helmer, "An

Abbreviated Delphi Experiment in Forecasting," in Jungk and Galtung, eds., *Mankind 2000*, 360–367, which predicted that fusion would be economically competitive by about 2003 (page 367).

43. Brown, "Technological Denudation," 1031.

44. Willard E. Hawkins, "The Dwindling Sphere," *Astounding Science-Fiction*, March 1940, 99–111 (quote on p. 111).

45. For the ocean as a frontier, see Gary Kroll, *America's Ocean Wilderness: A Cultural History of Twentieth-Century Exploration* (Lawrence: University Press of Kansas, 2008); and Helen M. Rozwadowski, "Arthur C. Clarke and the Limitations of the Ocean as a Frontier," *Environmental History* 17, no. 3 (July 2012): 578–602. Advocates of expansion also hoped to open up the polar regions as a third frontier, although it received less attention than the oceans and outer space. See for example Ritchie Calder, *The Inheritors: The Story of Man and the World He Made* (London: Heinemann, 1961), 275–279.

46. "Tracts on British Fisheries," *The Quarterly Review* 9, no. 8 (July 1813): 265; "Address of Professor Huxley, F.R.S, Delivered Monday, June 18, 1883" (London: Williams Clowes and Sons, 1883), 16; and Hawthorne Daniel and Francis Minot, *The Inexhaustible Sea* (London: MacDonald, 1955), 261. Minot was the founder and director of the Ocean Resources Institute at Woods Hole.

47. Callum Roberts, *The Unnatural History of the Sea* (Washington, D.C.: Island, 2007), chapter 12; and United States Department of the Interior, *Report of the Bureau of Commercial Fisheries for the Calendar Year 1967* (Washington, D.C.: U.S. Government Printing Office, 1969), 1–2.

48. National Academy of Sciences and National Academy of Engineering, *An Ocean Quest: The International Decade of Ocean Exploration* (Washington, D.C.: National Academy of Sciences, 1969), 2; and Robert C. Cowen, *Frontiers of the Sea: The Story of Oceanographic Exploration* (Garden City, N.Y.: Doubleday, 1960), 241.

49. Cohn, *1999: Our Hopeful Future*, 133; Sir Alister Hardy, "Will Man Be More Aquatic in the Future?" *New Scientist* 7, no. 175 (March 24, 1960): 730–733; Hardy, "New and Richer Marine Harvests Forecast," *New Scientist* 21, no. 379 (February 20, 1964): 482–483 (quote on p. 483).

50. The marine biologist was L. A. Zenkevitch. Vassiliev and Gouschev, eds., *Life in the Twenty-First Century*, 112. For a remarkably similar statement by some American counterparts, see Daniel and Minot, *The Inexhaustible Sea*, 4.

51. Speculative sea farming techniques appear in Calder, *The Environment Game*, 79; Daniel and Minot, *The Inexhaustible Sea*, 261; "The Futurists"; Hardy, "Will Man Be More Aquatic in the Future?" 733; and Cohn, *1999: Our Hopeful Future*, 133–134. Arthur Radebaugh, "Closer Than We Think: Hydrofungal Farming," *Chicago Tribune*, March 18, 1962. T. J. Gordon and Olaf Helmer, *Report on a Long-Range Forecasting Study* (Santa Monica, Calif.: RAND Corporation, 1964), 12–13.

52. Rosin and Eastman, *Road to Abundance*, 71.

53. Cohn, *1999: Our Hopeful Future*, 136.

54. Rosin and Eastman, *Road to Abundance*, 71 and 70; Cohn discusses contemporary

efforts to extract minerals from ocean water on page 136. Not everyone was as optimistic as Rosin and Eastman. Arthur C. Clarke wrote: "Many people have been hypnotized by the fact that a cubic mile of seawater contains about 20 tons of gold, but they would probably find richer pay dirt in their own back gardens" (Clarke, 148).

55. Hardy, "Will Man Be More Aquatic in the Future?" 730; Edward A. Link, "Working Deep in the Sea," in Calder, ed., *The World in 1984,* 104–105; and Asimov, "Visit to the World's Fair of 2014." For Sealab and its competitors, see Ben Hellwarth, *Sealab: America's Forgotten Quest to Live and Work on the Ocean Floor* (New York: Simon & Schuster, 2012). Also see Athelstan Spilhaus's call for sea-grant universities, which became a reality in the United States in 1966, and the contemporary comic book *Undersea Agent,* in which the United Nations builds an underwater city "dedicated to the peaceful research of the problems of how man is to live under the ocean when the land areas become too populous to hold him." Athelstan F. Spilhaus, "Man in the Sea," *Science* 145, no. 3636 (September 4, 1964): 993; and Tower Comics, *Undersea Agent,* January 1966, 9.

56. Frank H. Winter, *Prelude to the Space Age: The Rocket Societies, 1924–1940* (Washington, D.C.: Smithsonian Institution, 1983); and Howard E. McCurdy, *Space and the American Imagination* (Washington, D.C.: Smithsonian Institution, 1997), especially chapter 2 (the Gallup poll is discussed on p. 33). For the Soviet Union, see in particular Asif A. Siddiqi, *The Red Rockets' Glare: Spaceflight and the Soviet Imagination* (New York: Cambridge University Press, 2010.)

57. McCurdy, *Space and the American Imagination,* chapter 2. Although the United States and Soviet Union dominated efforts to explore space during this period, Europe developed an "astroculture" too. See Alexander C. T. Geppert, ed., *Imagining Outer Space: European Astroculture in the Twentieth Century* (New York: Palgrave Macmillan, 2012). Perhaps the science fiction writer James Blish captured the mood best when he wrote: "We are going to scatter the West throughout the stars." James Blish, *They Shall Have Stars* (1956), in Blish, *Cities in Flight* (New York: Overlook, 2000), 119.

58. Arthur Radebaugh, "Closer Than We Think: Space Mayflowers," *Chicago Tribune,* August 16, 1959; *Lost in Space,* season 1, episode 1, "The Reluctant Stowaway," aired September 15, 1965; Garrett Hardin, "Interstellar Migration and the Population Problem," *Journal of Heredity* 50, no. 2 (March 1959): 68–70; Dandridge Cole, *Beyond Tomorrow: The Next Fifty Years in Space* (Amherst, Wisc.: Amherst, 1965), 96 and 98; and Clarke, 84.

59. The Soviet efforts are discussed in Cole, *Beyond Tomorrow,* 110; Carl Sagan, "The Planet Venus," *Science* 133, no. 3456 (March 24, 1961): 858.

60. Gregory Benford, *The Wonderful World of the Future that Never Was* (New York: Hearst, 2010), 196; and "He Offers a Look at Future," *Daytona Beach Sunday News-Journal,* September 3, 1961, 4B.

61. Cole, *Beyond Tomorrow,* 102–103, 111.

62. Radebaugh, "Closer Than We Think: Mining on the Moon," April 12, 1958; Gen-

eral Dynamics Corporation, Astronautics Division, *2063 A.D.* (San Diego, Calif.: General Dynamics, 1963), 46; Clarke, chart on p. 233. Radebaugh's image originally appeared as a mining operation on Mars in an ad for National Motor Bearings in *Fortune* (April 1954), 211.

63. Wernher Von Braun, "Exploration to the Farthest Planets," in Calder, ed., *The World in 1984*, 1:39; Gordon and Helmer, *Report on a Long-Range Forecasting Study*, 40–41; General Dynamics, *2063 A.D.*, 9; and Clarke, chart on p. 233.

64. Clarke, 82 and 83. For the influence of the American frontier experience on science fiction portrayals of space exploration, see Carl Abbott, *Frontiers Past and Present: Science Fiction and the American West* (Lawrence: University Press of Kansas, 2006).

65. Brown, *Challenge of Man's Future*, 6–7. Samuel Ordway characterized the two groups as "Conservationists" and "Cornucopians" in *Resources and the American Dream*.

66. Marston Bates, *Expanding Population in a Shrinking World* (New York: American Library Association, 1963), 20; and Cohn, *1999: Our Hopeful Future*, 85–86.

67. Robert Jungk, *Tomorrow Is Already Here*, trans. Marguerite Waldman (New York: Simon and Schuster, 1954), 7; and Cohn, *1999: Our Hopeful Future*, 21.

68. Robert L. Heilbroner, *The Future as History: The Historic Currents of Our Time and the Direction in Which They Are Taking America* (New York: Harper and Brothers, 1959), 179–181.

69. Ramachandra Guha, *Environmentalism: A Global History* (New York: Longman, 2000), 19–24. Quote is from Mohandas Gandhi, "Wardha Letter II," *Young India*, December 20, 1928, 422.

70. Brown, *Challenge of Man's Future*, 257.

71. "Text of President Johnson's Speech at Dedication," *New York Times*, April 23, 1964; and Asimov, "Visit to the World's Fair."

72. Compare the cover of America's *Popular Mechanics*, July 1957, with that of China's *Kexue Dazhong* [*Popular Science*], no. 9, 1962; James MacDonald, "Food in 2000 A.D.," *Daily Gleaner* (Kingston, Jamaica), December 4, 1969, 25; and "Soviet and Other Science Fiction," *Times Literary Supplement*, March 2, 1967, 172.

## Chapter 5. A Choice of Bad Endings

1. J. B. Bury, *The Idea of Progress: An Inquiry Into Its Origins and Growth* (London: MacMillan, 1920), 5 and 6.

2. Lance Morrow, "Epitaph for a Decade," *Time*, January 7, 1980, 38; Robert L. Heilbroner, *An Inquiry into the Human Prospect* (New York: W. W. Norton, 1974), 19. Also see Leo Marx and Bruce Mazlish, eds., *Progress: Fact or Illusion?* (Ann Arbor: University of Michigan Press, 1996). For a taste of how prominent environmental concerns had become among those who spent time thinking about the future, see "Five Noted Thinkers Explore the Future," in *National Geographic*, July 1976, 68–74.

3. "Fighting to Save the Earth from Man," *Time*, February 2, 1970. For the origins of environmentalism in a global context, see Ramachandra Guha, *Environmentalism: A Global History* (New York: Pearson, 1999).

4. Thomas Robertson, *The Malthusian Moment: Global Population Growth and the Birth of American Environmentalism* (New Brunswick, N.J.: Rutgers University Press, 2012); and Paul R. Ehrlich, *The Population Bomb* (New York: Ballantine, 1968), prologue. Even before the publication of Ehrlich's book, a RAND Corporation study had found a consensus among top population analysts that food production and distribution would be unlikely to keep pace with population growth through the first half of the twenty-first century. A minority of the analysts anticipated Ehrlich by predicting widespread famine and higher mortality rates. T. J. Gordon and Olaf Helmer, *Report on a Long-Range Forecasting Study* (Santa Monica, Calif.: RAND Corporation, 1964), 15–19.

5. "Commencement '69," *Mills Quarterly*, August 1969, 17–19. The quotes appear on pages 18 and 19.

6. "Running Out of Everything . . . ," *Newsweek*, November 19, 1973, 117; and "Facing up to Cold Reality," *Newsweek*, November 19, 1973, 109. For the environmental dimensions of the oil crisis, see Karen R. Merrill, *The Oil Crisis of 1973–1974: A Brief History with Documents* (Boston: Bedford/St. Martins, 2007).

7. Robert Poole, *Earthrise: How Man First Saw the Earth* (New Haven: Yale University Press, 2008); and Kenneth Boulding, "The Economics of the Coming Spaceship Earth," in *Environmental Quality in a Growing Economy*, ed. Henry Jarrett (Baltimore: Johns Hopkins University Press, 1966), 3–14 (quote on p. 9). For the rise and fall of the "spaceship earth" metaphor, see Robertson, *Malthusian Moment*, chapter 8. For the relationship between the space program and environmental movement during this period, see Neil M. Maher, *Apollo in the Age of Aquarius* (Cambridge: Harvard University Press, 2017).

8. Donella H. Meadows, Dennis L. Meadows, Jorgen Randers, and William W. Behrens, III, *The Limits to Growth: A Report for the Club of Rome's Project on the Predicament of Mankind* (New York: Universe, 1972), 23.

9. George J. Church, "Can the World Survive Economic Growth?" *Time*, August 14, 1972, 58. For a taste of the scholarly criticism around the time of the study's publication, see H. S. D. Cole, Christopher Freeman, Marie Jahoda, and K. L. R. Pavitt, eds., *Models of Doom: A Critique of the Limits to Growth* (New York: Universe, 1973).

10. Herman Kahn, William Brown, and Leon Martel, *The Next 200 Years: A Scenario for America and the World* (New York: William Morrow, 1976), 1, 151, and 176.

11. Harrison Brown, *The Human Future Revisited: The World Predicament and Possible Solutions* (New York: W. W. Norton, 1978), 9 and 272. Brown also worried about humankind's ability to manage its increasingly complex technological and environmental systems, a fear explored in Roberto Vacca, *The Coming Dark Age*, trans. J. S. Whale (Garden City, N.Y.: Doubleday, 1973).

12. *The Global 2000 Report to the President: Entering the Twenty-First Century* (Washington, D.C.: Government Printing Office, 1980), 1:1.

13. Julian L. Simon and Herman Kahn, eds., *The Resourceful Earth: A Response to Global 2000* (New York: Basil Blackwell, 1984), 6.

14. The quote is from a revised version of the book: Julian L. Simon, *The Ultimate Resource 2*, rev. ed. (Princeton: Princeton University Press, 1996), 66.

15. Paul Sabin, *The Bet: Paul Ehrlich, Julian Simon, and Our Gamble over Earth's Future* (New Haven: Yale University Press, 2013).

16. Ronald Reagan, "Remarks at Convocation Ceremonies at the University of South Carolina in Columbia," September 20, 1983, Ronald Reagan Presidential Library and Museum, https://www.reaganlibrary.gov/research/speeches/92083c); George Bush, "Address to the United Nations Conference on Environment and Development in Rio de Janeiro, Brazil," June 12, 1992, The American Presidency Project (http://www.presidency.ucsb.edu/ws/?pid=21075). For political support for growth in the postwar United States, see Robert M. Collins, *More: The Politics of Economic Growth in Postwar America* (New York: Oxford University Press, 2000).

17. Will Steffen, et. al., "Planetary Boundaries: Guiding Human Development on a Changing Planet," *Science* 347, no. 6223 (February 13, 2015): 736.

18. *Assessment for Decision-Makers: Scientific Assessment of Ozone Depletion: 2014*, World Meteorological Organization, Global Ozone Research and Monitoring Project— Report No. 56 (Geneva: 2014). During this same period, some scientists also began to argue that the blasts and fires from a nuclear war might throw so much soot into the stratosphere that they could potentially dim the sun and precipitate a long period of intense cold. The widely read article that began the popular discussion of "nuclear winter" was Carl Sagan, "The Nuclear Winter," *Parade*, October 30, 1982, 4–7. The Cold War played an important role in shifting scientific attention toward the environment and the possibility of environmental apocalypse. See Jacob Darwin Hamblin, *Arming Mother Nature: The Birth of Catastrophic Environmentalism* (New York: Oxford University Press, 2013).

19. Food and Agriculture Organization of the United Nations, *The State of World Fisheries and Aquaculture, 2016* (Rome, 2016); Callum Roberts, *The Unnatural History of the Sea* (Washington, D.C.: Island, 2007) (for cod levels, see pp. 211–212). Despite the troubled condition of wild fisheries, the total production of the oceans has continued to rise with the expansion of fish farming around the world.

20. For summaries of the science at different points in the debate, see Richard E. Leakey and Roger Lewin, *The Sixth Extinction: Patterns of Life and the Future of Humankind* (New York: Doubleday, 1995); and Elizabeth Kolbert, *The Sixth Extinction: An Unnatural History* (New York: Henry Holt, 2014).

21. Xiao Dong, Brandon Milholland, and Jan Vijg, "Evidence for a Limit to Human Lifespan," *Nature* 538 (October 13, 2016): 257; Stuart A. Thompson, "Welcome to Peak Olympics," *New York Times*, Sunday Review Section, February 11, 2018, 2.

22. National Academy of Sciences, Committee on Atmospheric Sciences, Panel on Weather and Climate Modification, *Weather and Climate Modification: Problems and Prospects: Volume I: Summary and Recommendations* (Washington, D.C.: National Academy of Sciences, National Research Council, 1966), reprinted in "Weather

and Climate Modification: Problems and Prospects," *Bulletin of the American Meteorological Society* 47, no. 1 (January 1966): 4–20 (quote appears on page 10); Victor Cohn, *1999: Our Hopeful Future* (New York: Bobbs-Merrill, 1956), 118; and Ritchie Calder, *The Inheritors: The Story of Man and the World He Made* (London: Heinemann, 1961), 296. Also see Roger Revelle, "The Long View from the Beach," in *The World in 1984: The Complete New Scientist Series,* ed. Nigel Calder (Baltimore: Penguin, 1965), 1:112–113. For the history of climate science, see James Rodger Fleming, *Historical Perspectives on Climate Change* (New York: Oxford University Press, 1998); and Spencer R. Weart, *The Discovery of Global Warming,* rev. ed. (Cambridge: Harvard University Press, 2008).

23. See Weart, *Discovery of Global Warming.* In the 1970s, there was more concern about global cooling than global warming. See Fleming, *Historical Perspectives on Climate Change,* 131–134.

24. See Andrew J. Hoffman, *How Culture Shapes the Climate Change Debate* (Stanford: Stanford University Press, 2015).

25. Tyler Cowen, *The Great Stagnation: How America Ate All of the Low-Hanging Fruit of Modern History, Got Sick, and Will (Eventually) Feel Better* (New York: Dutton, 2011), 9. Also see Robert Gordon, *The Rise and Fall of American Growth: The U.S. Standard of Living Since the Civil War* (Princeton: Princeton University Press, 2016), which argues that the technological innovations developed between 1870 and 1970 were more life-altering than those that have followed.

26. Mark Hanlon, "The Golden Quarter," *Aeon,* December 2014, https://aeon.co/essays/has-progress-in-science-and-technology-come-to-a-halt); Paul Krugman, "Things to Celebrate, Like Dreams of Flying Cars," *New York Times,* December 25, 2015; Peter Thiel quoted in Edward Luce, *The Retreat of Western Liberalism* (New York: Atlantic Monthly Press, 2017), 34; and "Why Don't We Have?" *Popular Mechanics,* accessed July 30, 2020, http://www.popularmechanics.com/why-dont-we-have/. Also see Daniel H. Wilson, *Where's My Jetpack?: A Guide to the Amazing Science Fiction Future that Never Arrived* (New York: Bloomsbury, 2007); and Ross Douthat, *The Decadent Society: How We Became Victims of Our Own Success* (New York: Avid Reader, 2020).

27. Spencer R. Weart, *The Rise of Nuclear Fear* (Cambridge: Harvard University Press, 2012); Heinz Haber, *The Walt Disney Story of Our Friend the Atom* (New York: Simon and Schuster, 1956).

28. Stephen O. Dean, *Search for the Ultimate Energy Source: A History of the U.S. Fusion Energy Program* (New York: Spring, 2013). For expectations that fusion would be feasible by the 1990s, see Arthur C. Clarke, *Profiles of the Future* (New York: Harper and Row, 1962), 142–143 and 233; and Kahn, Brown, and Martel, *The Next 200 Years,* 77.

29. Matthew D. Tribbe, *No Requiem for the Space Age: The Apollo Moon Landings and American Culture* (New York: Oxford University Press, 2014); and Ben Hellwarth, *Sealab: America's Forgotten Quest to Live and Work on the Ocean Floor* (New York: Simon and Schuster, 2012).

30. For a view of supersonic transportation from the American side, see Erik M. Conway, *High-Speed Dreams: NASA and the Technopolitics of Supersonic Transportation, 1945–1999* (Baltimore: Johns Hopkins University Press, 2008). The Soviet Union had its own version, the Tupolev Tu-144, which stopped carrying commercial passengers in 1978.

31. H. T. Orville, "Weather Made to Order?" *Collier's,* May 28, 1954, 25–29 (quote on p. 25); Fleming, *Fixing the Sky.*

32. Peter Moore, *The Weather Experiment: The Pioneers Who Sought to See the Future* (New York: Farrar, Straus and Giroux, 2015); Weart, *Discovery of Global Warming,* ix; Nicholas Bloom, Charles I. Jones, John Van Reenen, and Michael Webb, "Are Ideas Getting Harder to Find?" *American Economic Review* 110, no. 4 (April 2020), 1138; and Marcelo Gleiser, *The Island of Knowledge: The Limits of Science and the Search for Meaning* (New York: Basic, 2014). Also see Deborah Strumsky, José Lobo, and Joseph A. Tainter, "Complexity and the Productivity of Innovation," *Systems Research and Behavioral Science* 27 (August 2010): 496–509; and John Horgan, *The End of Science: Facing the Limits of Knowledge in the Twilight of the Scientific Age* (Boston: Addison-Wesley, 1996), which makes the controversial argument that all of the major discoveries have already been made.

33. Rachel Carson, *Silent Spring* (Boston: Houghton Mifflin, 1962). The futurist Walter Hahn credited Carson's book with introducing him to "modern futures concepts." Walter A. Hahn, "Futures in Politics and the Politics of Futures," in *What I Have Learned: Thinking About the Future Then and Now,* ed. Michael Marien and Lane Jennings (New York: Greenwood, 1987), 108. Jacob Rosin and Max Eastman, *The Road to Abundance* (New York: McGraw-Hill, 1953). The former site of Rosin's old employer, the Montrose Chemical Company, is now part of the Diamond Alkali Superfund site on Lister Avenue in Newark, New Jersey.

34. James Roger Fleming, *Fixing the Sky: The Checkered History of Weather and Climate Control* (New York: Columbia University Press, 2010), chapter 8; and Clive Hamilton, *Earthmasters: The Dawn of the Age of Climate Engineering* (New Haven: Yale University Press, 2013). For a twenty-first century proposal to build underwater seawalls, see John C. Moore, Rupert Gladstone, Thomas Zwinger and Michael Wolovick, "Geoengineering Polar Glaciers to Slow Sea-Level Rise," *Nature* 555 (March 14, 2018): 303–305. For a well-known environmentalist's embrace of geo-engineering, see Stewart Brand, *Whole Earth Discipline: An Ecopragmatist Manifesto* (New York: Viking, 2009).

35. For the decline of progress generally, see particularly Robert Nisbet, "Progress at Bay," chapter 9 in *History of the Idea of Progress,* rev. (1980; New Brunswick, N.J.: Transaction, 1994). Tribbe, *No Requiem for the Space Age,* links declining faith in progress around 1970 to the waning of "rationalism" and the waxing of "neo-romanticism." For the political consequences of declining expectations in the West after 1970, see Luce, *Retreat of Western Liberalism.* For public concerns about science and technology generally, see Pew Research Foundation, "U.S. Views of Technology and the Future: Science in the Next 50 Years" (Washington, D.C.: Pew

Research Center, 2014); and Martin Rees, *Our Final Hour: A Scientist's Warning: How Terror, Error, and Environmental Disaster Threaten Humankind's Future in this Century—on Earth and Beyond* (New York: Basic, 2003).

36. For an overview of apocalyptic thinking after 1970, see Frederick Buell, "A Short History of Environmental Apocalypse," in *Future Ethics: Climate Change and Apocalyptic Imagination*, ed. Stefan Skrimshire (New York: Continuum, 2010), 13–36. For the cultural and political costs of catastrophism, see Sasha Lilley, David McNally, Eddie Yuen, and James Davis, *Catastrophism: The Apocalyptic Politics of Collapse and Rebirth* (Oakland: PM, 2012).

37. See, for example, Robert Silverberg, *The World Inside* (New York: Doubleday, 1971); T. J. Bass, *Half Past Human* (New York: Ballantine, 1971); John Brunner, *The Sheep Look Up* (New York: Harper and Row, 1972); Philip Wylie, *The End of the Dream* (New York: Doubleday, 1972). For anthologies, see Frederik Pohl, ed., *Nightmare Age* (New York: Ballantine, 1970); Thomas M. Disch, ed., *The Ruins of Earth* (New York: G. P. Putnam's Sons, 1971); and Roger Elwood and Virginia Kidd, eds., *The Wounded Planet* (New York: Bantam, 1974).

38. The relationship between environment and dystopia in science fiction is explored in Brian Stableford, "Ecology and Dystopia" in *The Cambridge Companion to Utopian Literature*, ed. Gregory Claeys (New York: Cambridge University Press, 2010), 259–281. For environmental literature since the 1980s, also see Frederick Buell, *From Apocalypse to Way of Life: Environmental Crisis in the American Century* (New York: Routledge, 2003), chapters 8 and 9. Even historians have tried their hands at imagining civilization after environmental collapse: see Naomi Oreskes and Erik M. Conway, *The Collapse of Western Civilization: A View from the Future* (New York: Columbia University Press, 2014).

39. Also noteworthy, but less well known, were *Silent Running* (1971), about the destruction of earth's plant life, and *Z.P.G.* (1972), about an overcrowded and polluted future earth where people are banned from having more children (the initials stand for "zero population growth"). For TV, see the British series *Doomwatch* (1970–1972).

40. Other noteworthy movies from this period include *Children of Men* (2006), *Snowpiercer* (2013), *Elysium* (2013), and *Interstellar* (2014). For a sample of the scholarly attention paid to *The Day After Tomorrow*, see Anthony A. Leiserowitz, "Before and After *The Day After Tomorrow*: A U.S. Study of Climate Change Risk Perception," *Environment* 46, no. 9 (November 2004): 22–37.

41. J. K. Ullrich, "Climate Fiction: Can Books Save the Planet?" *The Atlantic*, August 14, 2014, https://www.theatlantic.com/entertainment/archive/2015/08/climate-fiction-margaret-atwood-literature/400112/. For an overview of the literature on how young people in the West think about the environmental future, see David Hicks and Cathie Holden, "Remembering the Future: What Do Children Think?" *Environmental Education Research* 4 (September 2007): 501–512.

42. See, for example, Michio Kaku, *Physics of the Future: How Science Will Shape Human Destiny and Our Daily Lives by the Year 2100* (New York: Doubleday, 2011);

Joe Quirk, *Seasteading: How Floating Nations Will Restore the Environment, Enrich the Poor, Cure the Sick, and Liberate Humanity from Politicians* (New York: Free Press, 2017); Peter H. Diamondis and Steven Kotler, *Abundance: The Future Is Better Than You Think* (New York: Free Press, 2012); and Steven Kotler, *Tomorrowland: Our Journey from Science Fiction to Science Fact* (Boston: New Harvest, 2015). One could also still find traces of the utopian strand of the development narrative in children's literature, as in "Future World: Homes," *Boys' Life*, June 2019, 18–19, which forecasts the spread of surplus human population to homes built on platforms over the oceans and suggests that they would cause little damage to underwater ecosystems. The presentation of environmental crisis as an exciting opportunity is discussed in Frederick Buell, *From Apocalypse to Way of Life*, chapter 7. Expectations of godhood appear in Kaku, *Physics of the Future*, 10, and Kotler, *Tomorrowland*, xvii.

43. For Star Trek as a techno-utopia, particularly in the context of *Star Trek: Next Generation*, see F. S. Braine, "Technological Utopias: The Future of the Next Generation," *Film and History* 24, no. 1–2 (February–May 1994): 2–18.

44. For a discussion of environmental themes in Star Trek, see George A. Gonzalez, *The Politics of Star Trek: Justice, War, and the Future* (New York: Palgrave Macmillan, 2015), 131–143.

45. Gerard K. O'Neill, *The High Frontier: Human Colonies in Space* (New York: William Morrow, 1977); and O'Neill, *2081: A Hopeful View of the Human Future* (New York: Simon and Schuster, 1981). W. Patrick McCray, *The Visioneers: How a Group of Elite Scientists Pursued Space Colonies, Nanotechnologies, and a Limitless Future* (Princeton: Princeton University Press, 2013), frames O'Neill's work as a response to the debate about environmental limits. For profit-driven space exploration in the twenty-first century, see Kenneth Chang, "Opportunity in Orbit," *New York Times*, November 28, 2017, D1 and D4; and Christian Davenport, *The Space Barons: Elon Musk, Jeff Bezos, and the Quest to Colonize the Cosmos* (New York: Public-Affairs, 2018). The quote is from Jeff Bezos, "Going to Space to Benefit Earth," May 9, 2019, https://www.youtube.com/watch?v=GQ98hGUe6FM&feature=youtu.be).

46. Stewart Brand, ed., *Space Colonies* (New York: Penguin, 1977) (the first two quotes appear on p. 36 and the third on p. 83).

47. Susan Nelson, "Why Are We So Intent on Moving Backward?" *Chicago Tribune*, November 8, 1970, Section 5 (Features), 7. For orientations to nostalgia as a phenomenon, see Svetlana Boym, *The Future of Nostalgia* (New York: Basic, 2001); Simon Reynolds, *Retromania: Pop Culture's Addiction to Its Own Past* (New York: Faber and Faber, 2011); and David Lowenthal, *The Past Is a Foreign Country—Revisited* (Cambridge: Cambridge University Press, 2015).

48. Alvin Toffler, *Future Shock* (New York: Random House, 1970), 343; Morrow, "Epitaph for a Decade," 38.

49. J. W. Rinzler, *The Making of Star Wars: The Definitive Story Behind the Original Film* (New York: Del Rey, 2007); James H. Carrott and Brian David Johnson, *Vintage*

*Tomorrows: A Historian and a Futurist Journey Through Steampunk into the Future of Technology* (San Francisco: Maker Media, 2013); and Asif Siddiqi, "From Cosmic Enthusiasm to Nostalgia for the Future," in *Soviet Space Culture: Cosmic Enthusiasm in Socialist Societies*, ed. Eva Maurer, Julia Richers, Monica Rüthers, and Carmen Scheide (Basingstoke: Palgrave Macmillan, 2011), 283–306. The artist Bruce McCall has built a career out of future-tinted illustrations of what he calls "faux nostalgia." See, for example, Bruce McCall, *Marveltown* (New York: Farrar, Straus and Giroux, 2008).

50. The quote appears in *Walt Disney's Guide to Disneyland* (Anaheim, Calif.: Walt Disney Productions, 1959), 18. John Wenz, "SpaceX's Gorgeous Vintage Posters Have Us Packing Our Bags for Mars," *Popular Mechanics*, May 16, 2015, https://www.popularmechanics.com/space/moon-mars/a15585/spacex-vintage-mars-travel-posters/; for NASA posters, see both the Visions of the Future posters (https://www.jpl.nasa.gov/visions-of-the-future/, accessed July 30, 2020) and the Mars Explorers Wanted posters (https://mars.nasa.gov/multimedia/resources/mars-posters-explorers-wanted/, accessed July 30, 2020); for the Arconic ad, see *Arconic—Jetsons*, YouTube video, posted by Silversword Media, May 29, 2017, https://www.youtube.com/watch?v=EdzVmRN2IfI; for the evolution of Tomorrowland, see Priscilla Hobbs, *Walt's Utopia: Disneyland and American Mythmaking* (Jefferson, N.C.: McFarland, 2015), 159. Disney's 2015 movie *Tomorrowland* also appeals to nostalgia by advocating the return to a vision of the future that looks a lot like a mid-twentieth-century technological utopia.

51. For ecotopias during this period, see Marius de Geus, *Ecological Utopias: Envisioning the Sustainable Society* (Utrecht: International, 1999); and Lisa Garforth, *Green Utopias: Environmental Hope Before and After Nature* (Cambridge: Polity, 2017). Garforth emphasizes the differences rather than the similarities between pastoral utopias and later ecotopias (see p. 17). Also see E. C. Otto, *Green Speculations: Science Fiction and Transformative Environmentalism* (Athens: Ohio State University Press, 2012). A few green utopias did appear between these two larger outpourings. See, in particular, Austin Tappan Wright's *Islandia* (New York: Farrar and Rinehart, 1942) and B. F. Skinner's *Walden Two* (New York: Hackett, 1948).

52. Aldous Huxley, *Island* (1962; New York: Harper Perennial, 2009), 259 and 177.

53. Nigel Calder, *The Environment Game* (London: Secker and Warburg, 1967), 189. Calder later expanded on some of these ideas in Calder, *The Green Machines* (New York: Putnam's Sons, 1986).

54. Ernest Callenbach, *Ecotopia: The Notebooks and Reports of William Weston* (1975; New York: Bantam, 1990), 47–48.

55. Marge Piercy, *Woman on the Edge of Time* (New York: Alfred A. Knopf, 1976), 62.

56. Ursula K. Le Guin, *Always Coming Home* (New York: Bantam, 1985).

57. Kim Stanley Robinson, *Pacific Edge* (New York: Tor, 1990).

58. Garforth, *Green Utopias*, 3.

59. John S. Dryzek, *The Politics of the Earth: Environmental Discourses*, 3rd ed. (New

York: Oxford University Press, 2013), chapter 7. Also see Jeremy L. Caradonna, *Sustainability: A History* (New York: Oxford University Press, 2014).

60. William B. Meyer, *The Environmental Advantages of Cities: Countering Common-sense Antiurbanism* (Cambridge: MIT Press, 2013); and David Owen, *Green Metropolis: Why Living Smaller, Living Closer, and Driving Less Are the Keys to Sustainability* (New York: Riverhead, 2009).

61. For an accessible overview of the sustainable city idea, see The Worldwatch Institute, *Can a City Be Sustainable?* (Washington, D.C.: Island, 2016). For detailed drawings of the sustainable city of the future in popular publications, see, for example, Mark Fischetti, "The Efficient City," *Scientific American,* September 2011, 74–75, illustration by Brian Christie; and Angelique LeDoux, "Welcome to the City of the Future," *Time for Kids: New Scoop Edition,* April 20, 2007, 4–5.

62. Utopian sustainable cities do not have a large footprint in fiction. For an exception, see Jonathan Porritt, *The World We Made: Alex McKay's Story from 2050* (London: Phaidon, 2013). For the model sustainable city, see Julie Sze, *Fantasy Islands: Chinese Dreams and Ecological Fears in an Age of Climate Crisis* (Berkeley: University of California Press, 2015).

63. Dryzek, *Politics of the Earth,* 155–163. The ecological economist Herman Daly considers sustainable growth to be impossible. See Daly, "Sustainable Growth: An Impossibility Theorum," in Herman E. Daly and Kenneth N. Townsend, *Valuing the Earth: Economics, Ecology, Ethics* (Cambridge: MIT Press, 1993), 267–273. For other critiques of sustainable development, see Frank Fischer and Maarten Hajer, eds., *Living with Nature: Environmental Politics as Cultural Discourse* (New York: Oxford University Press, 1999). Steven Pinker summarizes the ecopragmatist position in Pinker, *Enlightenment Now: The Case for Reason, Science, Humanism, and Progress* (New York: Viking, 2018), 121–155.

## Epilogue: Changing the Dream

1. Williams R. Catton, Jr., *Overshoot: The Ecological Basis of Revolutionary Change* (Urbana: University of Illinois Press, 1980), 7. The historian and futurist W. Warren Wagar published a fictional history of the future in 1989. Just two years later, the Soviet Union dissolved, forcing him to publish a revised edition. W. Warren Wagar, *A Short History of the Future* (Chicago: University of Chicago Press, 1989).

2. Ursula K. Le Guin, "A Non-Euclidean View of California as a Cold Place to Be," in *Dancing at the Edge of the World* (New York: Grove, 1989), 80–100 (quote on p. 85).

3. Olaf Stapledon, *Last and First Men and Star Maker* (New York: Dover, 1968), 75; and Harrison Brown, James Bonner, and John Weir, *The Next Hundred Years: A Discussion Prepared for Leaders of American Industry* (New York: Viking, 1957), 151. For an assessment of the long-term sustainability of scarce metals, even in the absence of a technological breakdown of some kind, see M. L. C. M. Henckens,

P. P. J. Driessen, and E. Worrell, "Metal Scarcity and Sustainability, Analyzing the Necessity to Reduce the Extraction of Scarce Metals," *Resources, Conservation and Recycling* 93 (December 2014): 1–8.

4. Lewis Mumford, "Summary Remarks: Prospect," in *Man's Role in Changing the Face of the Earth,* William L. Thomas, Jr. (Chicago: University of Chicago Press, 1956), 1150.

5. Lewis Mumford, one of the twentieth century's greatest students of utopian thought, admired the predictive power of the literature of the future. He claimed that anyone in the past who had been well versed in it would have possessed "an almost clairvoyant fore-knowledge of present-day society." Lewis Mumford, *The Pentagon of Power* (New York: Harcourt Brace Jovanovich, 1970), 212.

6. Rosalind Williams, *Notes on the Underground: An Essay on Technology, Society, and the Imagination* (Cambridge: MIT Press, 2008), 203. For a self-conscious attempt to reinvigorate the dreams of the development narrative through science fiction, see Ed Finn and Kathryn Cramer, eds., *Hieroglyph: Stories and Visions for a Better Future* (New York: William Morrow, 2014). In contrast, the online quarterly *Into the Ruins* (https://intotheruins.com) uses science fiction to explore "a future defined by natural limits."

7. Jacques Ellul, "Search for an Image," in *Images of the Future: The Twenty-First Century and Beyond,* ed. Robert Bundy (Buffalo: Prometheus, 1976), 27. Also see the collection more generally, especially Thomas F. Green, "Stories and Images of the Future," 35–44. For a discussion of how to apply ecological utopianism to environmental problems, see Marius de Geus, "Utopian Sustainability: Ecological Utopianism," chapter 4 in Liam Leonard and John Barry, eds., *The Transition to Sustainable Living and Practice,* Advances in Ecopolitics, vol. 4 (Bingley, United Kingdom: Emerald Group, 2009): 77–100.

8. For an attempt by historians to construct what these reimagined pasts might look like, see Christophe Bonneuil and Jean-Baptiste Fressoz, *The Shock of the Anthropocene: The Earth, History and Us,* trans. David Fernbach (New York: Verso, 2016).

9. For an overview of the many calls for a new consciousness, see James Gustave Speth, *The Bridge at the End of the World: Capitalism, the Environment, and Crossing from Crisis to Sustainability* (New Haven: Yale University Press, 2008), chapter 10.

# INDEX

Page numbers in italic type refer to illustrations.